What is the definition of a survivor?

Someone who spends the rest of their life asking why their life was spared in exchange for someone else's.

STAYIN ALIVE

How PTSD (Nearly) Stole My Life

David Cruickshanks

BOOKS

Stayin Alive
How PTSD (Nearly) Stole My Life

Published by Razur Cuts Books (2022), a subsidiary of Nameless Town

razurcuts.com
razurcuts@gmail.com

ISBN: 978-1-914400-71-1

Edited and typeset by Dickson Telfer
Proofread by Gillian Gardner

All photographs courtesy of the author
Jacket design by Dickson Telfer and stonedart

Printed and bound by Martins the Printers, Berwick-upon-Tweed

BOOKS

For Becky

A brief, post-edit conversation
between editor, Dickson Telfer
and author, David Cruickshanks

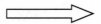

DICKSON

I meant to ask – how did you end up fighting in the
Falklands at the tender young age of 17 anyway?

DAVID

Well, I was due to join *HMS Nottingham*, a shiny new
destroyer with gas turbine engines, but I came home on
weekend leave and my mum said 'The Navy are sending
a Land Rover to pick you up to join *HMS Fearless* in
Plymouth'. I just laughed and said I'm not James Bond.

A few hours later, two sailors appeared in a Land
Rover and deposited me in Faslane to pick up my kit and
head south. A week later, I was leaving Plymouth
harbour on a landing craft bound for *Fearless*, which was
anchored out in Plymouth Sound and had just returned
from a stormy Caribbean tour. It turned out that another
sailor had taken seriously ill and I was his replacement.
As I approached the older, steam-powered amphibious
assault ship, I realised that only a few years ago I had
been playing with the Airfix model version of *Fearless*.

The ship was heading for arctic exercises in Norway
and then onto the Mediterranean, where it trained young
officers how to navigate, so we had the best of all
worlds. I thought I had cracked it when I heard the
deployment after Norway would be wall to wall
sunshine.

A month later, as we sailed down the north coast of
Scotland, news came through of the Argentine invasion.
I'll never forget when the ship's company heard that The
Falklands had been invaded. The first question was
'Whereabouts in Scotland is that then?'

As I was only 17, I was officially asked if I wanted to go to war and I said yes. I think I'd have been too embarrassed to say no and, deep down, I was hoping for a diplomatic end. The momentum of war can put incredible pressure on governments though, and backing down can seem like weakness, so off I went.

DICKSON

... Jeezo ...

With a little help from notes, letters, press cuttings and photographs, this book is based on memories spanning a 40-year period. It is therefore not possible to accurately recall the specifics of who said what and the exact words used. Additionally, where appropriate, pseudonyms have been used for some of the characters you'll meet in this book.

The important facts in *Stayin Alive* are as relayed, but occasional colour has been added for pace and entertainment purposes. If any misrepresentation is present, this is entirely unintentional and as a result of memories being clouded by the expiration of time.

Stayin Alive contains use of naval language, vocabulary and terminology, some formal and some informal (the latter referred to as Jackspeak), as well as some regional Scots. Where it was felt appropriate, definitions have been provided in footnotes throughout. There is also an A-Z glossary at the back of the book (pages 345-353) with the corresponding page number of the first or sole usage of the word, term or phrase.

Foreword

by Anna Smith

In a daily newspaper, when your news editor sends you on a foreign trip, you up your game and ensure you don't make any slip ups. It doesn't matter if it's a pre-arranged agreed feature interview, or a war zone. Back at the news and picture desks, they don't care if you do it with mirrors. Just don't come back without it. Don't mess up. So you don't. Or if you do, you'd better pray that you can pick up the pieces before any of the grown-ups back home get wind of it. And we always do. Reporters and photographers, for the most part, stick together. They're a team, they cover each other's backs. They work, on no matter how arduous the job is, and they can usually manage to have a laugh and a glass of wine at the end of a long slog of a day.

Most of the photographers I worked with were top hands, experienced, and had been around the course many times like myself. So making it happen was seldom a problem we couldn't solve. When I first encountered David Cruickshanks, I thought at first he was a work experience boy just in for a week. But after a few jobs with him, I could see that this diminutive, scrawny lad with the somehow worried frown lines and the biggest, whitest smile, was actually very good, very astute and plucky enough. I was still surprised though, when they sent him off on his first foreign trip with me to Romania at the height of the orphanage scandal in the wake of the fall of the dictator Nicolae Ceausescu regime and all the ugliness that surrounded it.

On the plane to London to pick up our connecting flight, David started talking to me, and surprised me by telling me about growing with an abusive father who beat him when he was a child. I was taken aback by his frankness, and even more so by his seeming need to open up to a relative stranger about this trauma. I wanted to hug him. I already knew David was a Falklands war veteran having served on *HMS Fearless* as a fresh faced young teenager, so there was always more to him than meets the eye. But when he told me of this childhood cruelty, I could see that perhaps this is why he has that look about him, older than his years.

We got to London ready to board the afternoon flight to Bucharest when suddenly David looked even more worried and stressed. 'What's the matter,' I asked. 'My passport,' he answered. He had a passport alright – it just wasn't his. It's was his fiancée, Becky's. What? It could be a sacking offence at the *Daily Record* not to carry your passport. And to be fair, he did have one – just not his. I could see David was mortified to the core, but I told him don't worry, we can handle it – hoping we could! But we had to break the news to desk back home in order to get his passport to London pronto! I called them, played it down, and Eric Craig, the sympathetic and highly professional picture editor swung into action.

Becky raced to the *Daily Record* office with his passport, and photographer Willie Thornton took it to Glasgow Airport and gave it to a British Airways passenger heading to Heathrow. Panic off. But the decision was made for me to go to Bucharest alone and wait for him. Unfortunately, the only flight David could get was to Budapest in Hungary, which he duly did.

I waited in the Buchar hotel for him, worried sick that he was travelling alone on his first foreign trip. I was relieved when David turned up the next day, but with his own edgy tale of travel. He'd arrived at Budapest towards midnight in time to catch the last train to Bucharest. He'd then sat for hours on the freezing carriage until the train finally left for Budapest. Throughout the journey, were armed police checkpoints where he had to part with money – common practice in some of these corrupt regimes, but the kind of nervy stuff that makes you terrified if you are alone. He arrived tired, and even more worried looking! But from that day my respect for him just grew. I'm not sure if I could have done that myself in a foreign country, especially the way Romania was at that time. I liked this guy a lot. We had a great week working, picked up some good features for the paper and a few laughs - in fact some of the scenes I later used in my crime novels.

Over the years, I've watched him grow to become an award winning photographer and more. He left the *Daily Record* a few years later and became a snapper in demand in Fleet Street. I know he has struggled with mental health issues over the years, but David has dug in. He's done the lot, from skinny, abused kid to decorated Falklands veteran. From having a photograph in the National Gallery in London, to stand-up comedy.

We teamed up again a few years ago for a trip to Kosovo with a charity so I could visit victims I encountered from the reporting on the war there in 1999. We picked up some good spreads on a worthwhile trip.

David has been to hell and back, and he's still standing. He doesn't know it sometimes, but he's Fearless, like the warship he served on during the Falklands war. This book is a testament to his life, raw and moving, but throughout, David's spirit and humour shine through.

Anna Smith
February 2022

Beat Surrender

1985

CRACK! The back of my head collides with a solid surface.

Only a few moments before, my girlfriend and I were relaxing on the faux leather settee watching a programme about sharks on the telly. We were still at the getting to know each other stage, though we'd been neighbours growing up. I'd always thought Joanne was out of my league; after all, her dad worked in computers. I was finding *The Undersea World of Jacques Cousteau* a bit tedious, so I changed the channel. It was this small, seemingly insignificant action that led to my flight from the settee to the dining table on the other side of the living room.

Although I'm conscious, at least for now, I'm not really in control of my senses, and the threat of imminent death remains a possibility if I don't act quickly. He pulls my hair and I instinctively laugh; no-one has pulled my hair since high school.

'Joanne! Out! Get out!' I scream while gripping the wrist of the hand that now contains clumps of my hair. I glimpse the screwed-up confusion on Joanne's face through the crook of my dad's arm before she turns and bolts for the door. I can't imagine what she's going to tell her mum when she gets home, but it's not going to be about sharks, that's for sure. I parry a fist and try to roll off what I now recognise as the living room table, simultaneously doing all I can to fend off further blows. I engage my core and lever myself up off the veneer, protecting my face as best I can to minimise damage. I'm not bothered about my face, but I've just had a knee operation at the Royal Navy hospital in Gosport and bursting the stitches isn't an option.

His body weight pins me to the table, although he's breathing hard now, which makes me think he might be tiring. I strain my neck towards the window and look for a weapon on the sill, but all I can see is cars bathed in the sodium of streetlight, the same streetlight that loomed over me when, as a toddler, I slipped on the ice one morning and rattled my skull.

I twist the other way, aware that my right knee is now vulnerable. His hand slips on my sweaty left wrist and I seize my chance, rolling onto my left hip bone as he attempts to land another blow. I manage to get purchase on the edge of the table with my left hand and prise myself up to a precarious sitting position. He's a dead weight. I breathe hard and fast, like I'm mimicking his breathing to lull him into relaxing his grip. Fuelled by a cocktail of adrenalin, determination and fear, I strain the sinews in my left arm and force him back, my right hand gripping his other wrist. I need to get my legs onto solid ground to avoid a severe beating or worse.

I take a deep breath and scream which jerks him backwards. He definitely wasn't expecting that. I wriggle hard, twisting my bad knee and sending a pain signal to my brain, but it quickly numbs the sudden burn of ripped stitches and switches back to survival mode. Miraculously I've done a reverse jack knife onto the carpeted floor which helps me gain some traction and my hands are finally free.

We gasp into each other's faces. His chin is shiny with spittle, his thinning grey hair matted with sweat. I look deep into his eyes, searching for some human connection, but they're as dead as the sharks he worships.

My wrists sting and, looking down, I realise his sharp nails have pierced my flesh and discharged fresh blood. I want to retaliate with words – something that would diffuse the ticking time bomb opposite me – but nothing comes to mind, so the breathy, sweaty stalemate continues for a while longer. Suddenly I'm thinking *It's funny how fights in movies are full of whacks and thuds, but real fights are silent tests of power perforated with strangulated grunts.*

I give the window a momentary glance as rain begins to spatter against it, before returning to the monster confronting me. The snarl on his lips surrenders to gravity and his shoulders slump as his breathing normalises. He wipes sweat from his forehead and spittle from his chin. In that moment I toy with letting it be, telling myself *You're better than him, David. You're better than this fucker.* Then five words change everything.

'You'll never amount to anything,' he growls through what's left of his yellowing teeth.

I look over his shoulder to the living room door and then I look back and my lips curl into a smile. I see his eyes flicker with confusion and I notice him swallowing hard. He's scared now. I know he expected me to cower like I've always done, but this time I slowly and deliberately navigate my way around him, our eyes still locked. As we come shoulder to shoulder, he looks down and succumbs to what sounds like a sigh of defeat.

I limp to the kitchen and open the door to the boiler cupboard. At the foot of the hot water tank are my heavy leather boots. At this moment, I'm still not sure what I'm going to do next, but at least I'm no longer worried about his actions.

As I lace up my boots, I think back to a time when I was about ten and came home with wellingtons that were soaking wet on the inside after I fell into the local pond. My mum told me to fill them with newspaper and hide them from my dad, because if he saw them, I'd get a beating. I tore up some old newspaper and did as she suggested, but I forgot to hide them, and my dad found them beneath the water tank. He interrogated me for what seemed like hours before putting me out my misery by beating me across the arse with a tough leather belt. No matter how hard I tried to be good, I realised he would always find an excuse for a beating, so I stopped trying. I began to welcome the beatings; the first blow that snapped the tension straight out of my body, signalling that it would all be over soon; until next time.

I make sure the boot laces are tight and try out my bad knee by stomping on the kitchen tiles. There is blood seeping through my jeans, but the pain is bearable and comes as a kind of release, and I realise there's much more at stake right now than burst stitches.

I go back through to the living room where he's still standing, propped up by the table. I grab his arm and spin him around to face me. I'll never forget the startled look of fear in his eyes as I drag him out of the front door and into the pissing rain, my heavy leather boots squelching on the surrendering grass, the rain backlit by the sodium streetlight adding a sickly glow to his punctured face.

Start!

1975

Mum shouts me in from the back green. 'David?'
'What?'
'Tea time!'
'Coming,' I reply. This is lie number one.
'David?' she shouts again, her tone a bit more aggressive this time.
'What?'
'Tea!'
I've got time for one more attack. The machine gun nest has to be taken at all costs. I've selected the elite commandos to lead the assault. The nest is well dug in at the foot of mum's geraniums. Behind them, a company of less well-trained German infantry lie ready for action. The commandos must get through or the rest of the allies will be pinned down in the sand pit. It's make or break.
'Right men, you know what to do. Jimmy, you take the left flank.'
'Yes, sir.'
'Tommy?'
'Sir!'
'Straight up the middle, Tommy, and no dilly-dallying.'
'Sir!'
'David!' Mum yells for a third time.
'What?'
'I'm not going to tell you again!'

I move the plastic troops forward double quick. 'I'm coming!' I shout, maintaining focus on my battalion.

'Right, not a moment to lose, you all know what to do.'

'Yes, sir.'

'Then get on with it, and good luck.'

My language is peppered with the clichés of old war comics and *Commando* books; of heroes called Tommy and cowards called Fritz, whose dying screams were always *Gott im Himmel!* Or, if they were Japanese, *Banzai!*

'David, if you don't come in here right this minute, I'll tell your dad as soon as he gets home.' Mum serves a match point ace in our game of verbal tennis.

'Coming,' I reply, exhaling the word like a dying hoover.

I clean my dinner plate in three minutes and a few seconds judging by the white clock on the kitchen wall. It sits like a Polo mint on a sea of green woodchip wallpaper.

The chips for my dad are bubbling in the pan. With any luck, Mum will trip and the pan of hot bubbling liquid will turn his face into molten putty. I'm in a hurry to get back to the battle, but my sweet tooth needs a fix.

'Mum?'

'Aye,' she replies, scrunching her apron, shoulders tense, ready for anything.

'What's for pudding?'

Her shoulders relax and she smooths out the wrinkled cotton with its lacy frill. 'Arctic roll,' she smiles.

'Can I get chocolate sauce?'

She lets out a sigh and looks at the Polo mint clock. 'Hurry up then, and only if you have peaches with it.'

'But I don't like peaches,' I gurn.

'Yes you do, you had them at Auntie Jean's last week.'

'But I didn't like them.' I make a gagging sound.

'Pack it in. No peaches, no chocolate sauce.'

'But, Mum.'

'Right, out of my sight, you're getting nothing.'

'Aw, Mum!'

'You wait till your dad gets home.'

The colour drains from my cheeks. 'I'll have the peaches.'

She scoops out the peaches from the tin onto my arctic roll. I consider about moaning about the arctic roll getting soggy, but then I think about my dad and what mood he might be in, and decide to eat the soggy sweetness instead.

Things hadn't gone well with the attack while I was away. The machine gun nest was pouring fire down onto the beach (sand pit) and the battalion was taking heavy losses. I rustle up Tommy using another commando with a radio moulded to his back.

'Tommy, why are you stalling man? Get up there!' I rage, pointing in the direction of German tracer fire.

'They have us pinned down sir, request air support!' he pleads.

'Okay Tommy, I'll call in the boys in blue, you sit tight. And Tommy?'

'Sir?'

I lower my voice in case Mum hears me. 'When that machine gun goes, I want you to annihilate those bastards!'

I clutch the undercarriage of the Airfix P51 Mustang as it swoops and strafes the machine gun nest lurking within the geraniums. With my other hand, I pick up a clod of earth and drop it to resemble the impact of the

23

Mustang's 1,000lb bomb. Bodies fly into the air as dirt peppers the Pampas grass. I land the aircraft and return to the carnage. There are soldiers scattered all over, some with no heads, a crater replacing the machine gun nest. Tommy lies close to the nest. It looks like he's collateral damage from the air strike, killed by his own side.

I take out Mum's lighter, which I nicked from the mantelpiece, from my school trousers' pocket and flick it into action. *Those bastard Gerries are gonna pay for killing Tommy.* I make up my mind there and then that Tommy had bought it, having heard this phrase recently in a war film on telly.

The flame licks at the German machine gunner's head, searching for a hold. A slight wind pushes the flame onto the tip of my index finger and I yelp.

'Is that you, David?' Mum shouts from the kitchen.

'It's alright, Mum. I just caught my finger on the Pampas grass.'

Lie number two.

'Is it bleeding?' she asks, her voice rising with concern. I imagine her shoulders rising too.

'No, it's okay,' I reassure her.

I circle the soldier's head with the flame again and this time it catches. His face bubbles and I can smell my own burning flesh. His blazing head soon becomes nothing more than a stump. I want to see him melt into a pulp, right down to his little plastic stand, but I can hear my dad's bike being bumped down the stairs and I know within three seconds he'll see me. I bury the German and smooth his grave over with my hands. The battle for geranium hill is over, for now.

My home is an end-terraced house with a close that has steps up to it and steps down at the other end to get to the back green. I try to spend most of my time outside, especially when my dad's looking to catch me doing something wrong. When he does catch me, he pins me up against the wall and interrogates me as to why I peeled the wallpaper in my bedroom wall, or why there were bogies[*] behind the headboard, or why I had given Mum cheek. Sometimes the interrogation takes hours, sometimes minutes, but it still feels like hours, the tension in my neck, pinching the blood flow to my floundering brain. I'm transfixed as he demands answers to questions I never have the right answer for and half the time I can't hear them because they're drowned out by the pounding of blood in my ears. For this reason and the subsequent beatings, I prefer to escape my home as often as possible, which is probably why I'm in the school playground at eight in the morning with a plastic football and a packet of sweetie cigarettes.

I live 5.2 seconds from my school, South Parks Primary. I ran it in 4.8 seconds once, when Brian the bully wanted a square go[**] outside the gates after school. Having witnessed the face-kicking and hair-pulling a square go entails, I wondered how much it hurt and if it was better or worse than Dad's interrogations. In many respects, a square go is exactly like my dad's interrogations, where the person who wants it is sure of the outcome, or at least they're the favourite.

Subsequently, I encountered two of these square goes and lost them both with varying degrees of damage, though nothing worse than a bruised nose and lots of crying, but what I hated most was the tension that would grow and grow and then fracture me, like faults in

---

[*] nasal mucus rolled into tight balls, like organic Blu-tack
[**] fight

Tectonic plates. The problem with me is that I had no inclination to punch or kick anyone, ever. With this attitude, growing up in Fife should have come with a council health warning:

Residents must be reminded that the kicking, punching and head butting committee meets tonight (Thursday) in the Council Chambers. Anyone failing to attend may be subject to square go induction classes.

The only difference with my dad's attitude to casual violence is that he waits so long before he hits me that I'm a trembling mess just waiting and praying to be slapped out of my misery before I pass out. I can always smell the disease in his gums as he spits accusations at me. Some of the spittle ends up on the wallpaper, but no-one gives him a row for making a mess. He is immune from prosecution.

Dub, dub, dub, dub.

The tyres bump down the last steps and the latch on the gate opens, making me jump.

'What have you been up to today?' he says, staring straight at me, his hair salt and pepper from decorating.

'Just school,' I reply, shifting my eyes around his face nervously.

'After dinner we can go for a cycle if you like,' he suggests, pulling a battered tartan flask out of his cycle bag, dark hairs protruding from the backs of his multi-coloured hands.

'Aye, fine.' I fixate on his hands, scared that making eye contact might trigger a flick or a slap.

'As long as you've been behaving yourself, I'll take you up Falkland Hill.'

I look up as far as his chin. There's a turquoise blob on it that looks like a willy[*] and I let out a snigger.

'I have. Ask Mum.'

Lie number three.

He fiddles with his bike, leans it against the wall, then pulls it back to make sure the frame isn't getting scratched by the brick. He does this several times before he's satisfied. Then he takes his Tupperware piece[**] box from his cycling bag and disappears through the back door, the blackcurrant bush shivering as his taut, sinewy frame brushes past me into the kitchen.

I don't mind cycling up Falkland Hill. After all, when he's cycling, he can't be thumping me. I get my bike out of the shed just as he comes back out. *Too late.*

'Put it back, you're not going.'

I wince as a pedal catches my shin. I have my back to him and I'm holding my breath, waiting.

He always does this. Changes his mind on a whim, builds me up, and then takes everything away. No reason given, no reason necessary. One day, maybe a few years from now, I'll sort him out. I'm biding my time. Mum knows it too. I notice the way she stiffens when she catches me looking at him.

The back door thuds shut. I take out the lighter and rub my thumb against the metal wheel. It sparks up and I hold it to my thumb. The tears trickle down my face, stinging with hate.

---

[*] penis
[**] sandwich

I've Changed
My Address

1976

Despite being only 12, I fantasise about joining the Royal Navy at a time when bright kids are probably fantasising about going to Oxford or Cambridge. It's weird to think that I was born only 19 years after World War II. It feels like my childhood is taking place on a different planet, but there's still a huge emphasis on kids "joining up".

I don't fancy the army. My cousin, Ian, has joined the Argyll and Sutherland Highlanders, but I'm terrified of being bullied and Ian has told me plenty stories that make my hair even curlier. I've already suffered a belly full of bullying – at school, at home, on the football field, down the shops, you name it. When it comes to fight or flight, I am in the run-like-fuck category. The Navy definitely seems a much more civilised option.

Lured by an advert in the *Daily Record* depicting three sailors in their tropical uniforms smiling at a map below the Athens Acropolis, I'm pretty sure that I want to get out of Glenrothes and see the world. The catalyst is our new neighbours across the road, the Whites. Alan, who's a year younger than me, becomes my friend and top toy swapper during the hottest Scottish summer I've experienced so far.

I cut out the advert and sprint the 2.8 seconds between my house and Alan's to check out his latest stuff and quiz

Alan's dad, Baz, about the Navy, because I know he's a sailor. I knock on the mint green of the White's ex-council door. Alan opens it after 3.7 seconds.

'Where's your dad, Alan?' I quiz, standing on the door step of number 51.

'Malta, I think,' he replies, anticipating my next question, looking over my shoulder as if he's expecting his dad to miraculously appear.

'When does he get home then?' I press further, looking beyond him and into the hall of his five apartment* semi-detached ex-council house to see his wee brother, Martin, singing in his pyjamas, using his mum or sister's hairbrush as a microphone.

'June, I think,' Alan answers, flicking round to check out his brother, then back at me, like his brother singing into a hairbrush is the most natural thing in the world.

'Can I borrow your armoured car for my Action Man?' I ask, with an air of desperation.

'Naw, but I'll do a swap if you give me the Nazi Commander's cap,' he relents, letting out a sigh as if he's so used to fending off seemingly endless questions from his wee brother, that fending off questions from brand new friends is a cinch.

'Only for tonight, though, cause my dad'll flip if he sees I've got something I shouldn't have,' I reply.

'It's okay,' Alan says, 'I've got Scouts anyway.'

He turns, heads past Martin on the stairs and, after some banging and crashing, returns with the armoured car. Martin doesn't miss a beat as his big brother tries and fails to wrench the hairbrush away with his free hand.

---

* 1970s Scottish colloquial term for number of rooms

I run back to my house and hide Alan's armoured car under the bed. Several swaps later, over the next couple of weeks, Alan's dad, Baz, appears.

Baz is a top bloke. For a start – unlike my own dad – he speaks to me without shouting. Every few months, he comes home, arms bulging with presents and tattoos, and with sea stories by the dozen. As the summer sun kisses our milky white bodies and touches up the tan borders around the back of our necks, he kicks a football about with us, teaches us how to fight, explains the rules of cricket to us, and even forgives me when I accidentally split Alan's head open with the willow bat. He also takes us on car trips to the sea or the safari park. Alan's wee brother comes with us so we have someone to bully.

Then, just when we're used to Baz being back, he's off again. 'Bye, boys, see you next time,' he says, getting into his maroon Ford Anglia.

I'm all consumed by the White's unique lifestyle, like the proverbial rose-coloured spectacle wearer. Hell, my specs are crimson with adoration! One night, when Baz is on leave, Alan and I sit beside him in the living room, watching the non-rented colour telly. Two monkeys are doing something we all laugh at, none of us quite sure why. Then it goes a bit quiet and I feel my neck burn.

'I'm gonnae join the Navy, Mr White,' I whisper, gawping at the naughty monkeys.

'Good for you, son,' Baz replies, in his soft Anglo-Scots voice. He turns to me and smiles.

My own dad had never said 'Good for you, son' in his life.

Dreams of Children

1976

I'm not quite sure when the darkness ends but, like a punch-drunk fighter, I hear a bell ring and the solid, brain-deadening black becomes dotted with tiny silvery fish that flitter away to reveal a blue sky as the volume of the ringing increases.

I'm flat on my back and the heaving up and down of my chest means I'm still alive. I feel a warmth return from my legs up to my stomach, like a cloud being vaporised by a ravenous sun. My ears gradually adjust to a mixture of screaming and laughing, and then it recedes as all the other kids including Darren Haldane are swallowed up by the school. Playtime is over.

How long was I dead?

Primary school has been one long kick in the head contest, one I was never destined to win. When I take a beating at school, inevitably one follows at home. There are flashes of insight when I know my dad is different from other dads, but I can't work out why he hates me so much and I can never ask him, so I take my anger and frustration out on insects and worms. I can't bring myself to fuse leather with someone else's skull in a fight with another kid, so I end up being the skull on someone else's leather.

I had thought that after the long hot 1976 summer, I would now be a grown up secondary school pupil with an Adidas bag, Adidas Gazelle trainers and the neckline of an Adidas top protruding from under my school uniform – and the beatings would stop dead like a 90-year-old's heart. They definitely will stop. After all, I'll be a teenager soon, just not soon enough.

Darren Haldane is a head case. Don't just take my word for it, everyone in our year is terrified of him and that includes most of the teachers.

One day, I walk into school and the most beautiful girl asks if she can kiss me, then the gym teacher says, 'David, we've made you captain of the school football team,' followed by the head teacher calling me to his office and congratulating me on becoming the school's first chess grandmaster.

Unfortunately, this isn't what happened. Instead:

'Do you want to see Jackie Penfold's tits?' Darren Haldane says.

He doesn't wait for an answer. Instead, he frogmarches me over to the bike sheds where Jackie can be found holding court, her cigarette conducting an imaginary orchestra as her more than ample mouth moulds a mundane story into a movie script. But then she stops quite suddenly, her pals and hangers-on unsure what's going on. I see a flicker of fear in her eyes as her brain registers *psycho*. Mid cig flick, Darren Haldane grabs Jackie's wrist and takes a long drag of her cigarette, eyes flickering as the smoke stings him and he struggles to look cool.

He elbows me in the ribs and nods to the cigarette. I'm about to shake my head but the follow-up elbow tells me it isn't a request, so I take the smelly stick and inhale while Darren Haldane's piggy eyes lock on to my reaction. I almost laugh but the smoke makes my lungs panic. Thankfully, my coughing fit pleases him and he turns his porcine gaze to Jackie as the crowd tenses with anticipation.

Violet Bishop gives me a look that says *Thought you were brainy?* I look down at my worn out trainers.

When I look up, Violet has disappeared in a fug of cigarette smoke. The other girl, whose name I can never remember (but I do remember the flash of her white pants in our first year school photograph) trundles off, leaving a stand-off between me, Jackie and Darren Haldane the head case.

'Fancy a better buzz than that, Jackie?' Darren Haldane says, nodding towards the dead cigarette on the grey concrete.

'What?'

Darren Haldane grabs me around the chest in a monkey tight grip. 'Take a few deep breaths and then hold it,' he orders.

'I thought you were going to . . . you know . . . with Jackie,' I splutter.

'In a minute, you first.'

Jackie smiles. Take it easy, Daz,' she says. 'You won't get a refund if you break him.'

The head case cackles as Jackie's smile broadens. 'Right, deep breath and hold...'

As I take my breath, I feel a crushing weight on my chest and the little silvery fish appear like when you get gassed at the dentist. I'll have to wait to see Jackie Penfold's tits or maybe I'll never see them. There's a thrumming sound in my ears and I can just make out muffled laughter and a noise like the telly being switched off at midnight.

By the time I stagger into Mrs Gibson's room, the bell has long gone. Everyone stares at me. Violet's face registers shock and I think maybe I have a snotter on my face or something. Thankfully, Gibby, as she has been nicknamed, is probably still smoking in the staff room.

Darren Haldane bangs his desk, guffawing like a demented donkey. A few sheep join in. Jackie looks down at her chest and smiles. Darren Haldane lifts up his grey jumper and makes out like he has a bra. 'Want some of this, ya wee pervert?' he mocks, gesturing to his audience, waving his hands around like a conductor. 'Pervert, pervert, pervert...' He swivels round in his chair and eggs on the rest of the class. But, to my surprise, no-one joins in.

'Shut up, Daz,' Violet says.

In a flash, Darren Haldane scrapes back his chair back and leaps at her.

'Da-rren Hal-dane! Back to your seat!' Gibby roars, arriving just in time.

Darren Haldane slinks back onto his chair pretending to be just another unruly kid but there's too much of the coil left in his manically wound spring for this to be over; apparently nearly killing a scrawny first year pupil isn't enough for a demented Darren Haldane. Not nearly enough.

Sounds from the Street

1979

I wake with a start, breathless in the darkness. I'm too young and skinny to sweat, so my pillow stays freezing cold and dry. It reminds me of the time I vomited in my sleep after one Irn-Bru ice cream float too many. The orange stain on the pillow never came out. So much for all those washing powder adverts on the telly.

I jerk upwards into a sitting position, locking my elbows. As my eyes adjust to the darkness, I survey the walls within my box bedroom. The one nearest me is icy and has little nicks in the wallpaper pattern where I've etched out swirls and squiggles with my fingernails. Straight ahead, I make out the shapes of kneeling footballers, their hair in various states of curliness as they peer out from the gloom, wincing as their caught-in-the-headlights faces are blasted with the flash from the Panini sticker photographer's fancy camera. Their crooked teeth and smiles are trapped within a rectangular papery prison, desperate to stand up and chase a ball.

The whole house is silent. I stretch down to the jaggy Bri-Nylon carpet and focus on the clock radio. Almost midnight. I get out of bed and feel the carpet clinging to my feet. I pad towards the window and look out at the orange dustbins and the odd car interrogated by the solitary sodium streetlight.

It's an hour after the pubs have closed. Still no sign. I had fallen asleep to the voice of John Peel gravelling

35

over Siouxsie and the Banshees' new album, which I'd already bought from Edwin Donaldson, a shop that sells washing machines, hoovers and punk albums. On the million-to-one chance that my dad might see it, I'd removed the Parental Advisory sticker from the cover. Tonight though, he has other things on his mind. Tonight is wages night.

I flinch and catch my breath as the tiny hairs in my ears stand to attention. At first I think I'm hearing things. Sometimes the street is so silent, you can fool yourself into believing you can hear noises. It's like the darkness has a sound of its own. The tiny window in my room is open a fraction. The air catches the back of my throat like ice cream after getting your tonsils out.

Tap, tap, tap, tap, scrape. Tap, tap, tap, tap, scrape. The sound of well-polished shoes on the concrete pavement grows louder, penetrating the silence of the slumbering neighbourhood. I fantasise about frost and the hope he might slip on those shiny shoes of his, going down, banging his head, his skull splitting like coconut, the warm, sticky contents spilling out over the cracks, hissing and steaming in the freezing air, his stinking breath silent forever.

Tap, tap, tap, tap scrape. Tap, tap, tap, tap, scrape. Tap, tap, tap, tap, scrape.

I shudder and dive back to my single bed, pulling the covers over my head, wishing, just wishing, that one Thursday night it would be different. Then the sound of the cheap wooden door frame creaking in synch with a Yale key being turned signals that tonight will be like any other Thursday night.

Non-Stop Dancing

1977

There's a girl who rides to my school on a motorcycle. She parks it beside the teachers' cars and I always take a detour past the car park on my way to the red ash football pitch for a kick about in the hope of catching her taking off her red, white and blue helmet and shaking out her curly, mousey brown hair like she's in a shampoo advert.

One crisp, bright morning, I stop and stare as she shimmies out of her leathers to reveal her grey pleated skirt and matching tights. Her skirt has ridden up to reveal the top of her thigh. She catches me looking and her forehead creases in a mixture of consternation and curiosity. I jerk my neck, wincing as I look away, face red as the ash on the pitch, heart thumping in my chest, panicking that she'll tell her pals and I'll be a laughing stock.

I kick my ball about, staining it red on the moist, ashy ground, until the bell summons me to class.

In Mr H's engineering science class, I gaze blankly at a jungle of chalk on the blackboard as he drones on like tinnitus. Gradually, the chalk symbols fuse into the shape of Motorcycle Girl. She peels off from the blackboard and glides out towards me. Her hair blows in the air and I can smell apples and cinnamon. But as she draws closer, the smell shifts to rotten apples in vinegar.

'The answer is what, David?' Mr H bellows, ejecting me from my nirvana.

My face burns. If only the question was about the colour of Motorcycle Girl's tights, or how many stripes she has on her helmet, I'd be able to answer instantly, with great confidence and certainty.

Mr H's eyes bulge. 'Well, Cruick-shanks?'

I look up at him, and although I'm pretty scared of this boggle-eyed praying mantis with halitosis peeking out of a white coat, I can't resist the temptation to be funny. 'Is it 42, sir?'

He pokes out his neck like he's just clocked a juicy bug and then draws himself back to his full height, reminding me of his status. As he lifts his arm, the sleeve of his white coat slips down to reveal craggy, vein-ridden skin, but there's no lack of strength when he cracks the desk with his pointer. Thwack!

There's a synchronised thud as everyone's airborne arses return to their seats.

'Are you trying to be funny, son?' he asks in a deadly whisper.

Of course I am, I'm the class jester; everyone expects me to make them laugh in return for not getting my head kicked in. Bullies claim me for a fight just to listen to me wriggle out of it by making them double up laughing; it's my number one weapon.

'No, sir' I reply, scratching my suddenly itchy nose.

Mr H has never heard of *The Hitchhiker's Guide to the Galaxy* and that the answer to life, the universe and everything is 42. He bores into my skull with his bogglies. I imagine the cogged mechanisms crashing around behind his pupils, grinding away with the strain of pushing his eyes almost out of their sockets. Then he stands to attention as if an invisible wire has saved him from falling over. I think he's going to devise a punishment exclusively for me, seeing how everyone had shit themselves when he cracked the desk, but maybe he's surprised at his effect on the rest of the class and will file it away under 'unexpected effects of punitive techniques' to use when the next class comes in.

'Next time . . . pay . . . attention . . . boy,' he says, waggling a bony finger.

He turns away and then looks back over his jaggy shoulder as if he'd expected me to disappear His raised eyebrow confirms my suspicions, he *had* expected me to disappear and seems genuinely pissed off I'm still here. The whole class stare at me as if they too are in on the 'teacher makes naughty boy disappear' trick.

I can't disappear, so I just sit at my desk, a little, red-faced, freckly joker, in love with a girl on a motorcycle.

The next night is the school disco that marks the end of our first year. I cradle my chin and peer in the mirror at the wiry hairs springing from my spotty top lip like weeds on a putting green. My dad's razor juts out of his bright orange plastic shaving cup. Ears pricked to alert mode, I fill the sink, dip the razor in the water and slash the weeds away, delighted not to cut my lip open in the process. As I rinse the razor, I clock a few newly sprouted pubes between my thighs. I'm definitely keeping them.

The thumping bass draws me up the school assembly hall steps like the smell of my mum's baking. Half way up, I freeze as I meet the narrow-eyed glare of Darren Haldane, his head cocked to one side like a Rottweiler sizing up a puppy He scrunches the collar of my pink shirt between a nicotine-stained thumb and forefinger. 'A bit poofy, isn't it?' he sneers.

'I-i-is i-it?' I stammer. My neck stiffens, the pain still there from staring at Motorcycle Girl. Darren Haldane's breath could give Mr H's a run for its money. His long nose and tiny black eyes remind me of Dad's obsession with sharks on telly. I fantasise about sticking my fingers in his eyes like some diver had done in Australia when he was attacked by a great white, or so Dad had told me.

'Too right, Ah widnae be seen dead in it, eh, Greg?' Darren Haldane says, not shifting his gaze.

Greg, Darren Haldane's reluctant sidekick, looks at me and shrugs his shoulders. Darren Haldane, who must've seen the gesture out the corner of his eye, turns and sticks his face into Greg's personal bubble, to the extent that their foreheads are almost touching.

'Aye, Daz, a wee bit poofy Ah suppose,' Greg says.

Darren Haldane looks back to me. 'There ye are, even Greg says so.'

I panic that if I try to say something, my dry throat will betray me with a comedy squeak, so I turn, head back down the stairs and, under a warm, dark sky, I break into a run and make it home in four minutes flat.

'Is that you, David?' Mum calls from upstairs.

'Yip,' I shout back.

'I thought you were at the disco.'

'I forgot something,' I mutter.

'What?'

'Nothing. I'm away now. See you.'

'Don't be too late, and mind, enjoy . . .' Her words trail off as I run back into the darkness.

The assembly hall, the daily venue for rows of silent, stone-faced, uniformed kids listening to dried-out teachers telling us how important school is, has been transformed into an ocean of glowing faces, flashing orange, blue, green and purple under disco lights.

A girl smiles at me. An actual smile! I look behind me in case she's mistaken me for another boy, but as I'm doing so, she grabs me and sucks me into the heart of the dance floor, where all the girls that pervade my waking thoughts and unconscious dreams dance around me. I nearly trip over a handbag, but thankfully notice it at the last moment and manage to catch my balance. The girls giggle, their kaleidoscopic faces drawing me to them. I didn't think changing my shirt from "poofy pink" to banana yellow with blue houses on it would have such an effect.

The music drowns out their gossip as they cup hands over ears, then draw back, laughing. A tall, slim girl with glossy black hair and cat-like eyes holds her palms up in a motion I translate as 'dance here'. Her long, aquamarine silk dress clings on as she shimmies and sways.

I stand transfixed for a few moments, a rabbit in headlights, but then I start to move my feet. The girl with the cat's eyes laughs, but I don't care, my feet feel the rhythm; after all, your face can only stay red for so long and in this light nobody knows what colour it is anyway. After a few minutes, the girls form a circle around me, whooping as I get my Elvis hips on, and cheering and squealing at my moonwalk, which is almost Michael Jackson tribute act standard. I'm so caught up in the moment though that I dance straight into their handbags, scattering them across the floor, throwing a cloud of dust into the multi-coloured light. Thankfully, the girls are oblivious to the mess I've made and I'm too possessed by the music to care. A few of them point at

41

my feet and laugh, but I don't give a monkey's, or at least that's what I tell myself.

A few boys come over to see what's going on, Darren Haldane among them, arms folded, his laugh tinged with menace. He jabs the shoulder of one of the girls in the circle, but she moves away from him and starts to dance with me. She's so close I can smell her hair; it smells of coconut, which, mixed with Dad's aftershave, produces a heady cocktail. I drink it in and close my eyes. I'm in heaven.

When I open my eyes, the other girl has disappeared and Motorcycle Girl is inches away, looking straight at me. This time I don't look over my shoulder. My neck is burning, but I force myself to glance back at her. Sweat trickles down my forehead and I can feel my shirt sticking to the small of my back. I smile. She's closer now, smelling of bubble-gum and candyfloss.

She pulls me close and wraps her warm arms around the back of my neck, nestling her nose under my bum-fluff chin. I almost pull away, my heaving chest pressing against her satin dress. The heat is intense. Then the DJ plays a ballad, the frantic disco lights softening and cooling to the mood.

Feeling brave in the eclipse, I take a look around. The parquet floor is now a sea of swaying couples. When I turn back, Motorcycle Girl presses her soft, warm lips against mine. Praying my rushed shave hasn't left a prickly top lip that'll tickle or scratch her, I close my eyes and concentrate.

Her warm breath gives me new life, her inquisitive lips burrowing as our necks dance in little circles. Death can come any time now; things are never going to get any better than this. But then the music begins to fades, so to

42

be polite I make to break away, but *Will You?* by Hazel O'Connor starts up and she pulls me back towards her and we fumble momentarily, searching for each other's lips.

After we finish kissing, I have a quick peek over her shoulder. Swaying bodies are draped over each other, hands wandering into new territory unsure if they'll be repelled or welcomed, but willing to take the risk.

One of the lights catches the slumped figure of Darren Haldane, who's sitting on one of those chairs that kills your bum in ten minutes. He's leaning forward, elbows resting on his thighs, clenched fists wedged under his spotty chin, straining to see what's going on while trying to appear cool. I turn away in case he catches me looking. Motorcycle Girl reads this as a signal and kisses me again, this time going deeper.

'So ye think ye're Michael Jackson, dae ye?'

We pull apart to find Darren Haldane in our faces, shirt splattered with cola, looking for payback. The stain has nothing to do with me, but that doesn't bother Darren Haldane.

'Naw,' is all I can muster, my tongue numb from extensive exploration of Motorcycle Girl's fantastic mouth.

'Ah'll see you the morra. You're claimed,' he says, poking a bony finger into my collarbone. The words clang in my ears as he disappears into the crowd.

Motorcycle Girl turns back to me. 'Just ignore him David, he's an arsehole,' she says.

She called me by my first name! She actually knows who I am! I want to talk to her, but Darren Haldane has dried up my patter; the fear of tomorrow has struck me mute.

'Ah'm gonnae huv tae go,' is all I can manage, unable to look at her.

Three minutes and 52 seconds later I'm crashing through my front door, wiping my eyes and dragging thick, oyster-like snotters off my top lip.

I sit in my jammies, hugging a mug of cocoa, toast cooling on the coffee table. The images from the telly in the corner flicker on Mum's face.

'Well, did ye have a good time, son?' she asks.

'No bad,' I reply, sipping my cocoa.

'Is it cold outside?'

'No really,' I say.

Clear that she isn't likely to get much conversation out of me, she stands up and says, 'Right, I'll see ye in the morning, son. Mind and pull aw the plugs out.'

'Night, Mum,' I say looking into my mug.

She's gone in a melange of creaking stair, toilet flush and squealing door.

I switch channel, but it's adverts for Volkswagens and instant mashed potato. Suddenly, there she is – hairspray girl, her head thrust back by invisible reins, eyes closed, mouth slightly parted, poised for kissing, just like Motorcycle Girl. I can still smell her. A tear falls onto the milky, chocolatey skin of my cocoa.

Then an idea strikes me. I switch off the telly, pull the plug and think about Darren Haldane. I then continue to think about Darren Haldane all night in my freezing cold bedroom while I pick at the wallpaper and roll bogies.

The next morning, I pinch my secret weapon from my sister's dressing table. It takes me 12 minutes and 38 seconds to arrive at the school gates from my house. The foyer smells of earth, dog shit and floor polish. I look up at the clock. The bell will be going soon, plunging me into a riveting double period of maths.

'Surprise, surprise, look who it isnae,' comes a voice from behind me.

I turn to see Darren Haldane, flanked by Baldy Nicoll and Greg. I've had Baldy helpless with laughter on many occasions, so thankfully I've never felt his scuffed shoe leather on my face, but his stony fizzog* suggests he's received orders from Darren Haldane not to laugh, no matter what.

My stomach feels like I've been on the waltzers for a couple of hours and my heart's banging in my chest, demanding to be set free to avoid a hammering.

'Ah don't see ye dancin noo, ya wee poof,' Darren Haldane sneers.

My mouth runs dry, but I manage a constricted chuckle at Darren Haldane's limited vocabulary. Chest tightening, I brace myself for a fist to the face, but I know Darren Haldane likes to string it out, like the baddies in James Bond films. They all have a fatal flaw though – they always tell Bond how and when they're going to kill him and what they're going to kill him with.

I take a deep breath, clutch the canister and pop the pink plastic top. Amid the tension, I have a fleeting thought about mentioning to my dad that he should audition to be a James Bond baddy so I can watch him getting his arse kicked and then eaten by a shark.

'Ah'm gonnae wipe that smirk aff yer ugly wee kisser, Cruickshanks, so the lassies are no gonnae be looking at you fur a while . . . Whit the fuck! Aaaaaaaaargh, ma fuckin eyes! Jesus, Ah cannae see!'

---

* face

45

I turn the spray to Baldy but he backs off. Greg has a hold of Darren Haldane, who's twitching like he's in an electric chair. He peers through his little piggy eyes as tears stream down his face. Then he lunges forward and grabs me by the throat.

'You're gonnae die, ya little shite,' he spits.

There he goes again, telling me what he's going to do. I feel the blood thrumming in my brain, followed by nausea as his grip tightens.

'Ugh, whit the . . .' Darren Haldane whimpers, letting go of my throat. He drops to the floor, moaning and whimpering, hands clutching his crotch, face purple and glazed over. Greg is off and running and Baldy just turns and walks, shaking his head.

Motorcycle Girl stands tall, helmet in hand, smelling of bubble-gum and two-stroke Castrol. A Harley Davidson biker boot to the nuts had done the damage to Darren Haldane.

'Are you alright, David?' she says, taking my hand.

Her phrasing makes it sound sexy, as if she's saying 'voulez-vous coucher avec moi?'

'Aye, thanks, em, eh . . .'

'Frances,' she says with a smile. 'You know, your kissing partner from last night.'

I'm about to say something witty when Mr H appears 'What's going on here?' he muses, leaning over Darren Haldane, who's still paralysed with pain.

'Sir, David stuck up for me when this boy tried to steel my bike helmet,' Frances says, 'that's all.'

'Is that right, Cruickshanks?'

'Em, yes, sir,' I croak.

'Well done son,' Mr H praises, looking at me with a half smile. 'I hope you can continue this vigilance in our next class. And you, Darren Haldane, get yourself along to the Rector's office, immediately.'

'Ugh,' Darren Haldane squirms, face now looking like someone trying to hold in a fart.

'Come on, get a move on, son, that'll teach you to pick on a girl.'

Darren Haldane pulls himself up and shuffles off. Mr H walks in the opposite direction, sniffing.

'Thanks, Frances,' I say. 'My god, where did ye learn that from?'

'*Karate Kid II*,' she says with a smile. This soppy stuff is harder to do in daylight. I take a deep breath.

'The dance was good, eh?' I smile, looking into her mesmerising, swimming pool blue eyes, which have a glint of mischief in them.

'David?' she says, dismissing my question.

I brace myself for the line that goes "It was only a bit of fun, it didnae mean anything; in fact, I did it fur a bet. All the lassies bet me that I wouldnae kiss a scrawny wee turd like you".

'David?' she says again.

'Aye?' I look at my shoes.

'I've got a spare helmet. I'll drop ye off tonight and we can go bowling later if ye like.'

I beam, butterflies doing somersaults in my stomach. 'Well, I don't know, Frances, ye see, Friday's my night fur washin ma hair.'

***

What I'd thought of doing back then was nicking my sister's hairspray and spraying it in Darren Haldane's eyes. The reality was that Darren Haldane punched me in the face and burst my bottom lip. Motorcycle Girl did not come to the rescue and Mr H was probably crying in a corner somewhere, wondering why a decorated war hero had to suffer verbal bombardment from a bunch of shits that didn't know how lucky they were.

After checking for missing teeth, I ran home in 7.2 seconds and my mum, seeing the state I was in, rolled up the sleeves of her Bri-nylon jumper and almost beat me in a race back to the school. The next couple of hours were a blur as my mum fought my corner like a scalded ferret, dragging me around and pointing at me, then to the various teachers, to emphasise my human rights, while almost separating my shoulder from its socket.

I slumped down just in time for recorder class, but the antiseptic the recorders were dunked in stung my burst mouth and I was excused from playing. Darren Haldane was nowhere to be seen and the girls were acting as if all the snogging that went on last night had never happened. And thanks to my burst lip, there wasn't going to be a rerun any time soon.

Hey Mister

1980

'**C**ome here, son, Ah'll no bite,' Tam insists.
      Cautiously, I shuffle towards the middle-aged storeman with his air of benevolence, but something's not right. He lifts up his shirt and runs a hand down his bandaged torso.

'It's this,' he says, pointing to the crepe ruffled bandage. 'Bloody thing's always coming loose, and the wife's hands are too rough these days.'

'Oh,' I reply, flatly, not sure where this is going.

I look around at the racks of stores* Tam is in charge of. A day ago, I was cleaning toilets, scrubbing floors and emptying out ash from the boilers of a fire station for Margaret Thatcher. Thanks to the Tory Prime Minister's Youth Opportunities Scheme, I no longer get benefits and have to earn £23.50 a week as a janitor's assistant at Thornton Fire Brigade headquarters, even though I'll be joining the Navy in three months. Don't get me wrong, I was happy enough. Bob the janny was a natural comedian and a great cartoonist, and although my soft hands took some punishment from polishing and scrubbing everything that didn't move, the laughs and nonsense made up for it. Then someone decided I should get some work experience with Tam the Storeman.

---

* supplies

'C'moan, son,' Tam says, more forcefully this time. 'It's just a bandage'.

I edge forward and he takes it as a sign of consent. Thankfully, he turns his back to me. His breathing is laboured as I unravel the bandage, which seems to take ages. The bandage stinks of stale tobacco. Then Tam lets out a dry cough, causing me to flinch.

'Ye're daein great, son,' he says, encouragingly, taking a deep breath.

I stand rigid with the bandage rolled up in my hand. Tam turns round, smiles at me, and then puts a hand on my shoulder. 'Nice and tight now, son,' he orders.

I comply, and then the rest of the day goes by like nothing has happened. A few days later, I'm back with Bob the janny and a few days after that, I bump into JB, the other stores assistant, near the fire tower.

'I just told him to fuck off when he asked me, the fucking pervert.' JB crows. 'Mind you, where you're going, there might be loads of that shite.'

A Town Called Malice

1981

Every sailor, no matter how bright or stupid, does basic training. That's why they call it basic. The transformation from schoolboy to sailor begins the second I walk through the gates at *HMS Raleigh*, a shore establishment with a ship's name. It's the last time for six weeks that I'll be walking anywhere for a while. I'll be bimbling*, doubling** and – most importantly – marching everywhere from now on.

Raleigh is a chain link ferry away from Plymouth, a sprawling vibrant Navy town with the promise of an alcohol fuelled good time made to every passing Jack the lad. But, for the six weeks I spend in basic, it might as well be on Mars.

I arrive at *Raleigh* on March 2nd 1981. Funny how you never forget these things. It's cold and damp and is determined to remain like that for 42 days. I lose count of the number of soakings I get – on the parade ground, in the shower with my clothes on, on the cross-country field. The Cornish rain permeates my 16-year-old bones and never leaves.

Cornwall is where I discover my love of alcohol, balanced only by my hatred of the stuff. It's where I encounter mindless cruelty, unconditional friendship, tap water shits, and my first hangover.

---

* walking
** jogging

I realise very quickly that, at 5ft 6 inches and weighing less than nine stone, I feel vulnerable, but my dad's constant bullying has made me wary of making friends too easily, of giving up too much of myself only to be shot down in flames. I'm determined not to forge friendships without playing a game of mental chess first.

Hierarchies during basic training establish themselves as naturally as newly formed lava cooling on the side of a volcano. Leaders emerge, they aren't picked. I've been selected for Anson Division, which I hope isn't like being picked for Balfour, the shittiest house at my primary school. Our instructors, who are all seasoned petty officers and have years of understanding Darwinian evolution, are primed to sit back and wait for the survival of the fittest gene to emerge. They rarely interfere with the natural order of things.

My first experience of how not to survive basic training is on the parade ground, where somehow everyone has miraculously learned to march without any training whatsoever. I, on the other hand, must have slept through these instructions as, when it comes to stepping off*, I tick-tock like a windmill in full sail until the drill officer squeals our division to a halt. Divisions. That word still sounds like a fingernails dragging across a blackboard to me. Tick-tocking is when your right arm and right leg move forward together instead of your right arm and left leg. I know it sounds simple, but to me it might as well be rocket science.

If I can't march in synch, I can't pass out, and if I can't pass out, I can't be in The Royal Navy. Not just me though, my whole class. I'm oblivious to the hatred that's

---

* leading with the left foot from a standing position to begin marching

festering towards me by the rest of my intake. I bull* my boots, clean my kit, have the obligatory crew cut to foster solidarity, eat, drink and joke with my new shipmates, blissfully unaware that I'm about to endure several nights of organised thuggery.

I'm blissfully unaware of the first night-time assault until the next morning. In the middle of the night, four of my classmates, hidden behind makeshift masks, had tried to turn my bed upside down with me in it. Apparently, I had sat up like Linda Blair from *The Exorcist* (minus the revolving head), screamed at the top of my highest tenor voice and then went back to sleep. The invaders were so terrified, they all ran off. I only found this out in the mess hall at breakfast the next day, from a mate who had been woken by my screams just in time to catch some of the X-rated action.

The increasing pressure for me to perform on the parade ground is taking its toll on my health. There was a Rubella epidemic in week three, just before some of the most important tests like swimming and gas mask, which have already instilled an irrational fear in most of us. This is partly due to exaggerated stories of those who have gone before. My imagination is both a blessing and a curse and I begin to dream of drowning in the swimming pool wearing my gas mask. I'm sure others dreamed of similar things; there's always some new recruit shuddering and shaking in their bed and it isn't all masturbation. The Rubella epidemic heightens the tension and recruits fear being back-classed**. It would

---

* polish
** failure to complete a task, or sickness lasting five days or more, resulting in the recruit going back one week in basic training

53

only be for a week, but a week to a new recruit is life changing. He leaves behind his friends of, erm, three weeks – yeah, I know, totally irrational, but the real issue is joining a new class as an outsider, an alien. Unless you're brilliant at all aspects of basic, you'll never fit in with your new class. You don't wish back classing on your worst enemy. But I think my whole class wish it on me. The previous night's attack is just the beginning.

The next day on the parade ground, I tick-tock again and suffer a severe bollocking from Bucket Face, the drill officer. He's called Bucket Face because instructors insist on wearing their chinstraps on their hats regardless of whether there's any wind to potentially blow them off. It's just another way of saying *I am allowed to do what I want but you're not*. He's a Lieutenant Commander and his chin juts out like the bow of a ship. The top of his head, although hidden, tapers into a perfect upturned bucket shape, so the nickname Bucket Face stuck.

As we step off again, I do my marching robot impersonation and this time I know I'm in deep shit. We have a make and mend that afternoon back at the mess and we have to muster our kit ready for inspection. Four recruits ambush me and make it clear that showering with my clothes on is the least of my worries if I don't stop tick-tocking.

Whatever they had planned for me that night was to pale into insignificance. At 0200hrs, the petty officer instructor bursts into the mess carrying his marching stick. The lights flicker on and I squint at the sickly pallor of his tired and angry face, which becomes less tired as the fluorescent lights switch from stomach-churning green to white, by which time we've all managed to stand to attention, wearing ovies[*], carrying gas masks and with boots fully laced up. Someone yawns, although it sounds like a yawn of fear, the kind you get when you're so terrified, you forget to breathe. Our incensed instructor is so taken aback by this apparent subordination that he completely ignores it.

For the first time in my life, I notice my heartbeat and the thrumming of blood coursing through my ears. I stifle a cough and pray that I'll be able to mask it with some activity.

Within minutes, we're doubling up and down the parade ground in pitch darkness. The rain joins in so we can feel tired, scared, cold *and* soaked to the skin. I'm good at doubling, so if I'm being singled out because of my awful marching, it isn't much of a punishment. I actually enjoy it once I get my breathing and heart rate restored from terrified to slightly concerned. We double[**] up and down the slippery concrete in our best boots (now ruined) for what seems like an hour but is probably no more than 20 minutes. The crunching of hobnailed boots on rough tarmac, punctuated by the occasional barking of 'right wheel, right turn, left turn', takes its toll on some of the less fit recruits, who are now coughing and spluttering. This, thankfully, signals the end of midnight manoeuvres. The Navy isn't stupid; if we all end up in sick bay, there'll be no-one left to pass out.

Our instructor issues a half-hearted reprimand about our daytime drill performance, which comes to the attention of Bucket Face, who says we're the worst division he's set eyes on in a decade and is having none of it. I detect a tone in our instructor's voice that he

[*] overalls
[**] jog

doesn't agree with the severity of the punishment we'd endured, but he's outranked. Obviously he doesn't want to get out of his bed and run around in the pissing rain either, he's almost 40 for God's sake!

After our bollocking, we fall out. As we head back to the warmth and light of our mess, I make the fatal mistake of smiling, just as my instructor glares at me. His look of contempt says it all and I know I'm a marked man.

That night, I get another visit. I curl up into a ball as blows rain down upon my head and body. It's impossible not to cry out. I feel the weapon of choice cut into my back: the heels of worn out boots, which should've been in perfect shape for our kit inspection, ruined by the rain-soaked parade ground. The boots rip into my skin, softened a little by pillowcases, which muffle the sound of the beating, but not its ferocity. I yelp as a heel catches my collarbone and pain sears through my system. There's no point resisting.

Then it stops. And I've survived.

I feel like I'm living on borrowed time though. What will they do to me next time?

Next morning, I wake up coughing and spluttering and my legs are like jelly. I muster with the rest of our class, but my petty officer notices I'm not going to make the self-defence class without collapsing into a snotty heap. Reluctantly, he takes pity and orders me up to the sick bay with the jeers of the rest of the class ringing in my ears.

In the sick bay, everyone has gone down with German measles, except me. I have flu – proper flu though, not the skiving off work because you have a sniffle kind. The doctor orders me up to the ward. Well, he must've done, because the next time I'm conscious, it's 48 hours later and I've already downed half a dozen antibiotics.

I spend a whole week in sick bay without visitors, sexy nurses or get well cards. When I finally emerge, half a stone lighter, two miracles happen. I don't get back-classed, and when I step off on that rain-soaked parade ground, I can finally march.

Running on the Spot

1981

Now that I belong to the marching fraternity, thoughts of getting my head kicked in or my bed trashed at midnight take a back seat. I sail through the gas mask test and, despite my earlier fears, I almost piss myself laughing at the swimming test, which wouldn't have made a lot of difference – unless you believe those stories that urinating in a chlorinated swimming pool turns the water purple. Thankfully, I'm not *that* naïve, but I don't venture a piss, just in case.

The final hurdle before passing out is the cross-country run, a five-mile trudge around the sodden playing fields of *Raleigh*, with a tantalising glimpse of Plymouth on the outward stretch.

There's no point in describing the weather unless, like the Eskimos, there are 60 different ways to describe mind-numbing cold and penetrating damp, with a cheeky touch of drizzle.

We're permitted to jog on the spot in our pristine white plimsolls as they get mashed brown with each muddy stamp. This is in order to keep us from dying of hypothermia. I'm not even wearing socks, which means my feet are freezing, the only upside being I won't have to wash any white socks afterwards. I'm also sporting a white T-shirt that took me ages to iron, but now I'm wondering why I bothered.

My dad always tells me that I'll amount to nothing. Occasionally, his words take hold and paralyse me. This time, as I bounce about on the start line, I survey my classmates, counsel myself, and channel my inner Baz: *as long you don't fall, you'll be fine, son.* None of the other runners appear to have bionic legs, so it's just a case of doing my best and seeing what happens. I never made the cross-country team at school, which surprised me as several of those picked were clearly struggling with a regular pastry habit, possibly even a deep fried Mars bar affliction. There's a cup for the winning team, but as long as I don't make a complete tit of myself and manage to finish, I'll be content with passing out with the rest of my class and proudly wearing my uniform on the train journey home.

The shrill of a whistle signals the start and my heart needs no further coaxing. I quickly get into my stride. The route is four times around the football pitches, probably no more than five miles. I nestle in around the middle of the group and I'm prepared to stay there, but with every stride, more of my classmates appear to be going backwards. By the end of the first lap, I swear I clock my instructor smiling in my direction, which just confuses me. I carry on running, my lungs sucking in each damp bag of air. My legs and arms are numb with cold and the white of my plimsolls has been spattered by churned up mud, which has a faint whiff of manure about it.

By the end of the second lap, any white specks of plimsoll have disappeared completely and the freezing cold mud is working its way up my thighs. As I navigate the second turn in the sodden square, one of the other class trips and face plants into the mud. I try laughing, but it catches in my throat. I cough up some phlegm and attempt to spit, but only succeed in attaching the snot to my remarkably mud-free T-shirt. I resist glancing back at the casualty whilst trying to work the green slime off my T-shirt and keep up with what appear to be the race leaders.

The beginning of lap three sets off alarm bells in my head. My instructor *is* smiling, and it's a full-blown, toothy smile. Nothing I can do about it now though, just run. By the time I'm shifting down the back straight, there's only one runner in front of me. I have no idea how this happened. I briefly imagine everyone else playing a game of hide and seek at my expense, or the race is only three laps and everyone has gone in for a shower. It can't be this easy, can it? I shrug off the daydreaming and concentrate on one thing and one thing only. If I can keep this pace up and the guy ahead of me doesn't have a sprint finish, I could win.

I know I don't have a sprint finish, on account of coming last in every flat race I have ever run. At primary school, my mum has pictures of me coming last in school sports days, though I did win the wheelbarrow race in the summer of '76, but only because Campbell White (no relation to Alan or Baz) had grabbed my legs and lifted them so high that my hands weren't even touching the ground when we crossed the finishing line. Funny how neither of us won the dux for school sports that year.

No Campbell White this time, but I'm feeling good. With the exception of the gigantic bogey stain on my T-shirt, my freezing brown shins, plimsolls that will never see the colour white again, and arms that ache with every stride, I feel energised. The blond kid in front of me is tiring and there's only half a lap left. I smile to myself and even chance a look behind me. The rest are miles back and struggling. My God, I'm close to winning a race! The kid who couldn't march, who wouldn't amount to anything, who screamed like the wee girl in *Poltergeist* when his classmates attempted to turn him upside down in his bed, was about to come first. That's why my instructor is smiling, he's seen something my dad never has, a kid with the will to win, to never give up, a scrawny survivor who's determined to show everyone else that they'd better sit up and take notice.

I'm gaining on blondie with every stride and the home straight is closing in. I'm one bend away from glory. Just at that moment, I feel my left plimsoll being sucked in by the mud. I stumble and almost topple. A muscle deep within my left thigh twinges, threatening to snap. My back spasms and I can't control a yelp as I battle to remain upright. Thankfully, my mud-caked plimsoll clings on and – miraculously – I'm still running. Blondie gains a few yards, but the shock of nearly falling has dissolved and I know deep down that I have enough to beat him. I don't care if he has a sprint finish, there are only 300 metres to go and he won't be able to keep a sprint up for that time.

I focus on his blond crew cut, and then down to his mud-spattered legs, which are churning up what's left of the ground. Two strides later, I'm on his shoulders. My breath will be tickling his earlobes even if he can't feel it. I hone in on his rhythm and, like a fox with a rabbit, I sense he's struggling. For a second, I think about nestling in behind him for a few more strides, but I decide to just go for it. This is my day. I kick for the last 100 metres and my legs respond. At the finishing line, there's a tape, white of course, being held by two sailors who had given up. The pain of having to complete this task all over again is etched on their defeated, exasperated faces. I beam as I cross the line. I slam on the brakes, slump like someone's punched me in the stomach, and hog every ounce of air with what's left of my lungs. Three minutes and 21 seconds later, I'm mobbed by my classmates, who think bruising me with repeated thumps to my arms represents adulation. It's not much different to getting the shit kicked out of me really, just that they're doing it with a smile this time.

'Well done, Jock!' evangelises a voice I don't even recognise.

I'm released from the happy thuggers[*] and look up to see my instructor. Pride is registered across his face, a look I've rarely seen on a grown man.

'Thanks, P.O.[**],' I rasp, hands on hips, bent double, bursting with pride. I look at the ground and then up at him again. I return his smile, thumbing some mud away from my saliva spattered mouth.

'Better get back before you freeze to death, lad,' he advises, looking straight at me, then he catches himself and looks over my head. 'That means all of you,' he adds, before turning away and heading towards the accommodation block.

The group who'd planned to shower me in my clothes approaches me, and I instinctively tense.

'You've won us the cup, Jock,' one of them gushes, wrapping an ice cold muddy arm around my neck.

And I have. I bloody have.

---

[*] hybrid of thugs and muggers
[**] Petty Officer

Wasteland

1982

I cling on to the ship's guardrail as the North Sea swell does its best to coax my bile into making a public appearance. I look around the upper scupper[*], praying that none of the more experienced sailors appear and spot the green-around-the-gills pallor of the sea virgin. I swallow some salt spray from the force eight gale and gag.

I'm blaming it on the sea, but the six pints of Norwegian beer I had with my new shipmates last night might've had something to do with it. For the last four years, I've wished for nothing else than to be a sailor on board a Royal Navy warship. I'm hoping that my second wish of being put out of my hangover misery by being struck by lightning comes true.

Three weeks ago, I was marking time in Faslane, awaiting my instructions to join *HMS Nottingham*, a modern destroyer with bells and whistles on. After an emergency draft to replace another sailor, I'm on board *HMS Fearless*, an old steam powered amphibious assault ship that creaks and groans like my gran.

I joined the ship in Plymouth and headed straight to Norway. I'm the baby greenie[**] in a mess full of sailors who've probably known each other for years. My plan is

---

[*] top deck of a ship
[**] electrician

to keep my head down and my mouth shut. The trouble is I'm not very good at either.

When two of my new oppos[*], Sticky Green and Scouse Castles, take me ashore in Norway, I forget that I don't have an off switch where alcohol is concerned and worry that I'm just like my dad.

We sailed to Norway to carry out exercises with the US Navy to show Russia that we're keeping an eye on them. I'm not sure if Russia was paying attention, but The Royal Marines get to play war games, which stops them from beating us up for a while.

We're one day's sailing away from Portsmouth and I pray that my guts will hold on that long. There's been a rumour going around that some Argentine scrap merchants have landed on South Georgia and claimed it for Argentina. I have no idea where South Georgia is and I reckon no-one else on board does either.

'Awright, Jock?' quizzes Paul Calcutt, nudging me.

'Yeah, Paul,' I lie, taking in an extra deep breath, hoping it will distract my stomach from heaving.

'Sticky sends his regards,' Paul adds with a smirk, before he slopes off, seemingly unaware that the ship is lolling around like a balloon on a football pitch.

That's me fucked then. The whole mess will know I can't handle my booze. I retch at the acrid sting of sick at the back of my throat and distract myself by counting down the 17 hours and 42 minutes until we reach dry land. I think about asking someone down the mess if they know where South Georgia is, but they'll only take the piss.

---

[*] mates

64

To Be Someone
(Didn't We Have a Nice Time?)

1982

Back in Portsmouth, before we invade the pubs, there's work to be done. Half of the ship's company are due to go on leave, but not before the ship is tied up and shore cables have been connected, relieving the boilers of their duty to provide steam for the turbines and prepare them for cleaning. Cleaning the two giant boilers on board *Fearless* is similar to painting the Forth Rail Bridge: as soon as you've finished, it's time to start again.

The organisational skills of the ship are a marvel to those uninitiated, who gaze open-mouthed at the minutiae of tasks performed by inappropriately dressed sailors. The seamen, who are dolled up in their number ones[*] come into contact with grease-ridden hawsers and ragged ropes, which leads to time off for 'make and mend' afternoons. I know what you're thinking – wouldn't it be better if they wore overalls instead? But even the suggestion of such practical attire would destroy naval tradition, leading to a completely inappropriate number of lashes followed by a tattoo on your foreskin. The activities of the seaman contain an element of showmanship and, not unlike the royal family, their tasks are performed in front of spectators who are made up of

---

[*] dress uniform

sailors' families waiting at the quayside and disinterested French tourists who had obviously missed all the trains up to London.

The engineers and greenies (I aspire to become a fully-fledged greenie, but right now I'm a mere junior) carry out their tasks in ovies, so our make and mend time is taken up with the far more pressing task of finding the nearest pub.

The six-ton crane whirs overhead. The metallic arm prods the air like a giant Dalek looking for a victim, the ridiculous whisk used for trying to kill Doctor Who replaced by a conventional hook which could kill the Time Lord in one fell swoop, but instead benignly searches for items to pick up from the quayside.

Provisions are brought on board in crates; beer first, followed by some of the less important items like bread, milk and spuds, while Scouse and I, who normally manage to shirk activity of any sort, wrestle with the shore cables, connecting them up to the supply boxes. Red first, then yellow, and finally blue, before power from the dockside relieves us of the burden of watch-keeping. Boring! Just to enlighten you, switchboard watch-keeping means listening to a frequency of 60 hertz for four bloody hours during any given 24-hour period. But the boredom is alleviated by the porn drawer. If I say the hinges are well oiled, well, you get the message.

'Fancy a pint, Jock?' Scouse whispers.

The bastard knows I'm on duty and that I'll have to stay on board to perform some meaningless task, like fighting a fire or something. I'm pretty sure the Portsmouth Fire Brigade would win hands down against me and a two-gallon fire extinguisher with a rusty release pin.

'Think I'll pass on that one, ya miserable Scouse git,' I reply, feigning bravado, but inside I'd have given my right arm for a night of clubbing on Joanna's sticky carpet. Experienced sailors crow *You have to be pissed and desperate to end up in there, mate,* but to the drunken virgin sailor, it's a gilt-edged chance to lose your cherry.

Scouse winks as he heads towards the mess, arms already out of the sleeves of his ovies in anticipation of a major piss-up. As the last cable is connected, I troop down after him and sit on my bunk in my boxer shorts with my ovies at my ankles. This isn't some kinky initiation ceremony performed on baby sailors after returning home, more a tried and trusted method of preventing my bed cover from looking like a giant oil rag. As I sit contemplating an extremely boring evening, Scouse smiles down benevolently, his icy blue eyes betraying a slightly warmer heart.

'Don't worry Jock, if Ah don't trap a bird, I'll share a Chineeesey wid ya,' he says in his pathetic mock Scots accent. Scouse is at least three years older than me and has two years' service, which to me counts as veteran status. He befriended me when I ran into a bit of trouble with some stokers[*] I'd called "fuckin bilge monkeys." I'd decided to get a little too cocky for my own good by bad-mouthing a beefy, imposing Geordie leading stoker who subsequently threatened to rip my arm off and beat me to death with the soggy end. Scouse persuaded him that choking me for a bit and me doing his laundry for a week would be punishment enough. After that, I learned to humour him.

It seems like making people laugh is a good strategy for not becoming the mess punch bag, although every time someone calls me Jock I feel like I'm responsible for an entire nation. When I go out on the piss, I'm getting drunk

[*] Marine Engineering Mechanics (MEM)

for Scotland and its reputation will rise and fall with my own. It's not just me though. Scouse is just Scouse, he's not Paul any more than I'm David. Every time someone calls me Jock, I also feel like I'm being put in my place.

Welsh people are called Taffs and I don't know what Irish people are called in the Navy because I haven't met any yet. There isn't a nickname for English sailors. Funny that.

Jess is about 25 but looks ten years older. His face has a battleship grey complexion but what fight there once was in him has been worn down by the mess hierarchy, let's call them the hyenas, followed more menacingly by the vultures, who take a sly pop at him on a daily basis and then chance more frequent face-to-face confrontations until Jess becomes no more than a verbal punch bag. Even I'm at it, the mess junior gobshite who hasn't even been in a dogwatch*, with the big Geordie as back up. I take on Jess and win.

My bed is also a makeshift couch, where everyone sits to watch the goggle box. There's always some stoker who's just come off watch who wants to stay up all night, drink beer and watch crap, which really pisses me off. I have to cajole, plead or bribe them to go to their pit so I can get some sleep. It's fucking unbearable.

One night though, I'd had enough. I came down the hatch to find Jess sitting in his manky ovies watching TV on my bed. I looked around; everyone had their heads down.

'Hey, gonnae get aff ma bed, Jess, I'm knackered,' I moaned.

'Fuck off ye wee shite,' came the reply. The emphasis placed firmly on the word 'wee'.

---

* a four-year period of senior service

'Ah may be wee, but Ah'm no a baldy bastard,' I replied, my relish for justice pulling me up to my full five feet six and a half inches.

It was enough to set off a chain reaction in the mess, like a football chant when your team is playing great and has just missed a chance – but you gee them up because you know the next chance is going to land in the back of the net. The voices gathered momentum.

'He's baldy, baldy, very-very-baldy, he's ve-ry baldy,' everyone chanted to the tune of a TV advert about bran flakes.

As everyone stirred in the darkness, the chant got louder. Jess's sunken face flickered with the light from the goggle box. The chant was in full cry; 15 men giving it 'baldy, baldy', the malice spitting out of their mouths like venom. Jess looked at me; he fancied his chances but he hesitated. I made my move. Legging it past him, I launched myself up onto his bed, deep into the recess and tossed his bedding onto the floor. I had attacked and successfully secured the high ground.

'If you want tae watch telly all night ye can fuckin sleep with the fucker,' I said, echoed by the kind of cheer that follows a bone-crunching tackle. I was ready for a scrap, but as Jess lunged out of his seat, Geordie's voice emerged from the darkest nook. 'Leave im alone man, or Ah'll break yer fuckin legs, ya baldy bastard.'

There was a boorish jeer. Trafalgar, Waterloo, Wembley were nothing compared to the battle of the bunkbeds, and I was the all-conquering general. For now.

Jess looked at me. I knew he hated me in that moment, but my determination to throw off the tag of whipping boy was stronger than his hatred. I had climbed one tiny rung in the mess hierarchy, and at that precise moment it felt like a million dollars – and just as the stockbroker made his million-dollar profit, Jess had just seen his million go straight down the toilet.

Jess was looking for a way back, but he couldn't rely on back-up. I often wondered why he didn't just corner me and kick the shit out of me when no-ne was watching. A few months later, we all moved into a mess exclusively for greenies as the stoker/greenie rivalry had reached boiling point.

Now I have a new pit, back on the bottom bunk, next to the telly. And now there are twice the number of sailors in the same confined space. Things are about to get juicy.

Mr Clean

1982

I'm floating across a green landscape, peppered with buttercups, the sky the blue of a million clichés and cloudless to boot. Up and over a hill I float; there's washing on a clothesline, blowing in the turbocharged air of a summer's day. The brightness is dazzling. The sun stabs at my eyes through gaps in the washing, and then I fall back into pools of shadow on the hard earth.

It begins to rain; drops of yellow, orange and then red fall from the sky. It's pleasant at first, but then thickens, splattering my face, causing me to gag. I open my eyes to see a fat red face emptying the contents of a night on the piss all over me and my bed. 'Maaaaaaac!'

***

'Where's Mac?' asks Scouse, as if he didn't know.

'Hidin,' says Big George, pointing out the obvious, cos that's what he's gonna get when Ah get fuckin hold of the fat bastard.'

Scouse looks at me, then back at Big George, who takes his cue as if a microphone has been thrust into his face.

'Last night, he only went and spewed iz load all over wee Jock ere,' he says, putting me in a neck lock while rubbing his knuckles over my shaved head, which hurts like fuck, but I laugh through it. The stokers and greenies have been pushed together again. Someone suggests

71

putting up a divider in the middle of the mess, like the Berlin Wall only with more barbed wire, but another greenie jokes that we'd have to shoot anyone trying to defect. Well, I think he's joking until I see others nodding.

It's important to maintain a manner of annoyance with Mac in order to conform with Big George's feelings. Mac isn't a bad lad, but he's tubby and, let's face it, with a mess full of blokes who have the sensitivity of an end of pier comedian, tubby spells nightmare.

The mess ladders rattle and we all stand to attention. Somebody shouts 'Rounds!' Rounds is when the duty officer or officer of the day comes to check the mess is clean and tidy, or at least that it appears clean and tidy as he doesn't really give a shit; it's a waste of his time, our time and time itself.

'3H2 aft* mess ready for inspection. MEM (L) Castles reporting, sir,' Scouse says.

'Thank you, Castles,' bools the young duty officer, who goes on to give a great impersonation of appearing to be interested in the welfare of the mess inhabitants while probably thinking he's missing out on a perfect hand of gin rummy back in the wardroom.

'Going on leave soon, gentlemen?' he asks.

'Yes, sir,' we reply in enthusiastic unison, thinly plated with sarcasm. After all, he'll be swanning off to some country retreat while most of us will be making do with a fortnight in a pre-fab council house.

'Well, enjoy yourselves,' comes the stock reply.

'Thank you, sir.' Scouse salutes and the officer does a lazy flick with his wrist and turns away.

'Tosser,' hisses Big George as the officer climbs the ladders out of earshot, or so he'd hoped. We all gawk at

---

* towards the back of the ship

the big Geordie as his face turns pink, but the ladders mercifully remain silent. Big George, probably feeling his reaction was a little premature, decides to leave the next ten minutes of mess banter to the lower echelons of the hierarchy. The ladders shudder once more, this time the shabby boots encrusted with potato peelings betray their owner. It's Mac, but he's brought a peace offering. Somehow, he's managed to balance a tray of sausage rolls, sandwiches and vol-au-vents down ten decks of ladders from the officers' wardroom where they all preen around pretending it's a floating gentlemen's club. If Mac was a girl with a cigarette dangling from his lips, his puppy dog eyes would spark a rush of twelve offers to light it, but he's clever enough to aim his apology at the big Geordie.

'Ye needn't think Ah'll be impressed by a few fuckin vol-au-vonts, Mac!' says Big George, his eyes feasting on the impressive carrion from the wardroom. It has to be said that Mac risks getting even deeper into the shit if he's found to have been stealing from the officers. I sit hunched on my bunk, waiting for the apology, but Mac hesitates on the bottom rung, unsure of Big George's next move. All eyes are on the big Geordie, some of the less benevolent ratings egging him on.

'Tear iz fuckin balls off and make a scrotum sandwich!' comes a throaty rant from Smudge, a six-footer from Stoke with a gift for insults. After the choking fit, he sucks on his fag and resumes breathing normally. The effect of the smoke mutes his outburst and Mac seizes his chance.

'Jock, I'm really sorry mate,' he squeaks, looking at Big George. 'I brought some stuff down.'

'It's no fuckin good enough, Mac,' I say, strutting around like a cockerel looking for a fight.

'Aye it fuckin is,' says the Geordie, regaining his territory, 'but ye can dhoby* Jock's beddin and ye better never spew up in here again or Ah'll sit on yer ed till it buwsts, ahreet?'

In submission, Mac drops his gaze to the messdeck.

'Right, let's get this lot seen off and Mac can get us some puddin,' Big George bellows. As we tuck in, Mac creeps up the ladders and back to civilisation.

I feel a bit sorry for him. Outside the Navy, Mac is probably respected by his friends and treated like a grown up. You can imagine him washing his car on a Sunday in sync with his next-door neighbour. His wife would call him (by his proper name, John) into the house to ask his opinion on what to buy a niece or a nephew for their birthday. Later, he would hold court in front of a dozen sausages, ten steaks and a few pork chops while his wife passes beer and wine to his chums. The sun would shine on his puppy dog neck, the beer helping to lull him into a state of euphoria. He'd catch the glint in his wife's eye and receive confirmation from his friends that the meat is done to perfection.

But the reality is he's probably standing on the grey asphalt of the flight deck looking out to the Portsmouth harbour landscape wishing he's on that housing estate, but the price you pay for a nice, comfortable life is living with these bastards!

---

* wash

News of the World

1982

'Jock! Jock! For fuck's sake ger up!'

I awake to find Scouse swinging on the bed bar of my pit. 'We're goin to war, mate,' he chuckles.

'Fuck off, Scouse!' I grump. 'Wait a minute, whit time is it?'

Scouse looks at his watch. 'Eight o'clock. What do you wanna know that for?' His eyes narrow.

'Cos I'm off duty and I'm gonnae get pissed tonight at the Mucky Duck while you're sat here havin a wank.'

Scouse laughs like someone in a movie who knows a lot more than you about how things end. Then he leaps off the bed bar like an Olympic gymnast and legs it up the mess ladders. At five to eight (Scouse had lied about the time), the tannoy sounds. The shriek of the seaman's whistle through the speaker could drill teeth. It's followed by an announcement in affected tones of English public school. 'The ship's company is required to muster on the flight deck at 0800hrs for a special briefing.'

In the Navy, you never want to be late; honestly, they could make a soap opera about it. In fact, Shakespeare could have added another play to his repertoire concerning the woe begotten plight of the jolly late sailor. At one minute to eight, I'm standing at ease on the flight deck in the disappearing haar of an April morning. My beret manages to conceal a very dodgy haircut courtesy of Scouse the Chinese barber, not to be confused with my

75

mate, Scouse Castles, who I wouldn't trust anywhere near my hair with a pair of scissors. The ship's Chinese barber is called Scouse Number One because he only has one style of haircut. If you ask for anything else, he slaps you around the head and asks if you have a girlfriend. Chinese barbers, laundrymen and tailors have been on ships for years doing all the jobs sailors hate, but why they're all called Scouse I have no idea.

'Ship's company, ship's company, ho!'

The young lieutenant brings us to attention. He assumes an air of haughty self-satisfaction as if the task comes off a little better than expected. 'Ship's company stand at ease! Stand easy.'

We silently comply.

'Now, gentlemen,' he says, his confidence reflecting his use of irony. We are a bunch of scabby comprehensive school rejects with all sorts of reasons for finding ourselves on the flight deck, mostly to do with lack of choices brought on by poverty or the need to escape from mental dads. He, on the other hand, sees this as a stepping stone to running his own estate. 'I have some very important news.' He looks down at the folder of the ship's standing orders and pauses for three seconds.

He raises his bright eyes to a captive audience. 'At approximately zero eight hundred hours British Standard Time on Friday April 2nd 1982, a party of Argentinian scrap metal merchants landed on the South Atlantic island of South Georgia, a British dependency, close to the Falkland Islands.' He pauses for a few more seconds. 'Simultaneously, a highly trained unit of Argentinian troops engaged a garrison of Royal Marines in the Falkland Islands' capital, Stanley, resulting in the capture of the garrison, the Governor, Mr Rex Hunt, and the Islands themselves.'

What the fuck does this have to do with us?

'The Argentinians have since failed to recognise the Islands as a sovereign dependency of Great Britain,' he continues, 'and have claimed the territory for Argentina.'

Oh, right, I see.

'The Prime Minister, the Right Honourable Margaret Thatcher, has convened an emergency meeting of the War Cabinet with a view to deploying a task force. This task force, once assembled, will sail from Portsmouth to the South Atlantic to recapture the Falklands and liberate its Sovereign citizens. God Save the Queen.'

He kind of overdid the last bit but, all in all, it was impressive. Murmurs begin to break the silence left by the Queen. I look at Scouse and see the hint of a nervous smile.

'Jock?' he says.

'Pipe down,' barks the duty chief, not wanting to be upstaged by the young lieutenant. 'Right, listen up, the duty watch will prepare to store ship. Six ton crane driver, close up[*]!'

Scouse is today's crane specialist. I look over and he nods, signalling that his role alone may secure a medal.

'Ship's company, ho!' The young lieutenant projects theatrically. 'Ship's company turn to the right in threes, right turn, dismissed.'

I can imagine the young lieutenant galloping off to the nearest phone to boast to Mummy and Daddy back at the country estate how wonderful he was at telling the troops they're off to war and how those long summer evenings spent with Miss Joan Hunter Dunn driving through the

---

[*] report to the designated area

countryside in Daddy's car will have to stand aside as the pressing task of getting ready to give the enemy a bloody nose takes over. Me? A chip? You've got to be joking. In reality, I haven't a clue what he did, all I know is that two days ago I couldn't tell you where the fuck the Falkland Islands are, but now I'm in no doubt. As the ship's company cannons off into various directions, Scouse remains motionless on the flight deck, stunned and silent. The butterflies in my stomach are shitting themselves.

Every Little Bit Hurts

1982

'Scouse, mate,' I chirp. 'Ah don't think anything will come of it.'

I wait for a reply, but nothing comes.

'Nah,' I go on. 'What they'll do is send over some bombers and threaten tae nuke the place.' But the words chosen to provoke a response fall on deaf ears.

I change tack. 'Did ye get fixed wae any women last night?'

Still no answer.

'C'moan and gie us a wee test drive on the crane then,' I plead.

'Jock? D'ye think ye could break ma leg so that Ah dinnae hae tae go?' Scouse says, in his rotten Scottish accent.

'Awa an bile yer heid,' I mock back, but as he looks up, I can see his tight lips and narrow eyes quizzing my willingness to perform such a task.

'I reckon if you dropped a hatch on me shin, that'd be enough and I could go home to the missus while all the little sprogs die horribly with their entrails spilling out.'

'Scouse, ye know Ah'd help ye any way Ah can but Ah dinnae hae the bottle for that kind ay nonsense. Why don't ye ask Smudge?'

'Because, Jock,' a slight smile unfurling, 'I would want to be able to walk once the break heals. If Smudge did it, I'd be crippled for life.'

'Are you trying to say that Smudge is a clumsy bastard?'

'No, Jock, I'm trying to say that he's the fucking ballet dancer of hatch droppers, what do you think?'

'Ah think you're fuckin mental,' I tell him. 'Anyway, Ah'm away tae phone ma mum.'

As I cross the gangway in search of the phone beside the dockyard pub, Scouse shouts down to me. I turn to see him about to go into the driver's compartment of the crane. He makes a sawing action across his right leg and then disappears inside.

'Mum, how's things? Nah, dinnae believe what ye see on the telly, they newsboys are jist trying tae hype it up tae make it mair excitin. We'll get half way down there and the Argies'll surrender, Ah'm tellin ye. Anyway, forget it jist now, Ah'm away tae store ship, but don't worry about me, Ah'm fine, see ye, see ye.'

My mum always tries to hang on to the conversation as long as possible but my gnat-like concentration span kicks in pretty damn quick. I'm always restless when I phone her; always dying to give her a bell but desperate to get off again, especially when she gives it the 'I love you, son' and 'look after yourself, son' spiel. Her voice was cracking a bit just before I put the phone down. Either she's worried about me, or Dad has set about her again. I swear I'll sort him out when I get back. *If* I get back.

Instead of going back on board, I bimble* off for a wander along the dockside. Several Type-42 destroyers are tied up close to us. They too have begun the store ship process, which is an absolute bastard. It's like building the pyramids but with fewer privileges.

A line of about 100 men, two feet apart, hump cartons, boxes, sacks and more fucking boxes from

---

* walk

lorries at the quayside, over the gangway, onto the flight decks and disperse said boxes throughout the ship to the fridges and store rooms. This is done in the style of 17th century firemen tackling the Great Fire of London with armfuls of buckets, and with about as much success. The heavier items are lifted on board by cranes. Therefore, if you're switched on, you become a ship's crane driver. That Scouse is one smart cookie.

When I get back to where *Fearless* is tied up, Scouse is spinning slowly to the left, stopping, and then spinning slowly to the right. The crane's jib pierces the blue sky, blocking and unblocking the sun with its superstructure. Pallets of fruit and veg sit impassively on the flight deck, awaiting their fate in the bowels of the ship. As I cross the gangway onto the flight deck, the crane stops and Scouse leans out from the door to give me his impersonation of Jack Nicolson in *The Shining*, where he puts an axe through the door, forces his face through the slit and shouts 'Here's Johnny!' to a terrified Shelley Duvall. I smile back at the nutter and then leg it down the mess to get my ovies on for storing ship.

As I strap myself into a fireproof navy blue one piece, the mess ladders shake as Scouse propels himself down into the messdeck. 'Jock, c'mon, Ah'll show ye where we can do the bizzo.'

'Ye're no still on about that, are ye?' Ah've got tae get up top and dae some liftin and shiftin.'

'Pleeeeeeease,' he says, like a child pleading for extra pocket money.

'Are you really serious aboot this?' I ask.

'C'mon,' whispers Scouse, the urgency in his voice hinting that he is, at this moment in time, deadly serious. We climb up one deck and Scouse opens the clips on the metal door leading to the tank deck. The smoke from the exhaust of the Eager Beaver[*] makes me feel like I know what it's like to be Smudge kick-starting his lungs with the first smoke of the day.

We cross a large open space in the middle of the ship, which only a day ago managed to belch out 40 Snow Cats[**], and head for a door on the opposite bulkhead. *Fearless* is like two frigates approximately 80 feet apart, with a large platform joining them together. Above and below the platforms are several decks and in the middle is a huge belly, which could be used to store anything from cars to tanks to drag queens' frocks for the ship's concert. The belly is joined to the flight deck by a ramp, and a second ramp containing landing craft that can be lowered directly into the water without the ship sinking.

Scouse pushes back the six metal clips, opens the door and closes it again.

'What the fuck are ye doin?' I snap.

'Shoosh, Jock, Ah forgot where Ah was goin. Down ere, mate.'

Scouse leads me deep into the dark recesses of the lower tank deck until we come to a solitary open hatch. We stare into it as if expecting little green men to emerge, but instead it's just the smell of a little green man's fart, a mixture of diesel and belched ale.

I wince at the reek and yelp as Scouse grips my arm. He realises his grip is stronger than he intended and lets go. I rub my sore arm while listening to his plan.

---

[*] informal term for a military tractor
[**] small, tracked vehicles

'Right, mate, this is where you get me off of this rust bucket, just drop the hatch on me ankle and they'll P7R* me.'

I continue to rub my arm while trying to stare him out, but it isn't happening. There's no getting out of this.

The hatch rises two feet from the burnished metallic surface of the tank deck like a square volcanic crater. The metal edges have been scraped bare of the surface battleship grey paint and red primer countless times by bored seamen, before being recoated with exactly the same layers of primer and grey. The metal surround of the hatch is only half an inch thick and the hatch cover, which clamps tightly around it, provides a watertight seal that can save your life by sealing off floodwater – or it could sever trapped limbs like cheese wire.

'You should consider tying yourself to one of the missile launchers, Scouse, it'll be safer,'

Scouse grabs me tightly around the throat and looks straight into my eyes; make that *through* my eyes and into the back of my skull, penetrating the silly remarks section of my brain.

'I mean this, Jock, I fucking mean it, alright? I need you to do this for me, okay mate?' His teeth are clenched but I'm not sure if he's hiding a smile or not. 'Please, Jock,' he says, slackening his grip.

'What happens tae me if Ah dae it?' I ask.

'No-one's gonna know, mate,' he says with remarkable certainty.

'But whit happens if jist as Ah drap it, you decide ye dinnae want tae dae it anymore? Ah'll be right in the shite,' I crow.

---

* medically discharge

'Ah swear tae ye mate, Ah won't. Now, can we just ger on with it?'

'Okay, okay!' I say, motioning for Scouse to release his grip.

'Just me ankle mind,' Scouse adds.

Now I'm thinking I should've got something in writing, some sort of get-out clause in case this goes horribly wrong.

'Jock!' he urges, a touch of desperation in his voice.

I rub my hands together as if warming them might produce a better result. 'Right, put it on this corner near the hinge,' I say, 'and mind and be still. D'ye want me tae count tae three so that ye can prepare fur it?'

'Naw mate, just do it.'

'Are ye gonnae look at your ankle or look away?'

Scouse looks to the skies. *Did he just say a prayer?* 'Don't know yet; will ye just ger' on with it!'

I look around, expecting the entire mess to jump out and shout SURPRISE! But they don't. I take a deep breath. 'Okay, right, Ah've never done anything like this before. Ah'm nervous.'

Above us, I can hear the gunning of diesel engines as a second Eager Beaver helps out the first to load on more stores. I check to make sure we're alone. Scouse has his right ankle wedged into the corner where the hinge side of the hatch will connect with his foot. His left arm holds onto a guardrail around the hatch, his other flits between his right side and his nose, which has begun to irritate him. He looks down and I turn to the hatch cover securing clip, which attaches the hatch to a post when it's open. I pull at the spring-loaded clip, but it won't budge.

'Fuck,' I whisper through gritted teeth.

'What is it?' Scouse asks.

'I might need a hammer,' I tell him, one hand on the hatch clip, the other stroking my chin.

'What for?' he barks, right up in my face now.

'It's the hatch cover,' I say. 'It's broken.'

'Ya fuckin wimp, give it ere.' Scouse jerks my hand away from the clip and grabs onto it.

I push him back. 'Dinnae call me a wimp, ya fuckin nutter ye!'

'Awright Jock, awright mate,' Scouse reasons, palms held up towards my chest, clearly stunned by my force.

I take a deep breath. 'Okay, jist dinnae call me a wimp okay?'

Nodding, he moves forward gingerly and manages to free the clip, holding the weight of the cover until I take over. Then he resumes his martyr's position. His pose reminds of the football game I had when I was a kid, *Striker*, where you pressed the footballers' heads down and their legs sprung back and then forward to kick the ball. Scouse looks like a *Striker* footballer who's been stuck in the kicking position. I smile at him but he's concentrating on his ankle. His shoulders heave in and out and I reckon his heart must be doing about 140. I decide to let the hatch cover go on a silent count of three. With his boots on, the worse scenario will be a fractured ankle, but he'll have to cope with the aftermath himself as I've got my escape route marked out. I'm not good with compound fractures; I still have memories of fainting when I saw my sister's appendix scar.

The hatch cover is getting heavy. I feel like I'm in charge of a grenade with the pin out, the pressure forcing me to make a decision on Scouse's future; a career as a professional footballer is out, that's for sure. I don't even know if Scouse is Liverpool or Everton. I begin to think of the noise it'll make when the metal slams down on Scouse's boot, twisting and contorting its shape like the slow motion shock waves on the crash test dummies' adverts. Will it stop there, or pierce the rubber and converge on the skin, rupturing ligaments and splintering bone like an alligator with an impala that you see on David Attenborough? I'd have loved to have been the cameraman who shot that footage; the unsuspecting impala being lifted clean out of the water and crushed between the jaws of the alligator.

'Fuck!' Scouse screeches so loud I nearly crap my pants.

'Right Jock, that's fuckin it,' he says, locking the hatch clip back onto the post. 'Ah ain't askin no Jock shitebag ever again to help iz mate out.' He lifts his foot off the hatch combing. I try to grab his arm, but he dodges me.

'Honestly, Scouse, Ah can do it, Ah jist lost track for a bit, Ah'm ready now, really, really ready, in fact Ah *want* to do it,' I reason, verging on begging.

'Too fuckin late, Jock. Ah'm sick of you fannying about,' he says, and bounds his way up the ramp into the blinding sunshine.

'Right Scouse, see you later, eh?' I say.

'Yeah, Jock, Mucky Duck for a sesh.'

'But aren't you on duty tonight?' I ask.

Scouse turns, but his expression is silhouetted against the sky, wrapped in smoke from the Eager Beaver. 'Not any more,' he says. 'Jess has done us a swap.'

I can feel him smiling, even if I can't see his sniggering face.

During the afternoon, I practise our 'putting out the Great Fire of London storing ship' technique alongside Smudge, a man of few words and much coughing. Lugging the boxes of tins is the worst. The sharp cardboard edges leave welts on my wrists and forearms, and with Scouse's earlier grip, my arms are the colour of battered beetroot.

Smudge is struggling, coughing hard. I take his mind off our hardship by suggesting we drop some of the stores over the side. Smudge goes one further, deciding that only really expensive items – fluorescent tubes, batteries and medical equipment – are worth the risk of getting caught. We bottle out of the medical supplies in case we really do go to war, but there are at least four boxes of fluorescent tubes lying among the silt of Portsmouth harbour. I never threw anything over, honest.

Boy About Town

1982

'Jock!' Scouse screams in my right ear. 'Are you comin to get laid or whah?'

The transition from Paul Weller's soulful voice in my earphones being replaced by a screaming Scouser causes me to jolt so much, I almost knee him in the face. 'Jesus Christ, Scouse, you scared the shit out of me!'

'C'mon, Jock,' he whispers, 'there'll be stacks of fanny down at the Mucky Duck.' His lips curl and the skin around his eyes crinkles. He looms over me, one arm hooked on the middle bunk's bed bar, wedging me into the bottom bunk with no escape.

I look into his eyes. 'Give us a minute to get a quick dhoby then,' I say, giving in. With Scouse, resistance is futile.

'Urry up then, wee man, or we'll end up wiv a couple o dogs,' Scouse replies with an air of seriousness.

'Let us get up then,' I say. His fag reek aftershave combo is making my eyes water. Scouse lets go of the bed bar and pirouettes back to his own bunk.

'Five minutes,' Scouse says, knowing that I'm a sucker for doing everything at a gallop.

Spurred on by the thought of trapping*, I'm in and out of the shower sharpish. Scouse laughs as I struggle to pull the drainpipe jeans over my wet arse, the energy I expend getting ready cancelling out any attempt I make to look

---

* copping off

cool. Fuck it. I leave the mess sweating, red-faced and nervously excited. We dive across the gangway, but the duty Seaman shouts us back to hand in our station cards.

'Don't get too pissed lads, we've got the Argies on Monday,' he reminds us, like it's a lower league football fixture.

We run down the gangway laughing, almost colliding with the concrete quayside, straightening up to avoid a clash with the officer of the day, who flashes us a look of disdain, one that gives away his assumed air of natural superiority, years of breeding and the correct school. *Warning – chip on shoulder alert!* Fuck it, we're off on the piss, nothing matters but the pursuit of the greatest number of pints in the smallest possible time. Three usually gives me enough courage to chat up women, but by four I've usually lost them.

Tonight it's going to be different though. Tonight it's time to exorcise the virgin right out of me with some holy water from the nearest boozer.

The night air makes me regret not bringing a jacket, but the only jacket I have in my locker would make me look like a ponce (it was a bit of an impulse buy).

Scouse and I strut like pubescent peacocks through the gates of the Royal Dockyard and become imposters in civvy street. The city of Portsmouth bristles with pubs, most of them imbued with the trappings of former naval glory in battle. Cap tallies, the black silk ribbons around sailors' caps embossed in gold with their ship's name plaster the walls behind the town's sailor friendly bars. It's in these areas that sailors are known to trade their cap tallies for drinks when they run out of money. There's always an air of tension in Portsmouth when civvy meets Matelot. Some pubs grudgingly accept their survival is down to the Navy, but it's also their main source of aggro as drink fuels the resentment between civvy piss artist and sailor, or Jack as he's known in civvy street, who has a reputation for throwing his money around.

Jack is young, free and single, even if he's married. The Navy looks after him: no rent to pay, no meals to fork out for, cruising around the world doing fuck all all day, all at the tax payer's expense. *He comes in ere, flashing his cash, shagging the local birds, givin them a dose, leavin them when they get pregnant . . .* Get my drift?

'Your round, Jock,' Scouse announces, propping his elbows on the bar of the grandly titled White Swan, deep within the hub of Pompey[*] pub land.

In reality, we are in the Mucky Duck, a boozer that had last seen a makeover to celebrate Charles Dickens' first novel. I mirror Scouse's body language; elbows on the bar, head swivelling to survey the scene. Jack is everywhere, sprinkled lightly with women (very lightly). I turn back to the bar. 'Two pints of lager, mate!'

The barman performs this task in monastic silence, but I've never seen a monk with such a burst nose. The drinks are banged down on the bar, spilling some of the contents. Burst nose smiles as if a deed has been performed according to the ancient tradition of the lager spilling brethren. I hand over my money, determined to smile back at him in case I can forge an immediate and lasting bond; well, lasting enough for him to be on my side in the event of a fight breaking out. He doesn't smile back so I about turn and commence a bar slalom manoeuvre.

'Cheers, Scouse,' I sing, gliding his pint across the bar like a curling stone.

---

[*] Portsmouth

Scouse scoops it up and smiles across the top of his glass at two girls tucked away in the snug. Surprisingly, the girls smile back.

'We're in, Jock,' he says, elbow flicking me. 'Let's go.'

I think back to the ankle in hatch incident. If Scouse had used the same conviction in his voice, I would've dropped the hatch, no messing. I try to grab his arm to explain that it's only my first pint and I'll bomb in the conversation stakes, but he's out of reach, completely focussed on his target. I turn back to the barman, order two more pints and down what's left of my first.

Matelots push and shove at the bar as the pub begins to heave. Once I have the pints, I cautiously make my way to the small table in the corner. Scouse has his back to me, his head nodding like the cutaway shot on a TV news item as he engages in what I take to be pre-mating dialogue with the two girls. I manage to shoulder my way through Matelots, now ten deep, without spilling too much beer. I make it to the table, miraculously with almost two half pints of lager. Scouse snatches both and necks them, finishing with a proud burp. The girls don't flinch.

'Joch,' he slurs, an affectionate variation on my nickname. 'Joch, this is Sharon and Linda.'

''Em nice names, Scouse, eh?' I say, trying to sound cool.

'Didn't ya get us a drink then?' Sharon protests.

'No, Ah'm sorry,' I say, avoiding eye contact as I sit down. Despite the awkwardness, I'm eager to watch Scouse's performance. I'm happy to just look at the girls as he does the chatting up. Hopefully they'll lock on to his patter and not notice my voyeuristic gaze.

'D'ya know gerls,' Scouse begins, 'dat me an Joch ere are goin ter The Falklands on Monday. We're goin down ter give them Aaargies some baaargy, in't that right, Joch?'

He doesn't wait for a reply.

'You do realise gerls that dis could be the last time that me an Joch are sat ere alive, like?'

Sharon shifts in her seat her skirt riding to reveal the top of a stocking. I'm mesmerised, but only momentarily.

'My dad's Argentinian,' Sharon announces.

Scouse looks at me. I swallow hard. An awkward silence follows. It's probably only a few seconds but feels like ten.

'Good one, Shaz!' Scouse blurts with a laugh that could shatter glass.

I laugh along. Linda looks at me, the thinnest of smiles appearing on her face. Much to our relief, Sharon joins in with the laughter. As she chuckles, she reaches down to pick up her bag. When she stands, her skirt rides back down her thigh. 'See you when we get back from the bogs,' she says. 'Can't let a couple of heroes die without a shag, eh, Linda?'

'He looks like a good shag might kill him,' Linda says, gesturing towards me.

Scouse for once is lost for words. I scramble for something to say, praying that whatever it is doesn't sound like I've prematurely ejaculated. 'Eh . . . I think we should get some more drinks first.'

Scouse casts me a sideways glance before returning to Sharon's skirt. 'Excuse us, gerls,' he says, 'me an Joch are just goin to the bar. Port n lemon an a vodka n Coke, is dat right?'

'Hurry up then or we might be gone when you get back, right, Linda?' Sharon says, with a touch of venom.

Linda makes no attempt to confirm or deny Sharon's threat, her shoulder length dark hair styled to slightly conceal her face – and now I'm thinking I'm going to lose my virginity to a Cleopatra lookalike.

Scouse stands up quickly, his chair scraping across the ground. 'Right, Joch, let's get the gerls them drinks!' he commands, gaffer-style.

I follow sheepishly, finding it difficult to shake off my fizzy nervousness. We carve a route to the bar like two grannies let loose in a jumble sale on pension day. As we edge nearer, Scouse tugs at my sleeve. 'She's got the sussies on Joch, did ya see er stocking tops?' he says, wide-eyed. 'The dirty mare.'

The black band around Sharon's thigh had transfixed me like a rabbit in a headlights factory. First there had been the hint that she had stockings on when she had laughed at Scouse's antics and her skirt rode up as she pushed back against her chair. This movement had revealed the black seam and the suspender clip, which sent a signal to my cock to be on standby. I had tried to look away from the tops of her legs and cast a nonchalant glance around the pub but my eyes bore down on them, desperate for the sight of naked inner thigh.

'Well? Did ya see em?' Scouse shakes me with both hands and I nod, grinning. 'Whose round is it? Yours. Right, pint for me.'

Scouse quickly swivels to glance back at our targets before swivelling back to me, his lips turned up at the edges again. 'Bet you a tenner Ah'll ave the knickers off er before the night's over.'

'Ah huvnae got a tenner, Scouse,' I laugh, 'but Ah believe ye anyway.'

'Well, you'll ave to get chattin to that other one Joch or they'll piss off, Ah know it, mate,' he says, digging me hard in the ribs.

'Okay, okay, Ah jist need another couple ay pints an Ah'll be brand new,' I reassure him.

Scouse orders the drinks and looks at me with a mischievous grin. 'After these, we're gettin laid, no excuses.'

I swallow hard and nod.

The barman thumps our order down. I clutch the two pints as Scouse picks up the port and lemon and vodka and Coke like a man on a mission.

I traipse behind him as we head back over. 'Awright ladies, ere's yer bevvies, get them down yer nechs,' Scouse says with a smile.

Sharon accepts hers gleefully 'Ta, Scouse,' she squeaks, like Barbara Windsor on helium. Linda barely lifts her head, her mumbling acceptance drowned in a sea of noise from the packed bar. I can see Scouse getting agitated with my poor chat up performance but I'm still mesmerised by Sharon's revealing skirt. I've got the kind of hard-on that could splinter mahogany. Linda has expressed no interest in me whatsoever so I'm content to sit back and fantasise about the contents of Sharon's underwear.

I experience temporary paralysis as Sharon shifts in her seat and places her black patent heels onto the metal arch underneath the table. Her skirt rides up even further this time and she opens her legs to reveal her pubic triangle. I look up and catch her gaze. Scouse is whispering into her ear but I'm getting the best view. Her ear is cocked towards Scouse's mouth but her eyes are on me. I look deep into her eyes for what seems like only a few seconds but the alcohol has begun to take effect so it's probably a good bit longer, possibly bordering on creepy. The last time I felt like this was my slow dance and snogging session with Motorcycle Girl and that was ages ago.

Come on, David, you can do this. All I need is a couple more beers, maybe even just the one, and I'm going to pop my cherry. To my disappointment, Sharon reduces the amount of flesh on show but my imagination is in overdrive. Scouse still thinks he's copping off with her, but I've got other ideas. Just one more pint and I'll be sorted. I'm actually going to get laid. Just one more pint.

A while later, having watched a bar stool take flight, somehow losing Scouse and the girls, and waiting ages at a kebab stall without acquiring a kebab, I take the two mile walk up the prom from Pompey to Southsea and into Joanna's, the nightclub that makes crotchless edible knickers look classy.

Along the way, I also manage to acquire my first packet of cigarettes.

The bouncer looks at me and shakes his head before letting me into Joanna's. The cold sea air has attempted to revive the few remaining brain cells that control walking and talking but the alcohol has killed off any chance of doing both at the same time.

Joanna's is Pompey's most famous après pub hangout for sailors. This is where Jack hunts for the women who manage to elude him during pub hours, a repository for the fulfilment of seedy fantasies, fuelled by excess booze and fumed up by fag reek. The only women that come to a place like this are looking for exactly the same as the men, the key difference being the men are mostly incapable due to brewer's droop. Joanna's is a dingy hive of multi-coloured flashing lights with a DJ, a sticky carpet and overpriced booze served in plastic tumblers to prevent serious injury. This said, I've never ended up here sober, so that description is quite likely suspect and not to be used as evidence in court or printed in a newspaper.

I peer through the smoky haze, but Scouse and the girls are nowhere to be seen. *Fuck.* After Sharon's pubic triangle performance, I decide to have a few shots to loosen me up. Big Mistake.

Supping lager from my plastic tumbler and sucking on a Benny Hedges, I move through the contorted couples on the dancefloor and select a corner where I can watch various acts of lustful acquisition taking place. I engage in one-way conversations with several girls and none of their boyfriends seem to mind. No, honestly, they really don't – even when I go to kiss one of the girls. And that's when the lights go out.

Absolute Beginners

1982

'Ye should av seen im, Smudge, ee was fuckin paralytic,' Scouse muses. 'Ye know dat little bird Ah know down at de Mucky, well Ah bet er a fiver dat she wouldn't flash er fanny at Jock under the table . . .'

'Duty MEM (L), duty MEM (L), report to the gangway!'

'Dat fuckin tannoy! Ah better go an see what the bastards want. See ya later, Smudge.'

'Hey, Scouse! Did you shag er?' Smudge's question flicks at Scouse's heels as he darts up the ladders to the gangway.

Smudge turns to me. 'Jawk! Ger up, ya lazy little bastard.' He shakes me, but I can't budge, cocooned in my sleeping bag. His breath could stop an alien invasion and I can feel the tickling vibrato of his voice as he nuzzles his future-cancerous mouth to my ear. 'Hey, whar've you been up to then? Trying to get yer end away, were we?'

'Gie's peace, Smudge, will ye?' I try to burrow deeper into the sleeping bag but Smudge is having none of it.

'Ye can't lie there, Jock, it's nearly lunchtime an Scouse as been coverin for yer scrawny little arse,' Smudge growls, his tone switching from soul to heavy metal. He scans the mess for someone else to pick on but his other favourite target, Jess, is down one of the refrigeration plants.

I know that a hangover and an ear bending from Smudge are on a par, so I prise my naked body from my stinking sleeping bag. As I stand, my brain feels like a snow globe being shaken by an excitable child. As the snow settles, I take a trip through the events of the previous night, but there's a 'do not pass go' sign after Joanna's. No doubt I'll find out from Scouse how I got back on board. Right now though I have to de-fur my tongue, but I know I'll throw up if I attempt the ladders.

'Could you get us a Coke, Smudge?' I ask, my voice fragile and pathetic.

'Fuck off, ye little get,' he nips.

'Does that mean no?' I say, looking at the floor.

'Ah wiz only jokin, ahhhh, ya bastard, ah wiz only jokin!' Smudge grabs my arm, which he uses to turn an imaginary key in the small of my back.

I grimace at the discomfort. 'Cheeky little fucker, aren't we Jock?' Smudge is so close I wonder if pre-cancer is contagious. Head pounding and arm smarting, I do my best to smile through gritted teeth.

When he lets go, I'm in no fit state to mount a counter offensive, especially since I'm bollock naked, but I'll draft up a battle strategy as soon as I have clothes and sugary pop.

'That was fuckin sore,' I say, the misery in my voice aiming to lull Smudge into feeling remorseful rather than looking for round two.

'That's just for starters,' he gurns. 'Wait till ye get dressed, Ah'm gonna give yer clothes a shower with you in them.'

Compared to what he's capable of, I reckon I'm getting off lightly.

The ladders rattle and Scouse appears, smiling, his hands locked together. He pulls them close to his chest as if he's about to release a genie. 'Sharon likes you, Jock,' he says, barely repressing a spasm of laughter.

'Gie's peace, Scouse,' I counter with a shrug, 'Ah'm no in the mood. Get us a Coke, will ye? Ah'm dying here.'

Scouse, more concerned with getting me up and working rather than helping a dying mate, legs it up the ladders and a few minutes later returns with the holy grail of hangover cures. I crack open the can of Coke and guzzle it like it's a vaccine for rabies. 'Ah heard you talking to Smu-udge.' I tell him, the last word a burp. 'I'm no bothered anyway.'

I sit back on my pit and let out a fart.

Scouse doesn't relent. 'But the other one really did fancy you,' he says, 'until you asked her in the bogs for a shag.'

'Lying bastard,' I mumble into my chin, stifling a vomit-laden burp. The alcoholic mist is beginning to clear, but I'm still not convinced.

'Please yourself, but drink dat cos there's sacks of spuds with your name on em up on the flight deck,' he beams, before burping his way out of the mess.

The rest of the day is spent making sure I'm no more than ten yards away from the heads[*]. Scouse occasionally pops up to see how a boy so worse for wear can still be alive. Later in the day, he gives me the highlights from last night's piss up. 'Great camouflage Jock,' he mocks, 'you could stand next to that bulkhead and no-one would know you're there.'

I look with concern at the bulkhead and then at the battleship grey of my shaking hand. The resemblance is remarkable and I'd find it funny if I didn't feel so close

---

[*] toilets

99

to death. Thankfully, Scouse's threat of lugging spuds into the stores doesn't materialise. Around four o'clock, he finds me loafing around on the flight deck. I must still look like I could easily lapse into a coma because he puts an arm around my shoulder and knuckles my cheek to show how much he cares.

'You didn't half depress dat Linda bird last night, Jock,' he tells me, 'goin on about how you an me might never get back from dem Argies. That's why Ah knew she fancied ye, well until you did the wobbly man impersonation. She spent ages holding you up, but when you spewed on her shoes, she said there was something she was dying to see on the telly and bolted.'

'Where the hell did you get to anyway?' I ask him.

Scouse turns to face me and puts his other hand on my other shoulder. 'Sharon and me ended up doin dat old horizontal boogie,' he reveals, eyes lighting up. I shrug his hands off and walk towards the tank deck.

'The *Invincible* and the rest of the task force are sailing tomorrer,' he shouts. 'Tuesday, it's us, an dat bloke from the telly's comin wiv us; cameras the lot.'

'Ah take it you're comin with us an all?' I shout back.

'Got no choice, ave I? Me best mate can't even do me ankle in to ger us off.' I turn, but he's gone.

There's a trace of fog as the day surrenders its warmth to the enveloping gloom. The heat and light from a nearby hatch invite in some wisps for a twilight tour of the ship. I feel the cold air begin to sharpen my senses. The perilous voyage through hangover straits is coming to an end.

At sunset, I seek out Scouse and help him switch on the ship's harbour lights. From the bridge, I can see the huge fleet of ships, their harbour lights twinkling. *HMS Invincible* dwarfs the smaller destroyers and frigates, but as I begin to think about sailing off to war, the tannoy blares out, 'Duty MEM (L), duty MEM (L)!'

Why are all the bloody ships in the Navy always looking for the duty MEM (L)?

As it gets darker, sailors who are lucky enough to live close to Pompey are returning from weekend leave. The mess is swelling up and with it comes the rise in volume: the unpacking of bags, the metallic banging of locker doors and the seemingly endless inane chatter. It begins to grate, so I grab my Walkman and seek solace at the stern, perching myself on a freezing metal bollard. The earlier fog has drifted away. The masts of the warships are now silhouetted against the sky.

The radar aboard the destroyer *HMS Cardiff* whirs around, casting its baseball catcher's mitt-like structure across the harbour. I listen to Simple Minds on my Walkman. The radar spins relentlessly, mapping out the contours of Portsmouth, looking for imaginary enemies. I wonder who has the unenviable task of scrubbing millions of flies and tons of seagull shit from the catcher's mitt. I wonder if the Navy could ever lose a ship because of the radar being choked up with so much crap that it can't detect enemy aircraft:

'Cause of sinking, sir, was a choked up radar, covered in shite it was.'

'Lieutenant!' barks the commander in charge of the inquiry.

'Yes, sir?' replies the baby lieutenant.

'Bring me the radar shite cleaning bod.'

'I'm afraid that's impossible sir, damn chap threw himself into the briney*. Couldn't bear to be brought up on a charge of keeping a disreputable radar, sir.'

'Very good, lieutenant. Dismissed!'

---

* naval bastardisation of brine

The next morning I'm close to singing with relief that my hangover has gone. I'm first up and immediately turn on the telly.

'Turn that bastardin thing off, ya wee shite!'

'Sorry, George, Ah jist wanted tae see if we're on yet, GMTV are coverin us.'

'Awright, but turn the fuckin thing doon.'

GMTV, short for Good Morning TV is new and shiny, a bit like me without a hangover: keen to present a bubbly, enthusiastic and knowledgeable front whilst actually knowing fuck all about anything.

'Cheers, George,' Ah say. 'Ah'll get ye a cuppa.'

'Fuckin wanker, get off me you little shit,' Jess moans. I'm sitting on Jess's bunk, inches from his manky feet. Mesmerised by what I'm seeing on the screen, I bounce up and down on his bed. 'It's on. Look, there's *Invincible*,' I say, pointing at the screen.

'Fuckin wankers,' Smudge coughs, 'fuckin won't go anywhere near the shitty stuff.' Smudge has an uncanny knack for prophecy and is on a roll. 'Fuckin Navy can't afford to lose that big bastard.'

Am I dreaming, or had Smudge become an intelligence officer during the night? The smoke from his first fag of the day is wisping its way towards me, so I get up to avoid having to put my gas mask on.

Sure enough, *Invincible* and that rust bucket *HMS Hermes* are grabbing all the TV glory. The editor cuts from the aircraft carriers' Harrier-laden decks to banner-waving women and children on the Southsea shore. Plenty of cliché-choked close-ups of kids with tiny union jacks. The camera zooms in to their little blonde-haired, blue-eyed features, closely followed by a blow-up page three girl with tears painted on her face, strategically placed next to anxious wives and mums at the quayside, just to add a bit of glamour. 'Tits out for the boys, ugly grannies to the back' I imagine the TV producer saying.

Invincible's stern merges into the greyness and the TV newsman brings his report to a well-choreographed close.

We switch the telly off and the mess descends into a contemplative silence. I wonder what our send-off will look like on a pixelated screen, or will the press have moved on to something else on day two? Perhaps an item on the cost of sending a task force to rescue a few hundred people 8,000 miles away. Why are the media obsessed with the cost of things over the value of people's lives?

Fuck! Big George's tea!

I steal a glance, but Big George is out of it, snoring for Great Britain.

Dream Time

1982

C ontrary to the 'All leave has been cancelled!' routine, most of us are given the day off. We're due to sail the next morning, so I'm still hopeful of a shag before the war. Scouse pesters me to go down the Mucky Duck, but I manage to slip away when he's in the shower. As I sit on the train to London, it's hard to imagine that several ships from a British taskforce have already sailed while I head for Pizzaland.

London is sunny and busy. First on my list is a new Walkman – I'll need something to stem the boredom of a long voyage, ideally something that doesn't consume 50 batteries an hour. I find a shop at the top of Tottenham Court Road, spend £85 on a Walkman and another couple of quid on four AA batteries, a great investment the shop keeper tells me. I wander back down The Strand towards a camera shop at the Trafalgar Square end and press my nose against the window.

This is what all amateur photographers do when confronted by a window full of shiny cameras and lenses; they lean forward, lemming like, feet gripping the surface of the pavement, upper half and eyes straining towards the shop, hoping not to get pulled in, yet desperate for an excuse to see the more expensive cameras inside.

Even if they just buy a filter or a lens cloth, it will allow them to mix with the photography elite. Unable to do the sensible thing and walk away, most of them topple into the doorway and, before they know it, they're in the heart of the shop destined to emerge several pounds lighter, often with something they'll donate to their camera club's Christmas auction. I fill my head with excuses as to why I really need a new lens . . . I can't afford to go to war without a new lens, I mean what if I missed a great photo opportunity?

I manage to push myself back from the window with its rows of Nikons, Canons and Leicas, as my stomach signals for food. I take a deep breath and exhale. My bank would be so proud of me, if they knew I existed. I'll just have to snap anything that moves with my Olympus OM10 and hope for the best.

'Thin and crispy tomato and cheese, sir?' the waitress sings. I look up and wait for a few seconds before answering; this is to engage her in sustained eye contact, which I read in one of my big sister's magazines is the key to a long-lasting relationship.

'Crispy?' she sings again tunelessly this time.

'Aye, that's me,' I say, fashioning a smile, but opting to leave the teeth out of it. I didn't want to seem desperate. Her enamel remains uncracked but I feel I'm in with a chance when she makes an excuse to come over to my table again.

'Parmesan with that, sir?'

I look up again but I'm too embarrassed to give her any more than a glance. 'Eh, oh aye, thanks,' come my words of profundity. I add a 'Cheers' as she turns and walks away.

'You're welcome,' she flashes back. Teeth! Definitely teeth! Bingo! I've made contact. I stab two eyes out of my pizza and eat them, and just as I'm starting to fashion a cut-out mouth, she comes over again. This woman is a nympho!

'There's your 7-Up, sir.' But before I get a chance to utter anything immortal, she's off again.

I look out the window. Life carries on as usual; beggars beg, standing, sitting and lying down. I wonder if prostitution really is the oldest profession in the world. If so, their terms and conditions need an upgrade. There's human flotsam drowning all around Leicester Square. Theatreland can't compare with the microcosmic street theatre from Pizzaland's picture window.

Students float past, laughing, carried along by a trail of invisible energy, their lives not yet tarnished by the nine to five. Idealism intact, they have a few more years of dreams before the tidal wave hits. The light begins to dim and neon signs from the Odeon cinema give a pink tinge to a tramp's bearded face. He stares into the window and I thank God that I've finished my pizza. I turn away, drain the dregs of my 7-Up and pay my bill to a different waitress. Tonight is not going to be the night.

My appetite for a film has gone, so I make my way to Waterloo station for the train back to Portsmouth. It's the long train, stopping at every station, but at least I have a new Simple Minds tape to listen to on my shiny new Walkman. The dry heat inside the carriage is irritating, so to take my mind off it, I fantasise that there's only one other passenger (a woman) in the carriage and that there are no connecting doors to any other carriages, so if she fancies me, we can't be disturbed.

She's diagonally opposite me, sitting four rows back, rocking with the movement of the train, every once in a while stealing a glance in my direction. She's a little older, mid-20s maybe. I keep looking up but I'm afraid of blushing, so I turn away and catch her reflection in the window. She's wearing a grey pinstriped business suit, cut sharply. Her padded shoulders momentarily remind me of American football, but her long blonde hair puts paid to any more thoughts of men wiping each other out whilst wearing helmets. Her fishnet stockinged legs are crossed, her feet syncopating to the rhythm of the train.

She bores into me with her sapphire blue eyes, daring me into making the first move, but I'm paralysed with the fear of rejection, worried that I've misread the signals. Those fucking magazines, making me analyse everything. However, it's my fantasy, so I decide to take the bull by the horns. I get up, walk over to the seat opposite her and ask if anyone's sitting there. She shakes her head. I sit down and place a foot close enough to her ankles so when the train hits a bend, my foot brushes against them.

After a while, she uncrosses her legs and leans back against the seat. She stretches her legs wide, causing her skirt to ride up and strain against her thighs. I lean forward, place my palms above her knees and push up, taking some of her skirt with me. Her legs open wider and I'm getting seriously horny. As the band of her stocking tops appear, I'm in heaven. She begins to tease me by asking for my ticket, her voice soft and sensual to begin with, but then it drops an octave and becomes huskier and deeper. She reaches forward and I think, yes! Orgasm city here I come, but instead of embracing me, she grabs my shoulder, shakes it and shouts, 'Ticket! Ticket please!'

I awake to find the ticket collector, a face full of stubble and paint stripper breath, hanging over me. I fumble about in my jacket until I find my ticket. He punches it and then shuffles off. *Bastard!* I'm never getting back into that fantasy now, although when I was a kid, I was able not only to get back into the same dream after I had woken up, but to interact with what was going on in my subconscious. God, it was so cool. I look out the window as the train comes to a halt at Havant, not far from Portsmouth, so there's no point dozing off again. I stick Simple Minds up full pelt on my Walkman and sigh out the arid air of the carriage. My fantasy will just have to be a chicken korma.

England
I Miss You Now

1982

'Glory grabbin bastards, eh, Jock?' says my chief petty officer, a fellow Scot referred to by everyone as Jock Blair, although never to his face.

'Aye, Chief.'

'Did ye see them all fuckin day yesterday on the telly? An they carriers, they'll no get anywhere near the shitty stuff. If anything, it'll be our arses on the line.'

I wonder if Jock Blair has ever spent four hours in a telephone box with Smudge, but it turns out to be the consensus amongst the ship's company that the aircraft carriers are glory grabbing bastards. I'm more pissed off that I'm not able to go up top to see our own send off, but Jock Blair and I are at our designated action stations. What for, I have no idea, but I think Jock Blair will laugh incredulously if I ask him so I just pretend this is what I suppose will happen to the greenies when we leave port.

I had joined the ship at Plymouth by boat so I don't know any better about leaving harbour; I had thought it might be a wee bit more glamourous than being stuck in a tiny compartment with a switchboard, a wind-up telephone exchange and the pungent smell of a rubber mat for company though. Oh, and the chief had brought along his cassette recorder minus a cassette. This adventure is not getting off to a particularly prestigious start.

The chief finishes his rant in our eight by four feet grey cell, flanked on either side by banks of switches and breakers, also in glorious grey. There's one seat and it isn't for me. I sit my bony arse on the manky rubber matt, designed to prevent you becoming a conduit for 440 volts AC if you're mad enough to go looking for bare electrical wires. Mercifully, the diesel generator next door is silent so I don't have to put up with the whining sound of the 60 hertz frequency it generates when flashed up[*]. There's one way in and one way out. Our way out is blocked by a two-inch-thick solid metal door which has six chrome clips wedged around it in a half nelson. This fucker could seal us in forever. I shiver as a flashback of Scouse's boot wedged into the hatch combing hijacks my consciousness. The sickly fluorescent tube leaks an excuse for light down onto the patches of brown lino not smothered by the rubber mat. Des res in this case means desperately in need of rescuing.

On the wall next to the door is the wind-up phone from a bygone era. You generate enough power to speak by winding it up, hence the name. When you make a connection, a coloured flag pops up in a glass portal like those old shop tills where the prices pop up in a window as you press down on the keys.

Only a few months ago I had seen the film *Alien*, in which the spaceship bristles with computers, androids and all sorts of technical marvels – and we're going to war with a windy-up telephone that's our only link to the outside world. Well, that is unless we sink. If this

[*] started

happens, the Navy will send details of our unfortunate demise by carrier pigeon.

'You and me could be holed up here for quite a time, Jocky,' Jock Blair says from his throne. This last nom de plume conveys my subordinate position. Not content to just demean my existence as an individual, but also to condemn me as a junior non-individual, confirms that this trip is going to be shite. I begin to have nostalgic thoughts about hangovers from Trondheim and Haarstad which prove how totally shit I expect the next few days to be. I sit back and dream of solitary confinement.

After about four agonisingly slow hours, during which the chief and I exchange about ten words, we fall out of action stations. The journey has taken us about a mile outside the harbour, but the media have to get their shots so we can't go too fast. The chief nods towards the switchboard door, signalling that our time together is up and I resist the urge to expel a sigh of relief.

I open the door clips, go through an empty messdeck, up a flight of stairs and open another hatch just under the flight deck. I climb the three steps onto the flight deck and bend my head into the wind, catching my breath. I look up at the grey-walled expanse that is Portsmouth, the lines of cheering onlookers having disappeared. There are no Union Jacks and the TV station and the paper with the page three stunner have cleared off too. Sailors retiring from Procedure Alpha dressed in their number ones are crossing the flight deck,

'Missed it mate, all them birds flashin their tits at us,' says a pock-marked killick* seaman.

---

* leading

'Naw, Ah managed tae see it all, looking through this scupper,' I say, pointing to the door leading up to the flight deck.

'Good, weren't it, Jock?' the seaman smiles.

'Great,' I reply without a stumble. *Birds flashing their tits? Maybe they'll have that bit on the telly.*

Life from a Window

1982

Afew days later, we have an NBCD* exercise. Basically, if you're into rubber then you'd love wearing the NBCD suit and gas mask, complete with rubber shoes, and prancing around simulating chemical or biological warfare. Now my face is encased in rubber and I'm cocooned in a room that smells of rubber, I begin to wonder if I could die from a rubber overdose.

'Yock, ee if ye an ontac the main witchbor?'

I throw Jock Blair a perplexed look, but it's concealed by the steamed up holes in my gas mask. 'Wha, Shief?' I reply, sounding like an actor in an advert for cold medicine. He doesn't give me an answer but motions to the switchboard phone and puts his index finger to the side of his gas mask to indicate that I'm thick. He rings up the main switchboard himself and I almost piss myself laughing when I hear him trying to communicate through a wind-up phone wearing a gas mask.

'I'm wick this thick little Jock,' I think he says. My god, we really have come on leaps and bounds since D-day.

I really want to shout through my gas mask 'Get away from her, you BITCH,' which is my favourite line from *Alien*, but I bottle it.

Jock Blair and I are stuck down at our action stations two days in a row, but at least we have a bit of variety in the form of an impromptu guess-what-I'm-saying

---

* Nuclear, Biological and Chemical Defence

113

competition. The chief takes it all very seriously though, so I disguise my laughter by making choking noises inside my gas mask. I can see he's becoming exasperated by the jumbled communication from Hotel switchboard that dribbles out of the Bakelite earpiece. The phone system is designed for use in an emergency, when the ship's power is down and you're waiting for the emergency power to kick in. It's basically a cock-up job and not a very good cock-up job at that.

Even though there are only two of us in the watertight compartment, I know Jock Blair won't dare remove his gas mask; that'd be cheating on the gas mask test, which has to last an hour. It's designed to show you how utterly pissed off you would be if you have to wear it for real. Actually, if it went beyond an hour, you'd probably end up with a rubber fetish.

November switchboard, our designated action station, is a compartment two decks down on the starboard side of the ship. This tiny space functions as an electrical control room for the ship's auxiliary and emergency power. The fluorescent lights make sure you never leave without a headache, especially when combined with the plastic air coughed out the vent by ageing extractor fans. Okay, it isn't *Alien* but there are enough switches and coloured lights to impress a girl enough to drop her drawers when there's a ship's open day, or so I'm told.

Against the bulkhead is a sodding great diesel generator which, when flashed up, can supply electrical power to our switchboard if one of the steam turbines stops supplying power to either Kilo or Hotel (the two main switchboards), so basically, if the shit hits the fan and we lose main switchboard power, we're the cavalry.

During action stations, the stoker next door starts up the generator and checks that it's able to supply power to our switchboard. This causes us even more discomfort as the diesel fumes snake their way into our tiny space. The generator is then run under load for a few hours and subsequently shut down. Me and the chief maintain the frequency of the electricity at 60 hertz, which we do by keeping an eye on a frequency gauge and adjusting it if necessary. If it goes five percent above or below 60 hertz, the diesel generator trips and we lose auxiliary power. When the switchboard is powered up, it gives off a constant whining noise, which you either become accustomed to or you book a room at the lunatic asylum for later.

We fall out of action stations sometime in the afternoon and are addressed by the captain on our closed circuit television system. I don't catch what he says, even though he doesn't have his gas mask on. Sometimes with officers it's hard to tell the difference.

The next week is taken up with fire drills, more exercises and flying fish. We've only been steaming five days and already the sea has gone through a colour metamorphosis; it's amazing how the different shades act like a mood gauge. About two days out of Portsmouth, the light grey of the water has darkened into foreboding graphite. Sharp waves cut up the colour and toss around the dirty white foam that chaffs against the ship's side. There are no highlights on the surface, the sun refusing to supply light or heat to such a vicious power as if the addition of these two elements would result in untold climactic chaos.

A week later, the grey depression dissolves with the arrival of an aquamarine sea scape, bringing a confused cheerfulness to most of the mess, but then none of us had been to war before so how did we know how to feel? Smudge's oily, olive skin is first to tan without any redness. I know if I want to get anywhere near his colour, I'm in for some serious sunburn.

After work, which involves lifting and shifting a giant ventilation fan near the galley, I take Tolstoy's *War and Peace* (yes, really) to a quiet spot on the stern above the landing craft dock. It's hot enough to strip to the waist and, after spending a month in northern Norway, this is heaven. I can't believe Prince Andrei is dead, after all that he went through with Natasha, the death of his wife and his father's decline into dementia.

I stop reading and look out over the horizon. As I bring my head down to read, below me, not two feet away from the ship's hull, are what look like hundreds of skimming stones on the surface of the water. The sunlight catches the sparkling of silvery scales, scales that belong to a shoal of tiny fish, their pectoral fins acting like wings to lift them over the breaking waves. Six days out of grimy Portsmouth and I've seen flying fish. Jesus Christ, this is really something. I become mesmerised by the trajectory of their shimmering, silvery flight. I watch until the sun sets, smiling the whole time.

At night, our CCTV newsman tells us that a total exclusion zone has been set up around the Falkland Islands and any Argentine ship coming within a two-hundred-mile radius will be sunk. I wonder if I'll see flying fish tomorrow.

Ghosts

1982

'Kind a music do you like, Jock?'
'All sorts really, Jacko, a bit ay The Jam, some Simple Minds and Bob Dylan.'

'What you want is a bit a northern, Jocky,' Jacko says stretching out the word: nawwwthen. 'Northern soul, cowboy, get it into yer bones.' He leans on his mop and looks up, momentarily reminiscing, before breaking into a dance on the ivory tiled floor of the heads. He slides gracefully around the floor, mop and bucket discarded into one of the traps[*] as he grooves through his repertoire. Every so often, he slides up to me and gives me a soft punch on the shoulder or the stomach, normally at the end of a spin. The imaginary music stops as quickly as it began, the dancing instantly replaced by whistling as Jacko resumes mopping like nothing remotely weird had just happened.

Andrew Jackson is a lanky, streetwise 20-year-old from Yorkshire, with that Yorkshire trait of believing that England is in Yorkshire and not the other way around. To describe him further, he's pretty much Shaggy from Scooby Doo, minus the American accent, ginger hair and being a cartoon. He's actually a lot cooler and more laid back than Shaggy, although admittedly I've never seen him running away from a ghost while trying to stop his canine buddy from stealing his hot dog. His hair resembles a

---

[*] cubicles

117

thatched cottage that's been dyed some sort of blond but his dark roots are now piercing through. He has a long, thin, bony face, his eyes kind but up for mischief. He somehow manages to get away with having stubble on his chin despite naval regulations stating that being clean shaven or a having a set* is the protocol. Along with Scouse, Jacko likes a laugh, mostly at someone else's expense but nothing too vicious – like the time he and Sticky Green told Scouse there was a job going for a sailor in Brussels, as a bodyguard to a European commissioner.

Jacko had all the senior ratings in on the joke and once Scouse was convinced the job existed, he decided to apply. Jacko, seeing that Scouse had taken the bait, complained to our divisional chief that he had seen it first and had a small arms certificate. Scouse, though, was full steam ahead by this time. The chief, who was in on the joke, had let it slip the post would have rent-free quarters for the successful applicant and his missus. Scouse then requested to go on a small arms course. The request form was signed all the way up through the divisional hierarchy. Feeling satisfied that the job was his, Scouse settled down after supper to watch CCTV where it was pointed out by the newsman on the telly that 'The stupid Scouser who fell for the non-existent post in Brussels was to look at the date on his request form.' April 1st.

'Gotta sleep down the switchboard tonight Jock, eh?' Jacko says, chewing on a fingernail. He has that knack of winding you up while giving you the impression that nothing could be further from his mind and in this respect he's cut from the same bolt of mischief material as Scouse. Sleeping down the main switchboard, which makes an

---

* a beard and moustache

even bigger whining noise than my designated action station, is torture.

Jacko leans over one of the tiny stainless steel sinks and nonchalantly squeezes a zit on his stubbly chin onto the mirror. 'Never mind, eh, cowboy,' he adds, waltzing off, straddling the hatch combing and heading downstairs into our mess. I follow with the mop and bucket, clanging the bucket against the hatch just to make a few people as pissed off as I am. I'm the duty MEM (L) tonight and this job is ten times worse at sea. At any time of night, you can be called upon anywhere in the ship to fix an electrical defect. Sometimes the window wipers on the bridge pack in, but this never happens unless it's a force ten gale. Or a starter motor might pack up, but it's never accessible or the wiring diagram's wrong. On *Fearless*, electrical faults are never simple and tonight it's my turn. Jacko has succeeded in getting right up my nose.

After rounds, made up as always of kidding on to the officers that we keep the place nice and tidy and that we like them, we settle down to watch *The Exorcist* on the telly. I can't help thinking that the main character; a possessed pubescent teenager played by Linda Blair could be some distant relation to Chief Jock Blair. It's quite imaginable that if Jock Blair gets angry enough, his head would be capable of doing a three sixty and spewing out green goo all over the place.

'Jock?' whispers Jacko.

'What?'

'Check for ghosts down the switchboard tonight, mate.'

'Fuck off!' I say, trying to sound like it's the last thing on my mind, but alone at night in the dark isn't my strong point. All those nights listening for my dad's footsteps have taken their toll.

'I'm serious,' Jacko says, putting on an air of being genuinely offended by my reaction. 'Smudge says he saw summit down there about a month ago. Says it's like a sailor from the Battle of Trafalgar. His teeth are all rotten and he's got one leg off. He swore he could hear the peg leg banging on the deck.' To illustrate, Jacko bounces up on down on one leg.

'Fuck off, Jacko!' is all I can muster. I try to laugh it off but my imagination is in overdrive.

'Don't say Ah didn't wawn ya,' Jacko smiles, returning to two-legged human status.

At half eleven, I climb up the two sets of ladders from the mess into the red-lit labyrinth of the passageway. I cross over onto the starboard side of the ship and down three more decks into Kilo switchboard. The switchboards are all named after the phonetic alphabet, in fact everything is: messdecks, car number plates and Foxtrot Oscar, which is phonetic for "go away!"

Most of the ship's company are fast asleep. The constant whirring of air conditioning harmonises with my dry lipped whistle as I climb over the hatch combing that leads to the switchboard room. The whirring slowly increases in volume with each downward step of the ladder until it's drilled into my brain. I can tell by the tone of the noise that the genny* is close to 60 hertz. I peer around the switchboard. Wee George, the other Geordie in our mess is finishing off the middle watch. He looks languidly round at me. Wee George could never swivel his coupon fast enough to do a Linda Blair, but his face could definitely star in a horror movie.

'Awright Jock?' I could have been a bug-eyed alien instead of a spotty, skinny, pubescent sprog, but Wee

---

* generator

120

George's expression would have remained the same. Nothing much troubled him, except perhaps a maily* from his girlfriend. He's always falling out with her and he would get a 'Dear John', then a month would go by and she would write a maily, begging him to go back with her. He showed me the 'Dear John' but he felt that the getting back together maily was private so I didn't ask any questions. Wee George, his blotchy, pock marked face, topped with greasy ginger curls is camouflaged by the 12 o'clock shadow of a raggedy beard. The good thing about Wee George is that he isn't aggressive, the bad thing is that he's a bit whiffy so I'm thinking I'll have to put my exclusion zone around him if I'm going to survive the night.

'Not much doin' then, George?' I ask.

'Nah! Borin as fuck really,' he replies, casually. I can see my skinhead in his large square glasses and I smile at my reflection. Wee George smiles back.

'That *Exorcist* was good the night,' I hastily add.

'Ah've seen it afore, man. Load of pish if ye ask me.' As he utters the words, I catch the full force of his rancid fag-laden breath. I draw back. 'That film couldn't even scare me wee sister, an she's only ten,' he adds.

That'll be the pleasantries out of the way then. I decide to make up my bed for the night, which is basically a stretcher with one jaggy blanket that lies flat onto the tiled deck at the far end of the switchboard room. I'm expected to sleep fully-clothed in my number eights** with my ovies and tool roll beside me. I hope that for just one night there will be no call outs.

---

* letter
** working uniform

I pull the scratchy blanket over myself and the rickety stretcher bed and fight for dreamy oblivion against the sonic torture of the generator.

'Jock, Jock!' It's fag-breath again. Jesus, it's worse than getting your toenails prised off with a rusty scalpel. 'Jock, man, ye're wanted doon the engine room.' Wee George is hangin over me like the grimy reaper. 'They're moanin like fuck, cos a lightbulb's gone oot near one o the bilge pumps an they canna see the readins.'

I interpret this as the stoker on the middle watch being a vindictive bastard who fancies gettin the duty greenie out for a laugh because it's no like they don't all have fuckin torches, do they?

'Aw right George, Ah'm fuckin goin.' At least it's only a lamp. I prise myself up from the bed and grab my tool roll. As I climb out of the switchboard hatch, Wee George's comment of 'grumpy little bastard' catches up with me and squeezes out into the red-lit passage ahead. I slip down the hatch into Hotel section and climb down the three decks of vertical ladders on the approach to the engine control room door. As I open the door, more high frequency sounds buzz my eardrums, as my eyes confirm my vindictive stoker theory. Stan the Man, an effeminate and theatrical stoker is smirking.

'Get you out of bed, did we, Jock?' Stan says, delivering the line as if he's on Broadway, emphasising the word 'we' to confirm the conspiracy. Stokers and greenies are like two rival football teams, the Navy's equivalent of Rangers and Celtic. Like any rivalry, the new boy fails to see what all the fuss is about. More to the point, how did it happen in the first place?

Like all other rivalry, it's inherently false because it changes with each situation. For example, the English counties of Yorkshire and Lancashire hate each other, yet when England play football, cricket or rugby, they unite to hate England's opposition. Then England goes to war and drags the other union countries with it. England and Scotland don't like each other yet they unite to face the Argies. What happens when England draw Argentina in the World Cup though? The Scots, Welsh and Irish unite to support the Argies.

So, here's Stan, who's English, a stoker, and gets me up at two in the morning to go down a stinkin noisy engine room and fix a poxy lightbulb.

'Nae bother Stanley, old chum, Ah wisnae gettin any kip anyway. Jist show me where it is an Ah'll have it fixed afore ye can say you're-a-shit backwards.' Stan's smirk weakens.

I revel in my new found self-control. Meanwhile, the watch-keeping chief stares at his bank of knobs and dials, dissolving the partnership with Stan and his failed wind-up. One-nil to the spotty wee Jock.

Stan turns and thumps the two door clips, allowing the smells and sounds of the two steam turbines and their auxiliaries to invade the comparative silence of the engine room switchboard. The venom in his actions surprises the rest of the stokers who are all subordinate to Stan's seniority of age, if not rank, and therefore resist the temptation to laugh at his forced machismo.

I put on my ear defenders and follow the vindictive stoker. He leads me through the ship's Meccano belly, down into the lower compartment, which contains the bilge pumps.

It's just me and him. His torch lights a few feet in front of us and grows brighter as we reach the source of the gloom. He turns and points upwards in the cramped, noisy, fume-filled midden. He glares at me as he pushes past. For an instant I tense, expecting a blow, but he only shouts something, which, through my ear defenders sounds like 'Fwukinwaashol.' I turn and give him the finger, but he doesn't see me.

Our handbags at dawn encounter over, it's time to change the lamp. I take the brass key from my tool roll and couple it to the lamp casing's retaining ring. The ring needs a bit of elbow grease to get it to release its hold on the glass cover and I can feel myself beginning to sweat with the effort.

At last, it gives way and I unscrew the ring, taking the weight of the cover as the retaining ring loosens its grip. I place the ring and the glass case down on the metal deck. Some of the glass from the broken lamp has collected in the cover and it makes a muted tinselly sound as I put it down. I look up at the exposed filament. By this time, I'm drenched. We're only a few degrees off the Equator and even though it's night, the humidity from the turbines and steam pipes creates a metallic rainforest.

Steam snakes out from tiny leaks in the pipework above me, before climbing towards the deckhead where it condenses and falls back into droplets. No wonder the ship is full of rust. I know there's no point in looking for a light switch in this scrap heap, so I dig out my thick red pliers from the tool roll and pinch the protruding live filament. The filament gives way but the bayonet-mounted base is still attached to the lamp holder. *Shit.*

My ovies are saturated with sweat by this time. The Navy regulations permit essential personnel in the engine room for twenty minute periods in tropical areas and I had been wrestling with this seemingly simple task for what felt like half an hour. I push the pliers up to the bayonet fitting and twist it round. Brute force is replacing logic and more of the fitting gives way. I'm straining every sinew up towards the lamp holder. The sweat from my shaven scalp runs into my eyes and they start to sting. I tear about with my pliers but it's not working. I should take a break, but I'm fucked if I'm going to let this poxy lamp beat me.

'Aaargh, fuck's sake,' I squeal.

My arm is gripped by an electric snake, darting up through my nervous system and straight into my heart. I let out a pitiful yelp and fall back onto the metal deck. I lie there, looking up and breathing hard, but happy to be breathing at all. I decide it's wise to stay where I am for a while. The engine room noises wash over me. Images of coming to in the school playground with the bell ringing dart into my head. I'm gasping for a drink, but I feel like I'm dying, so what's the point? I press my index and middle finger to my neck. The steady but rapid pulse tells me I'm one lucky bugger. Maybe I will have that drink.

I think about Prince Andrei from *War and Peace* after he's felled by a French Hussar, lying staring at the sky gasping like a stranded guppy, imagining that he's in heaven.

I take long, slow breaths and wipe my face with the sleeve of my ovies, my heart pounding from the shock. The burred metal deck I'm lying on glistens in the relentless heat. I look up at the light fitting, take one final deep breath and haul myself to my feet. I pick up my tool roll and retreat. I'm going to have to think of a story and quickly.

'That it, Jock?' whines Stan the Man.

'Naw, no yet Stanley. It's a wee bit tricky tae dae it in a oner.'

'Too much for yer soft little hands, is it?' he snorts.

'Aye, that's it Stan, old boy, give me a sewin kit an Ah'm in ma element.' I lean down to where the limers[*] urn sits and pick up a cup. 'Jist havin a wee drink. Have ye nae tea, Stan? Ah'm freezin ma erse aff in there.'

I neck the limers and burp close enough to Stan to make him flinch. 'Time for round two.'

The chief of the watch looks round and smiles. I wink at Stan and head back into the steam room. This lamp is getting fixed, even if it kills me.

---

[*] cold drinks

Heatwave

1982

Almost a month has passed since we sailed out of the gritty grey of Portsmouth harbour. *Fearless*, along with various others, is anchored off Ascension Island in the South Atlantic, four degrees off the Equator and 4,000 miles from the Falklands. The diplomatic seesaw is in full swing.

We're getting mail regularly and my mum has sent me some Bob Dylan tapes. The stream of hot days dissolve into the most spectacular sunsets. As the sun dips below the horizon, green is the first glow to emerge, overtaken by various shades of orange, then red, getting deeper and deeper and, like the watching of hands on a clock, moving without appearing to move. The deep red transforms into blue and merges with the sea, darkening it until all that's left are the reflections of the tiny lights from the fleet of ships that support us.

At night, sailors fish off the stern for sharks. During the day, I bathe in the crystal clear waters around the shores of Ascension. Tiny fish come up and kiss my tanned body as I splash like a toddler. Then they bite me.

The payback for going ashore is that I have to fill sandbags before heading back to the ship on a landing craft. It seems impossible to imagine that 4,000 clicks north, the joint task force HQ in London is preparing for a seaborne landing somewhere on the Falkland Islands, while 4,000 clicks in the opposite direction the Argies are flying shit loads of troops into Stanley, to fortify it against attack – and all this is happening as I write a postcard to a new pen pal while sunbathing.

News has been sporadic but now there's a bit more banter on board. Word comes through of attacks on an Argentinian sub in South Georgia, followed by the recapture of South Georgia with no loss of life. Morale is high. We seem to be winning the war and there's even some chat that we could be sent home. But on April 30th, the peace process fails. The Yanks side with us. Each new day brings stories of Argentinian losses. Sea Harriers attack the runway at Stanley and Vulcan bombers give it a good cratering. Without supplies from Argentina, the invading troops could easily perish. Things are looking good. It's like we're invincible.

Then disaster strikes.

The Planner's Dream Goes Wrong

1982

I lie in the sand as the crystal clear water sifts between my toes. I open and close my fists around the white powdery sand to the rhythm of the lapping water. The sun is mercilessly hot, but being so close to the water gives me a feeling of control, safety even. I pick up my camera and focus on my feet. It's so bright that I had to get my mum to send me a polarising filter to stop all of my slides becoming overexposed. *Fearless* is in the background, almost silhouetted against the bright blue expanse of sky and ocean. The tiniest of white clouds fight for their rapidly diminishing territory, the sun picking them off one by one. I decide to name one of the clouds Icarus and watch as it slowly dissolves into the blue. Around me are sailors and Marines, messing about on the makeshift beach and in the water.

The Marines are proving their bravery by diving through underwater arches formed by jagged rocks. Mortality hasn't yet entered the equation. Some sailors egg them on and one or two even dive in themselves. I'm the happy spectator. The medic's going to be busy if someone miscalculates by even a few inches. I content myself with lying back on my towel and smiling as more clouds vaporise. It feels for a few hours like I'm on holiday, but without having to pay for anything.

'Okay, playtime's over, fill two sandbags each and take them back on board!'

The Marine sergeant in charge of the beach barks this order as the small landing craft that deposited us on the shore in a festive mood returns as a harbinger of doom. As the landing craft gets nearer, helicopters jar overhead, their giant rotors blocking out the sun.

The Marine sergeant blasts us with his acid tongue. 'Fucking hurry up. I said fill two sand bags not build the bleedin pyramids!' The bow door of the landing craft belly flops onto the water, bashing it into submission. A second later, the craft's engines roar into reverse and choking black smoke belches out of the exhaust manifold. The reversing manoeuvre is too late and the bow door plunges deep into the sand before grinding to a halt. The sergeant aims a hail of expletives at the coxswain and I don't need telling to get on board pronto.

I don't pick up on any of the body language on board the landing craft that takes us on the ten-minute journey from shore to ship. I'm too busy pointing the camera at helicopters and various other ships. It's only when I'm back on board that I hear the news that *HMS Sheffield* has been hit by an Exocet[*].

The Argies aren't supposed to hit back. I'm stunned. How could one missile take out a whole ship? When I had drawn war scenes in primary three, it took me dozens of hits on a ship to sink it. *One fucking missile.*

Back on board, the news about *Sheffield* has stirred a hornets' nest. I perch on a bollard up on the focsle[**] as helicopters of all shapes and sizes bristle and swarm overhead. Somehow it doesn't seem right that I should be

---

[*] a French-built anti-ship missile

[**] forward part or 'pointy end' of the upper deck of the ship

basking in the sunshine in good health while thousands of miles away, lads my own age are being fried in twisted metal.

'Let's get down there and murder the bastards!' some cocky seaman blurts, holding court in a corner of the dining area.

'Sit fuckin down, fuckin gobshite!' The unmistakeable tones of Big George silence the mouthy sailor who shows no embarrassment playing second fiddle to the Geordie. 'Yiz dinnah nah what yiz are talkin aboot. Lads are dyin man, lads wae wives an bairns. Yiz wid all do betta prayin that them fuckin schemin politicians can get their heads the gither an sort it fuckin oot!'

Everyone who's been listening bow their heads and resume eating in silence. Scouse, who's sitting opposite me tries to make me laugh, pulling faces and gurning. I know if I start though, I'll be a target for Big George's anger. I feign a coughing fit, scrape back my chair and leg it down the corridor by the entrance to the galley. Scouse follows and we piss ourselves laughing.

There are no more runs ashore to Ascension Island. A monastic silence descends on the ship's company, broken by the hauling of the anchor and the vibration of the giant propellers. Playtime is over.

A week later, the ocean reverts to grey and the foamy heads on the waves roll lethargically. No hurry they say, plenty of shit flying around when you get there. My grey world is peppered with brightly coloured candy dots, but they haven't stopped the sleepless nights I've been having since the news of the sinking of *Sheffield*. I commit an empty smarties tube to the sea. The waves fold around it before dragging it under. The flying fish are gone, although

I imagine them in their thousands balancing on their tails and waving us off at Ascension.

A few days later we're issued with ampules of morphine and shown how to secure the mess for action stations in the event of an air raid or missile strike: just tie everything down and tape everything up. Mirrors are crossed with tape to prevent fragments of glass exploding into the mess. We laugh about being caught shaving during an air raid, well some of us do. The ship's company is ordered to wear gas masks for twelve hours and the usual jokes about sailors' gas masks being preferable to their faces are bandied about by the Marines. Damage control exercises such as firefighting and restoring emergency power in the event of an attack, which were part of our basic training and had been a little haphazard because of 'it won't happen to me' syndrome, now take on a gravity and exactness that would have had our instructors back at *HMS Raleigh* doing cartwheels. Preparations are subtly introduced into daily orders. War, real war, not the stuff of comics, is slowly but surely entering our lives and no-one is talking about diplomatic solutions anymore.

Three days before my 18th birthday, I get a maily from my joining up mate, Iain 'Cheesy' Mould, which starts Dear Dave, a name I fuckin hate. His brother is on *Invincible*, but Iain hasn't managed to get on a task force ship and he's gutted. He tells me that his mum and dad are sick with worry at the thought of one of their sons on an aircraft carrier that's sure to be a major target for the Argentinian Air Force. He wishes me luck and hopes that we can meet up soon.

Iain and I talk the biggest load of philosophical shite on the planet when we get together, and all without the aid of illegal substances – the usual *us against the world* pish. We

132

had both suffered setbacks in our respective naval careers. I had wanted to become an artificer but failed a basic exam at the careers office. Sixteen years old and on the scrapheap. Iain had passed the same exam. He then went into artificer training but couldn't hack it so he joined up with our class of Electrical Marine Engineering Mechanics i.e. folk who didn't fancy the greasy stuff of the bilge (where all the shit ends up at the bottom of the engine room).

It couldn't have been easy for him; any drop outs from the artificer branch were not popular with our lads. Thankfully, he was a good bit older than most of us and it stopped him getting too wound up about snotty little baby sailors and their tiny prejudiced brains. There was a degree of irony to our friendship though – after failing the exam at the careers office and subsequently visiting the unemployment benefit people, I bumped into an ex-sailor at a bus stop. I told him of my failed attempt to become an artificer. He then told me stories about his time in the Marine engineering branch; how you only did your six weeks' basic followed by another three months' training and then you'd probably be on a ship. Artificer training was four years of drilling, classroom work and shining your buttons. I was straight up to the careers office again.

'Wait six months and you can re-sit the artificer's exam,' urged the chief petty officer at Dundee. *Have you any idea what six months feels like to a 16-year-old?* I felt like asking him. I told him that I was no longer interested in becoming an artificer and that I just wanted to join up. Three months later I was at *Raleigh*. Six weeks into basic training, I was called in to see my divisional officer. He recommended I go across the road to begin artificer training. I declined.

Even at 17, I could understand the conflict going on inside Cheesy's head. You wanted to think you couldn't wait to get down there and sort out the Argies, but on the other hand, if your dick got shot off or melted off in the process, what good was the rest of your life going to be to you? That said, if you didn't (get your dick shot off that is), you could bring back stories of heroism, gallantry, sacrifice and maybe a bit of shagging thrown in for good measure. And not forgetting the possibility of rat-arsed drunkenness in Gibraltar before heading home into the arms of your loved ones.

I fold away Cheesy's maily and put it in the bottom of my locker behind my dirty laundry. Maybe people will stop him in Portsmouth and ask why he isn't down there. The worst thing I can think of is being in the forces during a conflict and not being involved.

'Fuckin ell wee man, your locker is stinkin.' Scouse ectoplasms the smell of stale cigarettes over my shoulder, coupled with sweat from his strenuous efforts in the engine room.

'Scouse, you smell disgustin,' but before I can say anymore, he's shouldering me out of the way and heading for my box of dhoby-dust* from the open locker. 'Give us some o this, will ye, Jock,' he pleads.

'Have the lot, Scouse, you smell like you need it,' I say, swatting the air around him while trying to breathe. I let Scouse take the box of powder knowing I would get it back. If I make a fuss, the whole mess might join in and take some of my precious powder, leaving me with an empty box, well, apart from a few stubbed out fags in it.

---

* washing powder

Dad, Christine, and me as a baby

Playing Happy Families – the full Cruickshanks complement outside a boarding house in Rothesay

Doing my best Paul Weller impression

Passing out from Anson Division, *HMS Raleigh*, 1981. That's me at the bottom right, circled

In Norwegian fjords, only a few weeks before the Falkland Islands are invaded. (L-R) Scouse Castles; Pete Martin; Andrew Jackson; me

HMS Fearless at Ascension Island on the day *HMS Sheffield* was hit in the South Atlantic by an Exocet

Trying to smile while posing against the door to one of the noisy engine rooms, which is also directly next to my mess. Round my neck hangs an ampule of morphine in case I get injured

A Sea Harrier makes a detour to refuel on board *HMS Fearless* in Bomb Alley

Me and Dave Moy posing beside the Sea Harrier on the flight deck of *HMS Fearless*

The hospital ship, *SS Uganda*, anchored in Port William, near Stanley

With Mickey Mouse at Disney World, Florida, in 1983

Get Yourself Together

1982

My 18th birthday is a disaster. I end up getting so drunk, I stagger into another messdeck looking for the heads and end up pissing all over their floor. The next day, I have to gather up enough courage to revisit the scene of the crime, apologise and clean it up. To say they weren't chuffed about what I did is to say that the Titanic had a slight mishap with an iceberg. Now I know how Mac felt after he threw his guts up all over me and then went into hiding. To make matters worse, the mess in question makes sure everyone's present before calling me down for punishment.

'Ya dirty little Jock bastard,' scowls a Geordie stoker who's pals with Big George, the other big Geordie stoker and giver of the famous galley speech on war and moral decline. The stoker has a twinkle in his eye and gives a rousing performance of self-righteous indignation. 'Clean that disgustin piss off our mess ya wee shite, and then fuck off out.'

Saying nothing, I fetch the mop and bucket. If I put my back into it and mop up in record time, it might endear me to those sympathetic to bouts of memory loss and bodily control malfunction brought on by intoxicating liquor. I keep my head down and mop hard.

'Watch me fuckin shoes, son,' murmurs one of the bearded, three-badge[*] leading hands. All eyes are burning

---

[*] denotes 12 or more years of service

into me; my face is getting redder, not only from the exertion but from embarrassment.

The stench of piss is rapidly giving way to disinfectant. After a while, the purging steam rises from the floor and I begin to feel better. I place the mop back into the bucket and I'm thinking my humiliation is almost over.

'One more thing, fuckhead,' rasps the big Geordie who's pals with the other big Geordie. I grip the mop again, showing the whites of my knuckles. 'Happy birthday Jock, ya dirty little shite,' he adds, with the hint of a smile.

I've never felt so relieved to be verbally assaulted.

The mess breaks into loud applause and cheering. I smile and search for a one liner. I found it half an hour later as I crossed the flight deck. For the record, it was: "If Ah knew yiz were all gonnae cheer, Ah would piss in yer mess every night."

'Hands to action stations! Hands to action stations!' The intercom rasps the most feared words a ship's company can hear. Almost a thousand sailors and Marines scramble out of their beds and throw on their anti-flash hoods, gloves and firefighting socks. The red lights overhead indicate that it's still night, or the early hours of the morning.

Ladders rattle with dozens of pairs of feet battering up and down decks accompanied by the dull thud of watertight hatches being closed. Men labour to breathe through their anti-flash hoods, like surgeons running a marathon in gowns and masks. The ship breaks out into a higher state of readiness and my heart quickens as I sprint up three decks, along the cross passage to the starboard side, down three decks and along the passageway, opening and then closing the doors, before finally descending one more deck and into the November switchboard. 56 seconds. Flat.

'Glad ye could make it, son!'

Fuck! How the hell had Jock Blair made it from the senior rates' mess down eight decks before me?

I'm bent over, hands on hips, trying to catch my breath. 'Big Mac blocked the hatch, Chief, and we were stuck for a few minutes before someone pinched his arse,' I explain.

'Shite! Get here fuckin' earlier next time,' he blurts.

Oh well, that was that excuse blown out.

'Anyway, forget it, let's have a game of Othello,' he suggests, tone instantly mellowing, but I can't look at his face, even if it's smothered in anti-flash cotton.

'Is it action stations for real?' I ask, hoping it takes his mind off his superiority complex for a few minutes.

'It's fuckin Chief tae you!' he says.

Anxious not to lose it completely, I repeat the question with due deference to rank. 'Well, dae ye see us flashin up the diesel genny, Chief?'

'Flashin up the diesel genny, Chief?' he mocks, banging the Othello pieces down on the polished lino. 'Anyway, you're black and Ah'm white,' he orders, shuffling the plastic discs on the board.

'D'you hear there?'

Our game is interrupted by the captain. 'Captain speaking.' Then, for almost a minute, nothing bar the static hiss of the ship's intercom. The chief's eyes meet mine and he frowns as if I should know what the captain is going to say next. I blush underneath my anti-flash and hope he doesn't spot it.

Mercifully, the captain pipes up again. He must have dropped his notes or maybe he just saw something interesting out of the window and got side tracked. 'The ship was put to action stations as a result of a sonar contact, thought to have been an enemy submarine, possibly from the Soviet Union. Intelligence suggests that information gathering has been passed from the Russians to the Argentine Navy and it was therefore vital that we reached the highest state of readiness in the shortest possible time.'

He rambles on in his marbled warble.

'We shall be falling out of action stations shortly and returning to defence watches. It appears from tonight's reaction times that we may need to brush up as we approach the exclusion zone. That is all.'

The intercom clicks off.

We finally fall out of action stations at four in the morning. I'm knackered and I had taken a hammering at Othello. Another four hours and I'll be up again.

It's May 13th; one of my school pals, Gregor McCallum, or Wee Man as he was nicknamed at primary school, turns 18 today. I wonder what he'll be doing. Going to the pub certainly won't be a big deal for him. He'd grown out of his nickname two years ago when he stuck the heid into Niall Corkell during a fight in the cloakrooms. From then on, Gregor just got bigger. I, however, remain a wee man.

The ship is now 1,800 miles from the Falklands. Reports come through of an attack on the aircraft carrier *Hermes* by 12 Argentinian Skyhawks, but Sea Wolf missiles shoot down two and the rest take cold feet. Scouse and I decide to open a few tins of beer after work, but for me it's never just a few.

'Come ed, ya little terrrd,' Scouse taunts. He's smiling and slurring his speech, rendering the anger in his voice impotent. He grips the fork tightly in his right hand and holds his other hand behind his back like a Cluedo murderer.

The scene is the galley. It's early hours in the morning and Scouse has picked a fight with a steward we bump into wandering around the ship. I'm thinking it's a random situation but maybe there's friction between them that's festered before coming to a head. Maybe Scouse has engineered my being here so if he's mortally wounded by a spoon or a whisk, I can drag him off to sick bay and be a witness in the subsequent attempted murder inquiry.

'Fur fuck's sake Scouse, we'll get done if we're caught like this,' I say. I used 'we' because he's obviously past caring. I look around the galley. Only the air conditioning units can be heard humming. The normally buzzing fluorescent lights of the galley during the day are silent. Patchy red light pools around areas of the tiled deck but the shadows have the upper hand. Imagine a ghost ship but with one thousand souls tucked up in a cavernous red bed.

We hate the stewards, sometimes more than the officers themselves. It has a lot to do with the relationship between them and the officers. I don't have a clue what it's like between them, but when does that ever stop a prejudiced preconception? Anyway, the steward looks oblivious to Scouse's antagonism. It's as if the unreality of it all has failed to register any sense of danger from his brain. If Scouse is looking for a witness, I'm not it; time for some shuteye. I leave the two cutlery wielding gladiators and head for my pit. They can spoon themselves to death for all I care.

'Joch! Are ye awake, mate?'

'No, Ah'm fuckin not,' I answer in the darkness. I can see the blood vessels at the back of my head, lasered by Scouse's torch beam.

'Joch, Ah've done it, Ah've fuchin killed im. Yell av t'help us, Joch, Ah've done im in.'

'Piss off, Scouse, get yer head down, for God's sake.'

My head is nippin, the beer buzz threatening to give way to a premature hangover.

'Joch, ger up!' Scouse shakes me violently, scaring me into action.

'Okay, okay, Ah'm gettin up, give us a minute.' I try to pacify Scouse with my tone, wary that he might actually have flipped. After the failed hatch incident, maybe he was seeking a more dramatic way to get off the ship. 'Turn the torch off, Scouse, you'll wake the mess.'

Scouse complies and leads me back up towards the galley, my head and heart pounding. My mouth is swollen and dry, a combination of fear and beer aftermath. I worry about my heart, especially after the electric shock in the engine room. Scouse looks round at me, the softness of his face gone, his eyes narrow and focussed. He opens his mouth slightly and I get a whiff of stale alcohol. He shines the torch from beneath his chin, which should provoke laughter but instead almost makes me lose control of my bowels. Scenes from *The Exorcist* play on my overactive imagination.

I must've looked terrified because Scouse switches off the torch, turns and carries on through the red glow of the ship's decks back to the area where we last came across the steward. He touches my arm, slowing us down a little. The hairs on the back of my neck are standing to attention. We creep across the passageway, skimming the lino in silence. Even the air conditioning seems to be holding its breath.

Scouse touches my arm again, firmly this time, and we both stop.

He heads to the corner of the galley where the potato peeler stands. I remember having fixed this machine a few weeks earlier; the fuse had gone but to make myself look good, I made up some cock and bull story about having to rewire the starter motor. Slumped in the corner where the potato peelings usually decompose lies a dark shape. Scouse looks round and motions for me to come forward. I shuffle towards the peeler. The dark shape regains contrast and I can make out the white of a man's torso peppered with what at first appears to be pools of greyish black reflecting from the overhead light, but when the pools glisten, I realise that the steward's oozing black liquid from his back. Scouse stands to the side as I move closer. I can't see a wound or a weapon, but there was that earlier cutlery incident. Jesus Christ! I turn to look at Scouse, but my peripheral vision catches movement.

'Oh, God!' I scream, as the steward rises from his slump, groaning in pain.

'Oh, fucking Christ, help me!' I wail, physically jumping in the air, like Scooby and Shaggy from *Scooby-Doo!* Then the lights come on, momentarily blinding me. Scouse, the steward and three other bastards from the mess emerge from behind mixers and ovens laughing their heads off. I'm not sure my heart can take much more of this.

'Bastards, fucking waste of ketchup!' is all I can muster, grasping at my chest.

Saturday's Kids

1982

No more pissing around for us. Forty Commando Royal Marines come on board. Four of them camp in our mess, complete with rifles and a GPMG*, just like the one my first Action Man had. The tension is palpable. They don't like us, we don't like them, but they need us to get them ashore and we need them to stiffen the Argies into submission. If they don't get ashore soon, they'll probably rape then shoot us.

The food is now pot mess, which is basically mince and anything else that can be thrown in and kept warm for days. Surprisingly though, it tastes okay. There's no conversation between us and the bootnecks**. They clean their weapons and sleep on the floor. We clean our teeth and sleep in comfy beds.

News comes through from *Hermes* of a helicopter ditching in the sea. We're all sleeping in our clothes. War correspondents are now on board looking terrified, as do the Chinese laundry men who were given the option to leave the ship at Ascension Island but, strangely, most of them decide to carry on. I say strangely, but what the fuck would I know what's going through a Chinese laundryman's head on the eve of the first major landing by British forces since D-Day?

---

* General Purpose Machine Gun
** Royal Marines

Today is the 20th of May; Ascension Day. Jock Blair and I are at action stations for real down at November switchboard. It's eerily quiet, as if the troops are tiptoeing around in their socks.

'Get ready for fireworks, Jocky,' Jock Blair says, feeling no pain, at least outwardly. Next door, in the usually empty mess, sit around 30 Marines in full battle order and next to them is Brian Hanrahan, a veteran reporter who's going to get his feet wet. We're all bathed in crimson. I keep meaning to ask why the ship is always red at night.

Through the bulkhead, I hear the spluttering engines of landing craft. I'd love to have a look but there's no chance. We're stuck down the switchboard for ten hours as the ship passes through Falkland Sound and into San Carlos Bay. The landing craft engines' tune changes as the coxswain battles to manoeuvre the four landing craft in and out of the ship's submerged belly. I hear the jarring of metal against metal as one of the landing craft scrapes alongside the innards of the partly submerged ship, battling against the swell of the bay, reminding me of the day we were hauled off the beach at Ascension Island after *Sheffield* had been sunk.

At 0700hrs, I have to report to the bridge for a briefing. I have no idea what it's about, but it feels great to get some fresh air. I look up at the star-encrusted sky; no cloud cover, which is bad news for us. My view is punctuated by the rotating radar on the ship's main mast. Orders are spoken rather than barked. The fresh air gives the scene a sort of dreamlike quality. I make out the silhouetted ridges of the hills overlooking the bay as the sun rises. On the opposite side, the sun works its way up the hills, revealing a landscape of tough grassland and boulders. The dark water glistens as the light from the stars bounces off each ripple, the sea having calmed since the swell of the early hours.

It's so, so silent. I look past the bridge, through the focsle and across a valley into the hills. I have no recollection of seeing any other ships or landing craft in the bay, yet I know that they must have been there as the main landing carries on well into the daylight hours. There must have been 20 other ships just sitting like us, waiting for dawn.

'MEM (L) Cruickshanks?' an officer's voice splits the darkness; his tone is a kind of Jack Hawkins meets James Bond.

'Sir,' I reply, aware of the seriousness of my tone. Well, there's a degree of bullshit to this – I'm not exactly acting out a part in a war film, but old shiny buttons is giving it big licks, so I think *why not?*

'Cruickshanks, you will be sea boats patrol, report to PTI Munnings on the Starboard quarterdeck at 0200hrs tomorrow morning.'

'Sir.' I nod boldly, but I'm still clueless.

So zee enemy has gotten hold of ze formula for heavy water and now I will have to parachute in and blow up ze factoree. I allow myself a moment of fantasy. If the officer had given me my orders in the middle of a bombing raid with explosions going off, it might have felt more like the real thing.

I suck in a deep breath. The cold sharp air stings the back of my throat and I cough, the result of the musty atmosphere from inside the ship mixing with the good stuff. I make my way down to November switchboard. I regret not taking the time to survey the scene as the darkness lifts, but I know Jock Blair will have his stopwatch running.

When I get back, the Marines are gone. 'Time for a wee game, Jocky?' Jock Blair says, Othello already out of its box, black and white pieces separated and ready to go.

He ignores the fact that anything remotely historic is taking place, in favour of playing a board game.

'Chief Blair, how long dae ye think we'll be here?' I ask, putting on my curiosity voice, the one that purveyors of useless information rise to pepper with semi-precious nuggets of opinion, rarely spouting anything worth listening to. But given I have no idea how long we're going to be cocooned together, I have to say something.

'Don't know, son,' Jock Blair replies, nonchalantly.

'Oh, right then.' Shit, he hasn't taken the bait. Perhaps he just wants to concentrate on beating the shite out of me at Othello.

'Take cover! Take cover! Take cover! Air raid warning red! Air raid warning red!'

Whoosh!

Up goes a missile, then another. They sound like our missiles. Shit, they must be our missiles! The whoosh of their launch is closely followed by dum! dum! dum! dum!

The dum! dum! dum! dum! could only be the two Bofors guns on either side of the bridge. More whooshes – other ships' missiles going off. Fuck's sake, something must be attacking us. They don't let them go for nothing, they're too fucking expensive. Small arms fire now, GPMGs crackle between the whooshes and the dums. Jock Blair and I are prostrate, anti-flash covering our faces, sucking air in through the mesh. My heart hammers against the rubber clad deck of November switchboard. Kicking off doesn't even begin to describe it.

The ship's stern shudders as it takes evasive action, the huge propeller screws churning frantically, flailing in an effort to zig-zag the ship out of danger. I'm no ship's captain but a ship zig-zagging at one mile an hour against a bomb dropping out of the sky at ten metres per second squared doesn't seem like fair odds.

I breathe hard, but the heat has nowhere to go. It has a kind of calming effect, like that night my mum hyperventilated when she woke from boiling potatoes in her sleep and the doctor gave her a paper bag to breathe into.

All I can do is cover my head with my hands and listen – as if a few bits of skin and bone could prevent molten hot twisted bomb fragments from piercing through my skull. I smell the rubber from the insulation mats inside the switchboard. I want to sneeze as the cotton anti-flash hood tickles my nostrils but it seems inappropriate during an air raid so I hold it and hold it and then, all is silent. The ship stops shuddering. My breathing settles, but my heart feels like it's one scare away from a cardiac arrest. Something has to give. Luckily though, it comes from my nose. 'Achoo!'

The chief and I get up. The look on his half-hidden face says *sneeze like that again and I'll kick your arse*.

It's hard to know what to feel as the whole thing had only lasted a minute. God knows how many bombs, bullets, missiles and rockets were fired in that short time. Jock Blair and I sit in awkward silence, until the captain breaks it with his crackly intercom chatter.

'D'ye hear there? Captain speaking.' He pauses. I reckon this is how they teach you to speak in posh public school. I get an Action Man for Christmas, they get an intercom set and received pronunciation lessons. 'Ourselves and the other ships in San Carlos water have just come under attack from the Argentine Air Force.'

No shit.

There's more officer talk from the captain, the sort of shite about collateral damage and splashing enemy aircraft as if it's just some big game. No doubt they'll write plenty of accurate, detailed, factual accounts of who did what to who, sorry, whom, but who gives a monkey's?

The attack is devastating. Ships protecting us are either on fire or smoking. There are reports of unexploded bombs on board *Ardent* and *Plymouth*. *Yarmouth* is also badly damaged. *Antrim*, *Argonaut* and *Broadsword* are collaterally fucked up, to use a non officer-speak technical term. Casualties are helicoptered to hospital ships and the makeshift hospital on shore at Fox Bay. There are reports of sailors melting into the metal bulkheads as well as horrific burns to survivors. Later on, Ardent sinks with the loss of 20 men; the havoc has happened in minutes and this is the first day.

Jock Blair and I saw none of the carnage, we only heard it and felt it. As darkness creeps into the bay, the decision is taken to fall out of action stations. The pair of us have been cooped up together for 24 hours. At least I had managed the luxury of half an hour's fresh air on the bridge and I'm still cursing myself for not paying more attention.

The ship reverts to defence watches and most of us troop back to our messdecks. There are no tales of who saw or heard what, and no outpouring of how terrified or exhilarated anyone is feeling. The whole mess is stunned, succumbed to a combination of fear and fatigue. The welcoming crimson light of night-time tranquilises everyone until morning.

I sink silently into my pit and beg for sleep.

I wake from my slumber and sit bolt upright. The light is still crimson. I look at my watch: 0200hrs. *Shit!* I'm supposed to be sea boats patrol and I'm adrift[*]. I've been asleep in most of my clothes, so I grab my woolly pully[**] and sling it on. I sit on the edge of the bed and run my fingers through my greasy hair, sighing at the thought of a few more spots erupting because of my shoddy hygiene. I stifle a yawn and the urge to pull the sleeping bag around my exhausted body. The mess is silent and stinking of men welded to their filthy clothes. A sudden claustrophobia grips me and the hairs stand on the back of my neck. I quickly realise I'm holding my breath, and dizziness is flooding my vision. I take a deep breath, grab my torch, burberry[***] and beret, and race to the starboard quarter-deck.

The freezing wind is blowing hard and there's a swell that whispers *wakey wakey* as I catch a gust of South Atlantic winter full in the face. Rain stiffens my body further and I ping into full alert mode. I glance at my watch. Nine minutes past two. Back home, lads my age are staggering from pubs into nightclubs, heading for kebab shops, or taking someone home on a promise. When they wake next day, it'll be football time. And here I am, 8,000 miles away in a bitterly cold bay in the middle of a war zone and things are about to get worse.

'Are you sea boats patrol?' rasps the petty officer.

'Yes. P.O.'

I can just make him out. He's stocky, arms folded and mouth set into a line that says 'do not cross'.

'You are fucking adrift, lad!'

---

[*] late

[**] a woolly jumper / pullover

[***] a traditional rain jacket exclusive to the Royal Navy, not to be confused with the designer brand

'Yes, P.O.'

'Don't 'Yes P.O.' me,' he barks. 'This is a bloody wartime situation. You can be court martialled for this offence, do you hear me?'

'Yes, P.O.'

'Do you see these two lads?' He points to the two bedraggled sailors getting out of the sea boat, one of them carrying an SLR rifle, the other some scare charges[*]. They look up at me on cue, eyes brimming with contempt for the scrawny little latecomer. They tie up the sea boat which nods against the ship's side as the swell gathers. It seems to be on the side of the pissed off sailors.

I meekly answer that I can see them. I don't mention the nodding boat.

'Well, they want to get into their nice cosy pits, not stand around waiting for adrift stokers.'

The bastard called me a stoker! I'm a greenie, not a stoker. I brush past the P.O. (who I'd always remembered in peace time as a cheery chap, bubbling with enthusiasm), climb down the rope ladder and slump into the sea boat which is now threatening to slip its mooring as the waves up the ante. Another seaman appears out of the darkness and joins me in the sea boat. The petty officer's contempt must have spread to him because he takes control of the scare charges and the rifle as he guns the boat's engine. I sit and put on a suitably guilt-ridden face, even though there's no chance of him seeing it.

The seaman motions for me to untie the bow of the boat, which pitches and tosses like an untamed stallion, but we eventually break free of *Fearless* and chug away from the hull and into the swell. As the bollocking from the petty officer recedes, the rain clears and silhouettes of all the

[*] underwater grenades

ships in the bay show against the star-laden sky. Their bristling defence radars work overtime; a carnival of movement without sound or light. This is what I had failed to see just a few hours ago standing on that bridge thinking *I wonder what today will be like?*

This close up, *Fearless* at sea level is an imposing sight against the night sky, again reminding me of the photographs I took of her at Ascension. The decks above us form into a giant metallic pyramid, albeit with guns and missile launchers sticking out of it. The seaman steers the boat further away from the ship's side and as we round the anchored bow, the wind gnaws at my burberry. My bones feel naked against the chill as the boat leers towards the ship's port side. The seaman fights to regain control.

I wondered if any other silly fuckers are playing sea boats merry-go-round at two in the morning. A few of my mates will be bouncing around at home by now, probably burning toast and setting off smoke alarms after returning from the pub in a shopping trolley.

San Carlos Bay is only a few miles long, but it contains the nucleus of the landing and the Argentine Air Force are aware that to destroy the ships here would be to wipe out support for the landing troops. The daylight hours had shown how vulnerable the ships were without good air defences. Some of the ships have missile systems which were built in the sixties. This means if you can remember firing them, you weren't really there. Bofors guns are relics of bygone days when the intended targets were propeller driven and it didn't exactly inspire confidence to hear a machine gun being used on a jet flying at nearly 600 miles an hour.

The choppy sea is a handful, but the seaman nurses the boat in and out of the swells and it settles into a steady rhythm. I begin to enjoy my little night out in San Carlos. It's not a pissed up ride in a shopping trolley, but it'll do.

From my briefing on the bridge, I find out that the aim of the sea boat's patrol is to discourage underwater activity by the enemy. The scare charges are dropped into the water close to the ship. If this brings any divers to the surface then we shoot them, at least I think that's what the gun's for. The seaman blows hot, fetid air into his fingers. I remain silent, mulling over the day's events. At least half the ships in the bay had received damage. *Will it be our turn tomorrow? Think happy thoughts, David. Think about kissing Motorcycle Girl.*

There's a dull thud that lifts my arse right off the boat's hard wooden seat. It's the explosion from the scare charge, lobbed in by the pissed off looking seaman. After the initial explosion, I'm too cold to ask the seaman if I can have a warning next time. I instinctively feel for the pulse on my neck but my hands are too cold to feel anything.

Shitting myself while bobbing around the ship's bulkhead has given me an idea for payback for my mates back at the mess. But it's dependent on having to do this shitty routine tomorrow night, and surviving another day.

Happy Together

1982

At breakfast, the ship's mess hall is buzzing with activity. Pot mess has been replaced by bacon, eggs and sausages. If I didn't know any better, I would say that this is to boost morale – or it could just mean that the grub is getting close to its use-by date. The seamen gunners are noisily recounting tales of near misses from yesterday. I sit with some surly stokers as we listen reluctantly to their alleged kills and splashes. They pose in their flak jackets and have written names on their helmets. Someone has seen too many Vietnam war movies.

I'm jealous that I don't have a helmet to write on though. It would have been great to fire a £30,000 missile and knock out an Argy fighter, instead of cowering in a smelly metal and rubber tomb, breathing through manky cotton, waiting to take a hit.

'Hands to action stations! Hands to action stations! Air raid warning red! Air raid warning red!'

The excited chatter is replaced by the assault course to action stations: boots on lino, boots on metal, hands on helmets, anti-flash hoods being donned, the opening of hatch clips, running, climbing, sliding, the closing of hatch clips, and murmurings of various emotions: concern, pride, excitement, terror.

I juggle a rubbery fried egg from my plate and put it into a roll. My assault course now contains elements from race day at school sports. I remember doing the wheelbarrow race with big Campbell White and the system we developed at South Parks Primary to win every time: Campbell doing the running, me pretending to paddle my hands along the grass. Taking my egg roll and a mug of hot tea down to my action station proves more of a challenge.

Christ, Jock Blair's here before me again. He must be kipping in the place.

'Bring me anything, Jocky?' he asks, looking at my roll.

'Naw, Chief,' I say, breathing hard.

'You better eat that quick,' he says, glaring through the anti-flash.

The yolk's running out of the roll and onto my anti-flash gloves, which are now a breeding ground for parasites with a fried egg fetish. I lower the mouthpiece of the cotton hood and stuff what's left of my roll inside. I push my half empty mug behind the switchboard, feeling it's too much to drink tea in front of a chief who has sacrificed breakfast to be first at his action station. Following this, Jock Blair and I lie down and put our hands over our heads.

I take in the now weary smell of rubber before the bombs come.

The whooshes and dums are more frequent than yesterday. The ship shudders as bombs explode in the surrounding water. Again, the propeller screws churn into evasive action. The vibrations drill upwards through the deck into my hands, muffled by the smelly rubber mat that separates me from the metal deck.

There's nothing to look at. Like a row of men pissing in urinals and averting each other's gaze, I cast my eyes down towards the rubber mat. If I look up, I'll see the soundproofed inner casing of the switchboard door. If Jock Blair looks up, he'll see the same. I count an interval of six dums in between whooshes. Dum! dum! dum! dum! dum! dum! Whooosh! Dum! dum! dum! dum! dum! dum! Whooosh! My heart pounds out the rhythm of the dums, leaping at every whoosh! I strain to listen for the roar of low flying enemy jets but can't hear them over the cacophony of outgoing flak. My chest fills with the vibration of the ship, my ears ringing from the aftermath of exploding shells and gunfire. The rubber mat suffocates any other smells inside the switchboard. It seems too hellish to die without breathing in a final drop of fresh air but our orders are to remain here until the shit makes a direct hit on the fan. I lie and wait, and wait, and wait.

The silence returns, punctuated with distant gunfire. The vibrations cease and the all clear is sounded as my heartbeat returns to something resembling normal. Jock Blair and I get up.

There's a softness in the chief's eyes that wasn't there yesterday. Maybe he's clocked that spot on my nose and thinks I've got enough to deal with.

'Next time, bring us something to eat, will ye?'

Okay, so maybe I misread that softness.

'Yes, Chief,' I say with a nod.

The attack lasts all of five minutes. There hasn't been much damage, but the Argy Air Force has suffered heavily. In three waves of eight aircraft, 15 are shot down, eight by Sea Harriers before they could get anywhere near us.

We stay at action stations all day but there are no more air attacks. After hours of boredom in a confined spaced, a small part of me craves the action of the raids. I start to beat the chief at Othello. I don't know how he feels about this and, to be honest, if it's making him visibly miserable, I wouldn't notice, thanks to the combination of his anti-flash hood and his general surly demeanour.

During the early hours, the seaman and I once again potter around *Fearless* under a starry sky. At 2am, much to my relief, the biting wind is biting somewhere else in the South Atlantic. The sea is calm and there's a diesel electric submarine alongside us; the long, black shape nestles against the grey of our assault ship. There's a red glow seeping out of one of the hatches like the end of a cigarette and I'm sure the pungent aroma of unwashed sailors is seeping out of the hatch. There's no noise from its 2,000-ton body and I wonder what it's been up to in daylight hours, but another scare charge lifts my arse off the boat's seat reminding me that this could be the perfect night for payback.

Most of the mess will be sleeping like babies after a long day at action stations. The war is running like clockwork, breakfast being the first casualty of peace. It must be laid down somewhere in the DIY guide to battle strategy: always attack the enemy before they've had time to eat. I can tell you – being hungry and scared shitless can really piss a person off. Tonight, I fancy adding sleep deprivation to my mess mates' list of woes. After all, I'm the poor sod detailed to rise at 2am and splutter round the ship aimlessly in a sea boat trying to kill non-existent Argy frogmen.

We are nearing the outer bulkhead of my messdeck, 3H2 Z, which lies right on the waterline; funny how the officers were never stationed near the waterline. Did I tell you I hate officers?

I pull out the pin from the scare charge and drop it close to the ship's side. The seaman then opens up the throttle and we leg it. I laugh as the shockwave lifts my arse out of the seat.

'You little dickhead, Jock, they'll troop* us if they find out.' the seaman says, clearly not seeing the funny side.

'Let's go round again,' I sing.

'Fuck right off' the seaman says. 'If we damage the ship, we'll be right in the shit.'

'I know,' I reply, 'we might even get sent home.'

'In your dreams,' he grunts, turning away from me, his breathing vapour tailing off as he exhales deeply.

We don't do it again, but the rest of the patrol goes quickly and I head back to the arid ventilation and red silence of the messdeck. My antics don't seem to have made much of an impact, so half of me is happy, like that time when my schoolmate Allan Fowlis and I put a boulder on the railway line at Kirkforthar, a tiny village in Fife. Once the boulder was in place, we ran back up the steep embankment and waited for a train. We waited and waited and waited. It seemed like eternity but it was only a few minutes.

I can't remember whose idea it was to run back down and push the boulder off but I was relieved when we did. Morbid curiosity makes you wonder *what if?* We had convinced each other that even if we'd left the boulder on the line, the train would have crushed it instantly. I suppose we'll never know. But if Allan and I hadn't seen sense and changed our collective mind, there's a train driver and three carriages of passengers whose lives could have changed course because two kids had a moment of madness.

---

* court-martial-style punishment

162

The Gift

1982

Sunday, May 23rd. The morning starts off quietly. Most of the flotilla had left San Carlos after the first landings on Friday and has only just started returning, with an armed escort of what's left of the frigates to Bomb Alley, our new name for San Carlos Bay. We'd gone to action stations earlier in the day for a missile attack. I froze as the words 'missile imminent' flew over the intercom. I never did find out what had happened that morning, but thank Christ we didn't become another statistic. Maybe the Argentine pilot who launched the missile decided he didn't want it doing any damage and ran after it.

Nothing more is said publicly to the ship's company about the alleged attack and no questions are asked.

We fall out of action stations quickly, only to fall back in even quicker. I'm starting to store food; after all, who knows what's going to happen? We remain closed up at action stations for hours without any activity. The chief and I numb each other's minds with Othello and my increasing rate of victory provokes a perceptible tension. Our anti-flash hoods and gloves now have lives of their own; they would lose their protection if they were washed, so the things crawling around in them are a protected species. November switchboard, that tiny room full of metal still smells of rubber but it's now playing second fiddle to bad breath and excessive flatulence. Who in their right mind has a rubber fetish? Apart from one half of Holland, that is. Someone told me they even wrap their cheese in rubber.

The chief flashes up the diesel genny and tests the circuit breakers, the smelly rubber room whining once more to the tune of 60 hertz. Mercifully, we shut down after only 15 minutes and the room returns to silence. I think he does it out of sheer boredom, now that I'm not such a pushover in the board game stakes.

The monotony is broken by a ham sandwich wrapped in clingfilm. So now we have rubber *and* clingfilm. We're only missing the chains and handcuffs for an S & M orgy involving sandwiches. There are now some men in the adjacent mess and they've decided it's lunch time too. I think about speaking to them, but they seem preoccupied. After a bit of work, I manage to free my sanny from its clingfilm prison. I look at it with anticipation before lifting it to my mouth.

'Take cover! Take cover! Take cover!'

I hit the deck. The ship vibrates to bone shaking and teeth clattering proportions as the propellers and steering gear slalom around the bay. This time the bombs are closer. There's a sequence of bangs, much louder than the outgoing fire. Shit, have we been hit? There's nothing coming over the intercom. How the hell do we know if we're sinking? Jock Blair gets up and takes action. He winds up the phone and clicks the little flag marked 'Kilo'. They confirm they've heard the bangs but thankfully there's no damage to report.

We lie on the deck for a long time. The air raids are incessant; it looks like today is a big day for the Argy Air Force. Internally, I begin to pray, first simple stuff – Oh Father, who art in heaven – but then I switch to a more pragmatic mode – Oh Father who art in heaven, if the ship is hit please make it near the bridge, and please leave the escape routes from November switchboard clear so I can escape. Please Lord, keep casualties to a minimum; if the ship has to take a hit at the stern, please make the bomb explode in the tank deck where there aren't many men.

Unfortunately, my prayers are answered; the bridge takes a hit from 60mm cannon fire. A Mirage fighter has broken through the picket ships out in Falkland Sound and almost chops the ship's mast in two. The piercing shells take out some of the bridge windows, which are two inches thick. Four sailors are wounded, a finger here, a scooped out calf muscle there. The casualties are minor, unless it's your calf muscle of course. That's the price the seamen pay for being able to see and fire back at the enemy. The ship retaliates and manages to take out two planes with the Bofors guns.

When the fighting stops, I'm actually relieved to hear we've been hit. It makes me think back to when my dad finally unleashed his belt and I could breathe again. Several other Argy aircraft have been splashed*. Reports come in of an Argy pilot bailing out within yards of the ship and getting picked up under guard by our medics, having sustained a broken hip.

We fall out of action stations at dusk, around 4pm. I rush down to the tank deck to watch the wounded pilot come on board. The medic, a wee Scots guy, is helping him. Beside the medic, menacingly, is a paratrooper. They make a strange threesome; the pilot's face ground out with pain, the consoling face of the medic and the *one false move and he gets it* face of the paratrooper.

---

* shot down over the sea and sunk

165

A few hours later, as we sit in the mess, drained of adrenalin, the captain reports the results of the air attacks; around 30 Argentine planes have been splashed. *HMS Antelope* has been hit and is on fire and the ship's survivors are being brought by landing craft to our ship. Then comes the order which freezes my blood: 'Standing Sea Fire Party will muster in the tank deck.' I'm still part of the Standing Sea Fire Party. It can only mean going on board *Antelope* and fighting the fires. Jesus, the Navy's getting value for money out of me.

One of the stokers pipes up. 'Jock, are you—'

'Aye Ah fuckin am!'

'Hey Jock, ya little gobshite, get yer arse doon that tank deck,' the big Geordie Buddha commands. The rest of the mess, tired and tense, look up at me.

'See you later, Jock,' Jess stammers, his face trying to convey empathy, but I'm too absorbed in my own anger to acknowledge his concern.

At 1800hrs, we muster in the tank deck near the landing craft apron. It's cold and smoky. I'm detailed as a BA* man. All around us are the accoutrements of firefighting: five gallon drums of foam; hose reels; breathing apparatus; asbestos suits. I wonder where the next of kin form is. We huddle together, stamping our feet to keep warm. My asbestos suit stinks of oil, making me itch. I scratch around my chin. My plukes** are just about ripe for bursting.

As the BA controller goes through the procedures, I chew on my fingers and nibble my nails, shit scared at the prospect of boarding a burning ship filled with explosives. I try to tune in to the man who's attempting to keep me alive but instead I wince as the bottom of a landing craft

---

* breathing apparatus
** spots

scrapes against the tank deck apron. The hydraulic bow door opens and 40 feet away around 100 orange-suited men stand facing me. Like robots, they wait for a command, silent and unmoving, their expressions hollowed out by the horrors of what they've witnessed. They look back at us with their lifeless eyes, exhausted from fighting uncontrollable fires and scrambling to the exits. They've seen their shipmates expend their energy in the hope of saving the ship, only to end up abandoning it a few hours later. The black on their faces is soot, etched around their cheeks and eye sockets, the white the imprint of fear and protection from the anti-flash hoods.

Slowly, they trudge off the landing craft in monastic procession. The orange survival suits weigh them down, almost tripping them up as they lumber towards us on the tank deck apron. As they get closer, a look of shame appears on some of their faces, as if they've let the side down.

The orange refugees shuffle closer. The scene resembles a standoff between two warring factions. We size each other up. It's as if they're our prisoners. As another ship's company, they are homeless. They have no messdecks, nothing on this ship is theirs and they have no desire to know us.

When the last man from *Antelope* leaves the tank deck, we begin loading the firefighting equipment onto the empty landing craft. I'm shitting myself. The drums, hoses, foam and nozzles are loaded in silence. Once the last of the equipment is on board, we stand back from the landing craft, waiting for the order to go. I consider bursting all my plukes in one go just in case I don't make it.

There is no shout of an order, more a whisper that snakes around the fire party. We aren't going. The captain has been informed of the imminent danger of a massive explosion from *Antelope's* ammunition magazine as an unexploded bomb lies in wait for anyone foolish enough to board her. Without prompting, we gather up the firefighting equipment and place it back onto the tank deck. If they reissue the order, they might have a mutiny on their hands. I try not to look too pleased in case fate sees me smiling and has a rethink.

Minutes later, I'm in the dining mess surrounded by the orange refugees. The acrid stench of smoke from their survival suits overwhelms anything coming from the galley. The dining area is silent. They just stand there in limbo, like a still from a horror film; not one of them takes off their survival suit.

In the morning, *Antelope* is a memory. She sank during the night following a huge explosion minutes after her survivors landed on *Fearless*. There's no doubt that most of us in the Standing Sea Fire Party would have burned to death if we had boarded her. I'm relieved of my sea boats patrol for one night, sparing me the images of her scalded body succumbing to the freezing oily water.

I see no more of *Antelope's* survivors, but there's no time for sentiment. The air raids resume as black sky is replaced by blue. I imagine them flying back in a passenger airliner, being served food by civilian flight attendants with smiles and soft voices, their introduction to stress counselling coming from someone with a badge who speaks four languages. They'll probably see a lot of people with badges.

The Great Depression

1982

'Take the gash[*] down the tank deck, Jock,' says Big George in more of a laconic manner than an order, though it wouldn't have mattered how he'd said it, I'd have to do it anyway. Still, indifference costs nothing.

I drag the gash down to the tank deck. Who would have thought that you still had to take out the rubbish during a war? From the tank deck I make out a little of the horizon, but there isn't much to see. It's daylight though and I'm outside-ish, so I'm grateful for that.

'Is that you, Jock?' comes a voice from behind an idle Eager Beaver.

'Aye' I reply, unable to muster any form of sarcastic retort. I worry that Scouse's sudden appearance hasn't made me jump out of my skin.

'Bad news about yesterday, all those blokes goin home an dat. Their minds could be fucked up foreva.'

'Jist think, Scouse, you could have been hame now if ye'd been oan that ship,' I reply, scrunching the top of the gash bag, feeling the sharp metal of the crushed cans.

I immediately regret what I've said, but Scouse eases my embarrassment. 'I know mate, but their minds must be knackered. It's a bit ov a high price to pay for gettin home errly,' he says, kicking a tyre with his steaming boot[**].

---

[*] rubbish
[**] a sailor's work boot

'Yeah, better stickin this one oot tae the bitter end, eh?'

'Exactly, an think ov Sharon an Linda at da Mucky, they'll be all over us war heroes, Jock.'

Scouse walks over and, without a hint of sarcasm, he punches me hard in the stomach. As the gash bag clatters to the deck, I squat, struggling for breath, forcing the panic down by thinking about Sharon and Linda. Perhaps they *will* be waiting.

Monday is a relatively quiet start to the week. Eight enemy aircraft are shot down as they bomb two of the main landing ships, *LSL*[*] *Sir Galahad* and *LSL Sir Lancelot*. Luckily the bombs don't explode, but they cause big problems for the onboard bomb disposal teams. *Fearless* comes under attack in Bomb Alley, but the damage is minimal.

It's a brief respite in the tragedy department though. We're going to action stations continuously. It's becoming a bit of an art form and now I'm beating Jock Blair at getting to the switchboard *and* beating him at Othello.

I imagine my mum back home blethering in the street to the neighbours. Before the war, she would have been getting, 'Oh Margaret, this bloody weather, it's fair gettin oan ma goat, an Charlie wiz up aw night wae diarrhoea an they kids next door, they're eywis runnin in an oot o oor gairden fur that baw o theirs. If it comes ower again, Ah'm gonnae burst it.'

Now though it'd be 'Oh, hiya Margaret, Ah see they rapier missiles are no half gien the Argies a hard time. Yer boy must be awfy pleased that they Super Etendards[**] cannae come in tae the valleys wae their Exocet. Ah read

---

[*] Landing Ship Logistics
[**] French-built Argentine aircraft

in the newspaper that the bombs they Argies were droppin wurnae gawn aff because the arming fuses are set too low. Hey Margaret, is it true that yir boy's a born again Christian?'

'Well, fur the duration of the conflict anyway,' my savvy mum would reply.

Bomb Alley is receiving saturation coverage from the Argentine Air Force. Word has obviously got back about the fuses for their bombs being set too high. Thanks to the BBC and *The Sun* newspaper, the bombs are not only finding their targets, they're exploding on impact too.

Tuesday afternoon feels like double maths followed by single geography. *HMS Coventry* gets caught and murdered at the mouth of the bay. She rolls over onto her side and sinks like a stone. Her survivors thankfully don't come on board *Fearless*.

Wednesday is quiet. I get a letter from Mum. Her ears must have been burning.

Thursday, the attacks resume but the bombs are aimed at the shore and result in heavy casualties. The port Bofors gun claims two splashed Argentine planes out of four shot down. The seamen are chuffed to bits and make sure we all know who's winning the war.

Friday is our day off. We sail out of the TEZ[*].

The mess is dark and silent and swaying in a South Atlantic swell. It's also quietly creepy. There are no alarms, no call to action stations, no pipes[**] of any kind. We're either ghosts or I must be dreaming. If I'm dead, heaven is bobbing soundlessly in eternal darkness. When I was a kid, I used to watch *Space: 1999*. It was less about finding strange new worlds and imposing your ideology on them

[*] Total Exclusion Zone
[**] calls

and more about the psychology of being cooped up in an artificial atmosphere trillions of miles from anywhere. There was always strange haunting music being played, complete with dream sequences, and the commander would regularly have to go against the grain to make life saving decisions, while the rest of the crew questioned his sanity. This is the kind of atmosphere I'm currently experiencing. Thankfully, my thoughts are interrupted.

The door slides open to reveal the profile silhouette of a bearded face. 'Bloody hell, it stinks in ere.' It's Bomber Wells and he has a point. That was one sense missing from *Space: 1999* – smell-o-vision. I suppose if the commander had personal hygiene problems then the crew might have said, 'Fuck it, he really stinks and there's no way that energy field is going to deflect such a huge asteroid. Clamp him in the brig and we'll do it our way, and get some bloody air freshener while you're at it.'

'Awright, Jocky?'

'Aye, Bomber, right you are.'

Bomber scares me in a "loveable rogue" kind of way. One minute he's charm personified but if you cross him he can sting you like a scorpion and walk away as if nothing has happened.

The line of light from the sliding door swells to a full rectangle as Bomber turns to go up the ladders to the upper decks.

'Close the fucking door,' comes a Geordie voice from the dark recesses of the mess.

'Aye, George,' I capitulate. Sailors are great sleepers.

Safely out of the firing line for the time being, it feels good to relax. I exit my pit and get some training kit on.

'Where you goin, Jock?' asks Big George.

'Jist doon the tank deck fur a wee run aboot, George.'

'Mad bastard,' he replies, mid rollover.

I leave the mess in darkness and head up two decks, over the cross passage, down three more decks and out of the small hatch above the heads. Not a soul. The Marie Celeste has a doppelganger.

I hate using the weights when no-one is about in case I drop the bar on my neck and die helpless, pinned to the weight bench, lonely, frightened and freezing, so I content myself with running around in circles on the tank deck. My circular motion is hampered by boxes of ammunition and out of date maps, but at least I'm making an effort. It's not easy working up a sweat in the freezing cold and the odd marine shuttling past must think I'm mental, but I'm beginning to get a dopamine buzz.

After my workout, I head up for'ard* for a dhoby. When I get to the showers, there's an armed marine outside. I scan him for any signs of a refusal of entry, like when I get to the front of a nightclub queue and the bouncer looks me up and down before saying "Sorry, mate, not tonight." But the marine's body language suggests more *In you go, pal*.

Inside the heads stands a fully armed paratrooper and two unarmed Argentinian soldiers. As the door squeaks shut, the two bare-chested prisoners look up from their basins and swivel, eyes falling on me. In their gaze I sense fear and worry, perhaps even a hint of loathing. After all, I'm five foot fuck all, weigh less than a bag of King Edward's and I make a ridiculous flip-flopping sound when I walk. I imagine them saying *We surrendered to men like these?* I flip-flop up to the showers at the top of the bathrooms, their heads swan down again to their wash basins and I disappear into the shower. I can't resist

---

* towards the front of the ship

173

poking my head out just in case they try to overpower the para, but he has them scared out of their wits. He scares the shit out of me too, and we're supposed to be on the same side. Soon after, the squeaking door signals their exit and I get the rest of my shower in peace. I struggle to shake off those looks of resignation though, and flinch at a sudden flashback of *Antelope's* survivors trudging onto the tank deck.

When I return to the mess, everyone else is up. Pits and sleeping bags have been zipped up and folded away, cigarette smoke is doing a hazy tango with body odour and the TV has been resurrected. It's some spiel about our few days in the TEZ and that 2 Para[*] have taken Port Darwin and Goose Green in some fierce exchanges with the Argentinian troops. The paras have captured 1500 men with just a few hundred troops. With this news comes a change in us.

After weeks of being cooped up, we're allowed up top. The weather, whilst miserable to most, is fucking awesome to me. The morning's swell has morphed into a queasy pitch and roll. The accompanying mist leaks droplets onto my face, while the exhilarating waves spatter the deck and then roll back into the scuppers. Shrouded in the mist, I can make out the shape of another warship. They must be our picket ship and I bet they're delirious at the thought of being a decoy ship for us.

The ships scythe through the waves in sync, a hundred yards apart. There's a signal coming from their bridge but I have no knowledge of Morse code so it could easily have said *Good afternoon, Captain. Captain of* HMS Antrim *here. Have you heard that rumour that Disney are thinking about opening a theme park in Europe? Over.*

---

[*] 2nd Batallion, Parachute Regiment

Ah, hello there, Captain. Captain of HMS Fearless *here. Away with yourself, man, you've been at sea too long. Get the ship's surgeon to check you for scurvy. Out.*

I make out a few ghostly shapes on the flight deck of our escort ship, which is suitable for one anti-submarine helicopter only. There will be no flying stations[*] today; the mist is great cover from air attacks. It's highly unlikely that planes from Argentina will attack outside the TEZ. Sometimes you feel so good you just know it won't last.

The fresh air is therapy for the suffocating confines of the messdeck. The ships continue to pitch and roll in tandem. I take deep gulps of fresh salty air as the wind batters my face, but I'm feeling no pain. Overhead, a few gulls search for a target, rising and falling, the feathers on their wings buffeted by the air pushing up from the crashing waves.

Tomorrow is Saturday; club night at The Exit, my local disco back home. It's an alcohol-free place but it plays good music and I find I can chat up women there without any stimulants, unless you count milk. I miss the place. I love it so much that when I forgot my membership card one night I attempted to blag my way in and almost got barred. My mum had to plead my case and I was let off with a warning.

I had met a new set of friends there. It was like my university in a way, a place I could go where everyone and everything is new. There was the hint of a scene. Bands came to The Exit to rehearse and I had always been into music, even to the point of studying for my O grades while listening to X-Ray Specs. My mum had even bought me an electric guitar on her and my dad's meagre income, but I

---

[*] when the ship's flight deck is out of bounds to all personnel except the flight crew and flight deck personnel

was shite at it. Still, it was good to know that the neighbours were interested enough to critique my performance. One of my better reviews consisted not of words, but three solid knocks on the wall. I took that as a sign of encouragement, but when the coppers arrived, I realised maybe the drums would be better.

Giant rotor blades shatter my moment of reflective calm. One of the Sea King helicopters is flashing up*. It's just a test though. The chopper remains resolutely chained to the flight deck, the power from the rotors pulling at the chains, causing them to vibrate like a bulldog shitting in the Arctic. The pilot jabbers into his headset. Checks are being made, controls tested. It seems to take forever. Eventually, the pilot signals OK and the engines shut down. I head back for the stuffy, warm, fag reek of subterranea.

Down in the messdeck, the talk is of more attacks on Bomb Alley. There goes that guilt thing again. Half of you wants to be there to help get them out of the shit, the other three quarters says *Thank fuck it's not us for a change*.

'Let's see yer girlfriend, Scouse.' I lean over to try and catch a glimpse of a photo of Scouse's bird, but he draws back and pretends to hide the letter.

'No, Jock, Ah can't, just in case yer ave a little dribble in yer kechs.'

I show no more interest in Scouse's letter and this annoys him a little. Nonetheless, she must be worth nearly getting your ankle chopped off for.

'Dem Argies are done for now, Jocky,' Scouse says, his eyes lighting up with revived mischief, them having been sucked dry by the emotional buffeting of the previous week.

---

* starting up

Two years ago, I had sat in the town park in Glenrothes. Beside me sat my girlfriend, Carolyn, although she didn't know she was my girlfriend. It was an intensely bright, warm day. The blues and greens of the sky and trees were saturated, threatening to spill out their colour onto the greys and whites of roads and houses.

It was May 10th 1980, which just happened to be both our 16th birthdays. Carolyn was a Celtic supporting Catholic, I was a Rangers supporting Protestant, and sharing our birthday was an Old Firm Scottish Cup final.

As we lay together on the grass with the sun nuzzling the backs of our necks, 50 miles away at Hampden Park in Glasgow, hundreds of men in perms wearing figure-hugging jumpers and baggy flared trousers were hurling bottles at each other, tearing clumps of curly hair out of each other's heads. That night, blood-spattered faces appeared on TV, defiance shot out of their misty, sectarian, bigoted eyes. Many innocents were caught up in the troubles, one of them a sports photographer who was close to death after suffering a neck wound caused by a bottle. He ended up scarred and partially deaf, when he was just doing his job. No-one knew who threw the bottle and many, on both sides, wouldn't care.

The radio placed between our bodies that summer's day turned our light-hearted banter about the merits of our teams into disbelief. Sure, there can be rivalry at football matches, but this was a senseless, out of control battle. We stood up and Carolyn picked up her wireless. The chances of any further intimacy quickly became zero. The shock of violence on such an awesomely beautiful day had destroyed our relationship. We never saw each other until Monday at school where talk of the riot at Hampden was as thick as smoke from a burning mattress.

The battle for Goose Green had sparked my memory of May madness in Glasgow in the name of a football match.

Back in San Carlos, after only two days at sea, the threat of immediate air strikes has been lifted and I permit myself a peep at a possible future.

I keep a copy of the ship's Daily Orders (a military schedule of the day's events) from Thursday May 27th, one day before 2 Para's assault on Goose Green. It reads *Action stations by day – defence watches by night if threat permits. Enemy aircraft losses to date: 75 aircraft, 9 ships.* There is a footnote next to these war statistics. *Lost one Parker biro, finder please return to Chief Petty Officer Myers.*

Sailors talk of veteran status being conferred upon them. It smacks of Vietnam and the lottery of that guerrilla war, where men were killed after one day in battle and others survived the year-long tour – but no-one can agree on who the lucky ones were.

I swear that the captain's addresses to the ship's company are becoming upbeat. The Argentine forces have lost too many planes in Bomb Alley, or Death Valley as it's now being called, to continue their strategic suicide. My diary tells me that I read a book called *Trial Run* by Dick Francis but I can't remember what it was about; probably some kind of horse sabotage.

Tonight, I have sea boats patrol again. It's been given the name Operation Awkward, although fuck knows why they couldn't have given it a name that instils greatness and prestige on those who carried out its mission. Perhaps they could even strike up a medal in recognition of its success in foiling submersible subversives from blowing up the anchored task force fleet. I imagine receiving mine from Her Maj in a glittering ceremony that also awards some council flunky who keeps dog shit away from the local swing park.

Cruickshanks, I now bestow upon you, for gallantry in the face of blustery weather and choppy seas, the bravado medal.

Thank you, Your Majesty. I will treasure this forever.

Off you go then. And ask the dog shit guy to come in.

Then off I'd march into the sunshine, a scrum of press photographers in tow and a gorgeous bit of fanny hanging off me, while the ceremony for lesser mortals continued.

May I present to Your Majesty, for services to dog shit prevention . . . step forward . . .

The water is smooth and oily black because *HMS Onyx*, the diesel class submarine, is alongside us again. The sleek black skin, bathed in milky moonlight, hugs the grey metal bulkhead of *Fearless*, which has earned some rusty battle scars. The seaman and I nod our usual courtesies and get down to the job in hand. His job is to steer the boat, man the rifle, detonate scare charges and keep a lookout for water-borne infiltrators. Mine is to look at the pretty tracer fire streaking across the sky some 50 miles away at Mount Kent where the marines and paras are engaged in severe bloody hand-to-hand combat whilst dealing with well dug in Argy trenches bristling with machine guns.

I have no inclination to swap jobs. The sky occasionally flashes as a flare betrays the Argentine positions. Men are dying in the most brutally cold way as the paras and marines relentlessly push forward, while adrenalin rushes to replace the lack of food and warmth needed by their muscles to function as killing machines. I wonder how hard it must be to fire a piece of metal welded by the cold to your freezing hands, even if your life depends on it.

As we round the stern for the fourth time that cold, black night, the flashes and flares cease. The seaman gently manoeuvres the sea boat along the starboard side and our reliefs take over. As they descend into the pitch black, I shout, 'You've missed the firework display!'

'Fuck off, sprog,' comes the skin-piercing reply.

Circus

1982

For the next few days we play second fiddle to the land battles. *Fearless* is being used by the knobs from the army, who have set up command for the entire assault. An atmosphere of quiet confidence is filtering down to the rank and file, and it has to be coming from somewhere. We are able to get up on deck now and survey the various ships in San Carlos Bay. The harsh winter sunshine makes definition and identification easy. Canberra, the giant white P&O liner who has managed to survive 'friendly' as well as hostile fire, languishes in the bay like a metallic Moby Dick. The water remains calm and I attempt a few photographs. A Harrier Jump Jet has landed on the flight deck and we muster around it, eager for a picture. Most people would settle for a snap of themselves with Rod Stewart or some other famous pop star, but our idol is a Sea Harrier with its life saving Sidewinder missiles.

There is no chance of a quiet corner of the ship to myself. The decks are buzzing with sailors all eager for a nosey at what they've been deprived of since the landings nearly two weeks ago; a chance to see what the hell we are fighting for. Bomb Alley is protected by hills on three sides with only one way in and one way out, unless you're an Argentine pilot in which case you won't need to know which way is out. The landscape resembles the little inlets in the Highlands and Islands of Scotland minus the sunken ships and downed aircraft wreckage. I peer down on the flight deck from the Seacat missile deck; Seacat is the only missile you can outrun with a decent pair of trainers. The officer piloting the Sea Harrier climbs into the cockpit. He has no intention of taking off just yet, pausing to soak up the adulation; milking his 15 minutes' worth. If I were him, I'd plaster the cockpit with crossed-out Skyhawks and Mirages, even if the only thing I had shot down was a weather balloon. Thankfully, no-one asks for his autograph, but I wish I had. Like the rest of the ship's company, I wander freely around the upper decks. The still water of the bay has broken into a ripple as a landing craft trundles into view.

There are about 50 soldiers on board, tightly packed behind two Snow Cats. There's a wail emanating from the landing craft but it isn't coming from the engine. A Royal Naval Lieutenant, standing on the landing craft's bridge, is playing what looks like a violin, but the music is hard to make out. As the landing craft chugs along parallel to me, I lift my camera and focus on the violinist, his bow glinting in the strong sunshine. Utilising my zoom lens, I capture another man leaning nonchalantly against the guardrail as if he's modelling the latest camouflage gear for a catalogue. A few others smile, then they're gone, and the music fades. I blink and look around for corroboration to what I've just witnessed, but there's nobody there. At least I have a photograph to prove what happened. I think.

'Much d'ye want for that camera, Jock?' the big Geordie asks, softly, as he closes his locker – but I know he's buttering me up.

I take a step back, tensing up. 'Ah don't know, George, it's worth a ton fifty.'

'A ton fifty, ye greedy wee bastard,' he blusters. 'I'll give ye a hundred fur it right now.'

'Let us think about it, will ye? Ah'm no sure Ah want tae sell it,' I reply, tucking the camera in the bottom drawer of my own locker. Thankfully, the conversation changes.

Keith Hallas, a class one greenie, emerges from his bunk and slithers out of his sleeping bag; his body odour escapes into the air to assault the ventilation. Exaggerating every movement, he sits up and stretches. He surveys the room like an actor gauging the audience before his piercing eyes lock on mine knowingly. This seems to happen in slow motion and, as a result, Keith has received due attention for his theatrics.

'We're off on a little jaunty around the islands tonight, boys,' Keith discloses.

'How the fuck do *you* know?' challenges the big Geordie, his emphasis veneered with contempt.

'Doesn't matter how I know, fact is we're droppin off some SAS round the corner.' Keith motions his head sideways as if to indicate that his left shoulder is the aforementioned corner. 'Insertions,' he whispers, revelling in his acquired knowledge, gleaned from the SAS on board. They had been seen, mostly at the NAAFI* canteen, languidly hanging around. Most of them have long or straggly hair. They aren't what you expect SAS to look like but then serial killers don't all resemble Hannibal Lecter.

Keith is a man of few words and even less bullshit. He had helped me out in Norway when I'd just joined the ship and felt vulnerable, as in *Could it be possible that someone might attempt to shag my arse?* vulnerable. One night, when the ship was tied up in Trondheim, Keith returned from a drunken night ashore and climbed into my bunk. I flipped, telling

* Navy, Army and Air Force Institutes

him to fuck off, but he pinned my arms to the bed. I thought the worst was about to happen, but all he did was impart the code of how to avoid being a victim for the rest of my naval career. 'If someone comes on to you, they're usually trying to wind you up,' he said, almost spitting into my face. 'The only defence is attack. If they kiss you, kiss them back – harder, longer and wetter. They'll soon get the message.' It was sound advice.

Sure enough, the captain announces that we'll close up to action stations at 1800hrs. Under the cover of darkness, the rusting grey lady chunters around the coast, dropping her precious cargo of *Who Dares Wins* badge holders. As they set off to commit mayhem around the Pucara[*] airfields, we slope back to San Carlos and eventually fall out of action stations at 0500hrs where I'm immediately ordered to switchboard watch-keep until 0800hrs.

Wait a minute, I haven't been to bed for almost 24 hours.

Grudgingly, I troop down to the switchboard. The only thing that'll keep me awake for the next three hours is porn. In the narrow sliding drawer in the middle of the switchboard, where the logbook is kept, are the well-used porn mags. My ovies are beautifully designed for surreptitious wanking. They also have plenty of pockets for bog roll and you can even stuff a porn mag down the side pocket and get away with it. Make no mistake, every sailor enjoys a good tug, but absolute misery befalls anyone who gets caught. One baby stoker was caught on film and his life from then on was hell.

Three wanks gone and it's still only half seven. Isadora has lost her sparkle, and even Kimberley, dressed as a slutty high-ranking naval officer, has lost her lustre. I'm now bored, tired, and tetchy. The whining machinery is

---

[*] an Argentine ground-attack and counter-insurgency aircraft

really grating on my brain, which is already mush through sleep deprivation and a masturbation overdose. As I drift, slumping forward onto the porn drawer, the whining dissipates, then . . . silence.

'Christ!' I jerk up from my slumped position just as the switchboard ladders judder with the weight of descending boots.

'Caught ye, Jock,' laughs Sticky Green.

'No ye fuckin didnae! Ma hands were inside ma ovies because they were cold. You know how cold it gets doon here?' I plead.

'Calm down, Jock, I wasn't accusin you of tossin yerself off,' he says, picking up one of the mags. 'I was accusin you of being asleep on watch.'

'Oh, well, that's alright then,' I say, panic simmering. 'Ye're right, Ah did nod off fur a wee minute there, but jist the once.' Then defiance stretches to desperation. 'Ye're no gonnae say anything, are ye, Sticky?'

'About sleepin on watch, Jock? Course not . . .'

'Ah, cheers mate,' I reply, relieved as fuck.

'About tossin yerself off, though, that's a different story.' Sticky thumps the porn drawer with the palm of his hand, then turns and legs it up the switchboard ladders.

'Bastard!' I shout after him.

I bite my nails for another hour before I'm relieved of duty and then walk back to the mess praying that Sticky decided to keep schtum.

The foot is off the gas in our war as the ground forces take over for the final push. Sporadic air attacks continue around the various bays and inlets but it's mostly fly swatting. There are new ships in the anchorage at San Carlos, the ferry *Atlantic Causeway*, two new Type 21 frigates, *HMS Avenger* and *HMS Arrow*, a Type 42 guided missile destroyer, *HMS Exeter* (God knows what the unguided ones are like), two landing ships, *Sir Galahad* and *Sir Tristram*, our sister ship, *HMS Intrepid*, and the frigate, *HMS Penelope*.

More troops are coming on board; this time it's the turn of the Welsh Guards. There's no room to move about the ship to carry out maintenance and most of our department fixed anything urgent weeks ago. No-one wants anything tampered with in case it goes wrong, so we're left to our own devices between action stations.

I busy myself writing letters and taking photographs. Some of my best pictures sank in the South Atlantic when the freight ship, *Atlantic Conveyor*, suffered a direct hit, although I'm sure no-one gave a shit about my pictures as several vital helicopters, equipment and men perished in the sea.

There is so much airborne activity. Swarms of helicopters line up behind the flight deck, patiently waiting to land. It looks like taxis lined up on Sauchiehall Street in the centre of Glasgow on the Saturday before Christmas. I photograph them, zooming in on the first one, which is inches off the ground. Behind it, another rises up and, behind that, another a few feet higher. The resulting picture is reminiscent of TV footage from Vietnam I'd seen as a kid. Funny how wars always end up looking the same.

The choppers cradle 105mm guns, slung underneath their bellies, destined for the mountains above Stanley. The Argies garrisoned there are subject to relentless shelling from the 105s and naval gunfire. Other, smaller helicopters perform numerous tasks, zipping around frantically between their bulk-laden brothers.

The 105s don't seem to work at night, so the naval destroyers move in closer to pick up the slack and shell their positions, ruining any chance of sleep for the trench-bound Argentinians. It must be absolute hell. These days, I obsess about food and how to fill in the hours between breakfast, lunch and tea, without having to resort to cleaning the mess or any other hard work.

'You're mess cooks[*] tonight, Jock,' comes the joyous news from Pete Martin, as the mess telly blares in the background.

'Cheers, Pete. Who else?' I ask.

'You and Jacko, who else?' he replies, casually.

It isn't exactly something to look forward to, but at least cleaning up the mess for rounds is something. Imagine in the middle of a life-or-death conflict, my choices for the day are wander around and try to look busy or hide until lunch.

'3H2 aft mess cleaned and ready for inspection sir, MEM (L) Cruickshanks reporting.'

What a palaver just to say we've cleaned out the ashtrays and mopped the piss off the floor.

The baby officer has a quick nosey around the tiny mess, motioning with a twitching nose that it needs some air freshener. Happy he's identified a failing in our personal hygiene, he wanders off to 3H2 for'ard.

The ship has become interesting once more. The Welsh Guards, at least 500 of them, are scattered throughout the ship. The main body of soldiers is tucked up in the tank deck with about a hundred more in the dining hall. Tonight, our mission is to join up with *Sir Tristram* and *Sir Galahad* and head for Bluff Cove, a tiny, strategic inlet where the guards will disembark and provide support for

---

[*] cleaning and preparing the mess for inspection

the marines and paras who are shattered after walking and fighting all the way from San Carlos to the hills above Stanley.

I decide to find out a bit more about them, so I head for the tank deck. It's not long before I bump into a six foot plus strapping soldier nursing a machine gun. As he cleans and checks all of its components, we strike up a conversation. This unlikely pairing of skinny wee runt and a white version of The Incredible Hulk chew the fat on numerous topics. The towering Welshman complains about his wet boots and clothes so I bimble down the messdeck for some dry clothes and we do a swap. His smelly, faded, soaking wet sweatshirt, commemorating his guarding of the Berlin wall in exchange for one of my beautifully knit, dry woolly pullies.

Okay, this is utter bull. I nicked someone else's woolly pully out of sheer pragmatism. They can always go to stores the next day and get another one. I sacrifice a pair of my firefighting socks that attract a few jealous looks from the other soldiers. The big guard and I talk about our hopes and fears, our girlfriends (I make one up), our lack of food and sleep and what pubs we'll get drunk in in our respective barracks. We close up to action stations at 2200hrs, so the big man and I shake hands.

'Happy landings,' I say, flippantly.

'Happy sailings,' he replies.

I never see him again.

'Hello, Jocky.' There's something mildly sarcastic in Jock Blair's greeting as I creak open the bulkhead door into the switchboard. In the Navy, you're never far from sarcasm.

'Hello, Chief,' I reply, as matter-of-factly as I dare.

'Another night out of yer pit, eh?' Jock Blair says, nonchalantly.

'Aye, Chief,' I reply. *Not taking any bait.*

'Did ye manage tae stay awake the other night? Ah heard ye had tae switchboard watch-keep after we fell oot of action stations?' he quizzes, clearly fishing.

'Aye, nae bother. Mind you, Ah wiz tired, Chief, but Ah managed,' I say, thinking I'm home and dry.

'They say masturbation can keep ye up all night, Jocky?'

Luckily my anti-flash hood spares my blushes, but my silence betrays me.

There's still no-one in the messdeck next door so Jock Blair and I only have each other for company and the conversation quickly dries up. The time slithers along like a no-legged centipede. It's over 70 miles to our destination and landing all the troops in squally weather is no picnic for the landing craft coxswains. This is purgatory, cooped up in here with a prospective mime artist.

Jock Blair gets some news through the windy-up telephone. Someone must have given the order for us to return before the other landing ships have unloaded their cargo of men and guns, so it's back to San Carlos for us.

We leave *Sir Tristram* and *Sir Galahad* and sail out of Bluff Cove through Falkland Sound, which separates East and West Falkland, and slip back towards the comparative safety of Bomb Alley before dawn breaks. It feels eerie as the ship makes its solitary way through the night. Rationale states that there is little chance of a ship being attacked at sea during the night, but out here, isolated in open water without any picket ships, I can't help feeling vulnerable. Still, several hours later, we're back in Bomb Alley. I can't believe a place where two ships have been sunk and every other ship damaged is my safe space.

The next morning is bright and clear. We go to action stations once and *Exeter* fires off two Sea Dart missiles. I lose the ampule of morphine I was issued earlier, receive the expected bollocking, and console myself with two 99s from the NAAFI's Mr Whippy machine.

Burning Sky

1982

Tuesday 8th June. The Argentine Air Force decide to have another big day of glory. We go to action stations for a missile threat at first but remain closed up for most of the day. *HMS Plymouth* is caught out at the mouth of the bay by five Mirage jets and is hit four times. Her weapons manage to splash at least two aircraft, but she limps into the bay's comparatively safe clutches, smoke belching out of her. Later on, it emerges that only one man has been seriously injured and the unexploded bombs are defused without further casualties. My mate from school, who had been at my fifth birthday party, is on board *Plymouth*. I wonder what the odds are of him being the one casualty.

Tonight, *Foxtrot Four*, one of the landing craft belonging to *Fearless*, is caught in a missile attack but we don't know how bad it is yet. I shiver at this news and look around the messdeck as other sailors try to take it in. Thoughts of our invincibility are shattered once again. The fragility of our existence creeps back into the ship's company.

Then news comes in that the landing ships we left in Bluff Cove have been hit by A-4 Skyhawks. Above that bay, a small Argentine radio station had been operating and sent the word back that two ships full of troops, without an escort or air cover, were just waiting to be picked off. The ships had sat in the bay for hours while the command structure dithered as to when they should disembark the Welsh Guards.

There's speculation that air cover, which should have been provided by Rapier anti-aircraft missiles, was impotent due to the wrong equipment being supplied. So, the ships sat and waited for someone to make a decision, but the decision was made for them. The Skyhawks had swooped in low, dropping their deadly cargo bang on target. *Sir Galahad* took the brunt of the attack and quickly became a fireball.

Every available helicopter is sent to rescue the troops. In time, we learn that some had jumped over the side and swam to life rafts. Others had managed to escape on a few launched lifeboats. Many had appalling injuries: limbs lost, first, second and third degree burns. Most will suffer trauma, that's without question. We sit in the messdeck numb with shock as pictures of survivors being winched to safety (some of them unable to don their orange survival suits, such is the ferocity of the attack) are relayed on the CCTV. Many of the survivors come on board *Fearless*. I stay well clear.

Then the news we'd all been dreading filters through. Six men from *Foxtrot Four* have lost their lives in the missile attack. A blanket of silence descends on the mess and smothers any smart-arsed comments about winning a war for the next few days.

Historians say that these things happen in wars. They talk of strategic miscalculations, command fatigue, logistical errors, even the weather. Veiled in their sterile language lies the ruined lives of survivors away from the censored images of the news cameras. Men who would relive the images of their comrades exploding into flames in front of their very eyes, their ears cocked to the sound of men screaming like wounded animals. Flashbacks of bodies burning and bursting, the smell of charring bones and sinew forever ingrained into their nostrils. Others, panic-stricken in the thick drowning smoke, would make it out of an assault course of twisted metal; some would see others almost make it, only to be sucked back down into a black, smoke-ridden hole.

Hundreds of soldiers will go through the rest of their lives afraid of darkness, of the smell of cooking, of being in public places, afraid to live and breathe. And equally afraid to die. Their nightmares will make them beg for daylight, before the cycle starts all over again. Over the next few days, we learn that 50 soldiers perish in the attack and 170 are injured.

Later that night, I arrive a few minutes late for sea boats patrol and am threatened with a court martial. I shrug off the attentions of the shrieking petty officer this time. I can't help thinking about the us and them rule. Two officers on board *Sir Galahad* have a pissing contest to see who has the authority to disembark the troops and because neither of them back down, fifty Welsh Guards die. I think of my big Welsh mate and wonder if he's alive. I hope he's one of the lucky ones, but I have no way of knowing. I fish the tatty sweatshirt out of my locker and smell it. I don't really know why, but it gives me some comfort.

The next few days pass by peacefully. It seems that even the atrocity at Bluff Cove can't halt the relentless march over the mountains towards Stanley. You could say that the bombing has acted as a catalyst to get the job over and done with. I'm sure the Welsh Guards are chuffed to fucking bits.

The final push towards Stanley belongs to the memories of the soldiers who fought in the battle, and a few days later I glean some fragments of information about the brutality of trench warfare from a para in Stanley.

The news of attacks is taking longer to filter through to us. I learn that four days ago (the day *Sir Galahad* and *Sir Tristram* were bombed), Scots Guards shot down four Skyhawks. I feel good about this, me being Scottish. The Argentine Army don't seem to have the stomach for a major battle, but their air force continues to punch holes in our ships. *HMS Glamorgan* takes a hit from an Exocet as she pummels the occupying forces at Stanley with her 4.5-inch gun. Nine men lose their lives as the missile rips through the port Seacat missile launcher and aircraft hangar.

The ground forces bombard the enemy positions during the day, which are heavily dug in. A shit load of shells fall on their positions from the mountains and from naval gunfire support. Once they've softened up, the paras and marines move in under cover of darkness. The thin line between success and failure in the battle for the Falklands now depends on individuals, how each soldier has prepared himself mentally and physically for what lies ahead. This is the stuff war comics are made of. Paras and marines going at the enemy, hammer and tongs, running, stopping, firing, waiting for support, running, stopping, firing, counting down the rounds in their magazines to avoid dead man's click*.

They'll do all this against well-dug machine gun positions. They'll press forward relentlessly as an enemy tracer finds its range, killing their best mates. They'll punch, kick, gouge, stab and head-butt their way forward, trench by trench, all in a cauldron of thick smoke, blackout and gut-churning, ear-splitting noise. The Argentine

---

* when the trigger clicks but there are no rounds left

troops, some of whom are conscripts, haven't come across this attitude to battle and know little of the regimental pride that's at stake for these guys. Professional, motivated, highly trained, angry as fuck soldiers against a cold, demoralised but defiant enemy.

The next two days are not the best for Argentina. They lose the battle for the Falklands and, worse still, their national football team is beaten 1-0 by Belgium in the World Cup. I wonder what Buenos Aires is more worried about – getting lynched for having a shitty football team, or losing a war.

Once the momentum of the retreat gets going, the Argentine troops snowball down towards Stanley, hotly pursued by the marines and paras. At 0200hrs, General Menendez announces the surrender of the occupying Argentine forces. There are 17,000 prisoners to disarm.

Down the mess, the pfffft of ring pulls signals our elation. No more filthy anti-flash hoods to wear. No more cosy chats with Jock Blair. No more Othello and no more freezing my bollocks off in a sea boat at two o'clock in the morning, although it looks like I'm going to have to get used to hangovers all over again.

English Rose

'We're off to da Mucky, Joch,' Scouse slurs, holding court beside the mess TV, having battered into the beer stash that we received two days ago along with some mail and a couple of Argy helicopters, which are currently squatting on the flight deck.

'D'ye think Sharon and Linda will be there?' I ask.

'Too right mate, I'll tell em both to meet us and don't bother with knickers, eh?' Scouse pisses himself laughing, but it's not his false movie laugh, it's his genuine war-is-over-and-life-is-fucking-great laugh. I can't help but join in. The rest of the mess thinks we're crackers.

The beer flows good style across every messdeck while the propaganda machine goes into overdrive. We're bombarded with newsreels of the captured troops being rounded up, searched and put in holding pens in Stanley airfield. They look pitiful. Some of them have bandages around their blackened faces, their eyes deadened to defeat. Their humiliation is probably mixed with relief that it's all over. I bet most of them never want to set foot on these islands again. They aren't the only ones.

I'm slipping into a boozy trance trying to keep up with the images on the newsreel when someone thumps me hard on the shoulder, or where my shoulder would be if I wasn't so bony. I turn just as the spray from the beer spurts out from the can into my face.

'Have another tinny, ye wee shite.'

It's Big George and he's feeling no pain. I've never seen him this drunk. I decide not to argue and, faking a grin, I wipe a beer and spittle combo from my face. 'Fuckin brilliant, eh, George!'

'Not fuckin bad, son.' he says, and I think I catch a glint of kindness in his eyes as his face crumples into a gormless grin.

**

I wake and instantly regret it. The euphoria of last night is getting the shit kicked out of it by some hangover hooligans. My head is numb, aching, then numb again. My temples are being crushed by an invisible vice. My eyes are so small that they can't manage one piss hole in the snow between them. The only good news is that I don't feel sick. Oh, wait a minute, I shouldn't have sat up. *Oh, ma heid!*

There's hardly anyone in the mess, which makes me think I must be late for something. Panic rises in my throat along with what's left of my bile. I'm desperate to lie down, sleep it off, get some liquids into me, but there'll be no chance; someone, somewhere will be looking for me. I crane my neck up to Scouse's pit. He's still in the land of nod. This makes me feel a whole lot better, for at least ten seconds anyway, before the second wave of nausea kicks in.

The smell of booze and fags mixed together would rust a galvanised stomach. My stomach, which is made of the kind of paper used to make lucky bags, stitched together with gossamer thread, throws its hand in. I don't even make it to the second rung on the messdeck ladder.

Bloody hell, David, why did you get yourself into this shit state?

Don't look at me, you're the one with the morbidly greedy taste for ale.

What a dick!

I'm consoling then cajoling myself, pressing my hands together, looking down at my pool of vomit. I hear muffled giggling from Scouse's bunk, but I know he'll be feeling like shit too, just braving it till I leave so he can then have a good honk.

I'm startled out of my lethargy by Sticky Green bounding down the ladders. Sticky stays in the for'ard messdeck with Bomber, Netley Nick and a dozen other stokers and greenies. I have come to the conclusion that their mess is mental. The stories around what they get up to make an orgy look like scones with the Queen.

'Jock, Nick wants you to have a go at some maintenance cards, alright?' Sticky says.

'Yeah, I'll be up in a minute,' I slur.

'Are you okay, mate?'

'Yeah, once I've died, I'll be right as rain,' I say, my guts following my voice into the open. I look down at the orange porridge and wish for the ground to open up and take me away.

Sticky screws up his face, lighting a fag to mask the reek. 'I'll find someone else for Nick, you get yourself squared away,' he says, picking a stray strand of tobacco from his lip.

'Cheers, mate,' I reply, caressing my stomach. Scouse laughs, but I couldn't care less. In fact, I don't give a fuck about anything apart from how to survive the next few minutes and the next few minutes after that. Once I've managed to steady myself, I grab the nearest thing to hand, which is one of my number eight shirts and mop up the stinking mess. The stench makes me wretch and my head feels like a German dam that's been attacked by a Lancaster bomber. I'll worry about washing the shirt later.

'Still fancy shaggin Shaz and Linda, Joch?'

I force myself to look upwards. The fluorescent lighting tap-tap-taps on my head like a demented woodpecker. Scouse swings his legs over his pit. He looks like shit with a grin. I force a smile back, praying that I've puked enough for one day.

Last night was a belter. The mad lads from next door had got hold of a guitar and murdered an entire song book. Even the watch-keepers, who were always grumpy late at night, stayed up and partied until they went on duty. We danced with each other. Jiving, pogoing, twisting and even slow dancing was the order of the night. Ship's rounds had been cancelled and that was our signal. The mother of all hooleys* was under way. There was so much beer swilling about on the floor that Jacko, king of the northern soul boys, could slide about to his heart's content. The mop that he usually danced with was replaced by Scouse, then Pete Nicolls, then me.

We were all shitfaced, the mess spinning like a merry-go-round. I remember the newsreels on TV with happy-faced marines interspersed with sad looking Argentine conscripts, the soundtrack courtesy of Wee George's ghetto blaster. Sticky broke a string on the messdeck's only guitar so it was Wee George's tapes after that, but we didn't care what we were dancing to. We were going home alive . . . probably.

'Look out Portsmouth, we're comin to shag all yer women!' screamed Jacko.

---

* parties

'An when we're finished, we'll shag all the men as well,' came an anonymous voice from the deepest recess of the narrow mess, sending us all into fits of laughter.

There were cans everywhere. Some had been crushed by hand and some lay alongside sticky patches on the lino, where stale dregs had seeped out and congealed. The ashtrays were riddled with beer-soaked fag ends. The party only finished when the beer ran out and that was after raiding everyone else's mess for more.

'Jock!'

I shudder in synch with the mess ladders. It's the voice of Jock Blair.

'Yes, Chief,' I answer, straining towards the ladders. I can see his boots and the bottom of his trousers.

'Get yer arse up here and start on these maintenance cards,' he barks.

'Okay, Chief,' I say, clearer and more articulate than normal, like a kid talking to his parents after guzzling ten cans of cider down the woods.

He must've sensed something in my voice. His shoes become his trousers, then shirt, then the anti-flash hood round his neck, then his chin, and finally his scowling face and short, black, wiry hair.

'Aw, Jocky, whit a state you're in,' he commiserates.

I slump my shoulders and dip my head in anticipation of a severe bollocking. My dad's voice is never far away from my head when a bollocking looms.

'Go on, get yer head down, wee man,' he says, his expression unchanging. He turns and heads back up the ladders. I think for one crazy moment that I must actually be dying and that Jock Blair thinks I'll haunt him, so he's let me off.

I lay down the sick-filled shirt and slither back into my sweat-laden, drink-ridden, parasite-infested sleeping bag and pray that sleep will come quickly.

Away from the Numbers

1982

We're off and running. *Fearless* has been getting spruced up to take a bow in the harbour at Stanley, but someone forgot to tell the captain that her draft is too deep, so we have to content ourselves with laying anchor in Port William. Always the bridesmaid . . .

I'm on my best behaviour and anxious to make up for my lack of effort after the beer-soaked hooley[*]. Jock Blair, being a shrewd old cookie, knows this.

'I need two volunteers to dig out some pumps from the LSLs at Bluff Cove,' says Jock Blair (the rumour is that there are still bodies aboard *Sir Galahad* and *Sir Tristram*). I shoot up my hand and Phil Brooks, known as Brooksy, shoots up the only other hand in a workshop containing 18 greenies.

'Alright you two, get your tool rolls ready. You'll accompany a Tiff[**]. Report to the flight deck at 1000hrs. Oh, and Jocky?'

'Yes, Chief?' I reply, groggily.

'Waken up!'

---

[*] party
[**] a skilled engineer/artificer

I say nothing, but he thinks he's achieved his goal of public humiliation. I don't give a fuck. I'm going flying.

At exactly 09:59 I report to the fairy[*] on the flight deck. It's a grey, cold and damp morning. I make out land, but nothing that suggests civilisation. Choppers are buzzing from every direction. My mind is clear and sharp. It feels good to be shot of the hangover. I vow that I will never drink again. This time I really mean it.

I stand with my tool roll, looking at the Sea King on the flight deck about half-way through her start up procedure. The rotors are just ticking over, but the gaps between the noisy whooshes become shorter. This is my first time in a chopper and I feel the familiar stab of adrenaline, but this time it's joy rather than fear. I really hope it doesn't get cancelled. Some of the guys have served on ships for more than three years and haven't had a ride on a chopper. I am wasted with excitement.

The fairy motions with his arms for me to come forward. I do that pregnant pause thing when you're going to do something for the first time and stand there like an arsehole waiting to be told again. It's the old "Right, come forward, step forward. No, not you; *you*." There you have it; you've made an arse of yourself. The fairy gives a signal for me to scuttle towards the Sea King, which is now champing at the bit. Even with ear defenders on, the muted noise draws attention to the sheer power of these things. If I'm hit by one of the rotors, I'll go straight to heaven without passing go or collecting two hundred pounds, although I'd have to collect my head before being allowed through the pearly gates, otherwise how else would I be identified?

---

[*] Air Engineering Mechanic

I use the step to climb up to the metal flooring. The crewman, who's sporting a dark visor and jazzy helmet, takes my tool roll, gives me a hand up and then hands it back to me once I'm safely inside. He smiles. I haven't seen a stranger do that in a long time. Maybe he knows I'm a helicopter virgin. Worse still, maybe he knows I'm a virgin full stop. I shuffle away from the smiling crewman with the jazzy helmet and strap myself in. He talks into his mouthpiece and looks out the cabin door. I begin to wonder what I would do if the helicopter ditches. I know that offshore workers in the oil industry back home go on survival courses that include helicopter ditching exercises.

Luckily, Phil Brooks appears at the cab door and takes my mind off the subject. The crewman smiles at him too. I wonder if we'll get in-flight refreshments and immediately laugh at my own silliness. But then the crewman hands Phil and I a Mars bar each. I can barely believe my eyes!

Phil and I sit squashed up together, a melange of tool rolls, life jackets cold weather clothing and gas masks wedged in around us. We don't try to speak. A few marines get on board, with their fixed 'fuck are you lookin at?' faces. They strap themselves in and stare at us contemptuously, because we haven't directly shot or filled anyone in. I feel like telling them I had sat next to someone who threw scare charges into the water but think better of it. The crewman jabbers back into his mouthpiece. We sit juddering inside the chopper for what seems like half an hour but is really only ten minutes. I know because I snuck a look at my watch, then thought I might buy myself a new one when I get home.

I smile as Sticky rocks up last, throws his tool roll into the cab and hoists himself on board as if he's an old hand at flying in helicopters. The crewman makes sure that we're all secure and gives us the thumbs up. Butterflies with boots on are parading around my stomach.

The roar of the rotors drowns out a shout from Sticky and we give up trying to talk, but the silly grins between us says *This is the dog's bollocks*. The marines sit across from us, rigid, grinding their teeth. Maybe they too have missed out on the battles and are just a shit-clearing detail. I won't be trying to find out. The chopper judders from side to side and the noise changes from whooshing to a muffled machine gun sound.

In 3.2 seconds, we're 100 feet above the flight deck. It feels like the last day of school times a million. The crewman senses that I'm green and keen; he must have caught me craning forward to catch a glimpse of *Fearless* shrinking. He beckons me forward with his left hand while his right stays on the trigger guard of the mounted GPMG. He's so lucky to look that cool. The safety belts allow me to leave my seat and still be attached to something solid. My brave pills kick in and I sit cross-legged, like a kid in his first school photo, beside the crewman-cum-gunner. The water of Port William races a few feet beneath before giving way to ground. I feel like the pilot has discovered I'm a winner in a *Blue Peter* competition and he's doing his damnedest to make my flight memorable.

After a few minutes, we round the coast and ahead lies Stanley. It looks peaceful and unscathed, just like a wee village in the Highlands. This is what we have come 8,000 miles and lost over 200 lives to defend. The church rises above everything else. Its tower says 'hit me' with such aplomb, I'm surprised it's survived unscathed. As we draw closer, I can make out the line of trucks and guns on the main street. I don't know if they're Argentinian our ours.

The pilot circles around for somewhere to land. The crewman signals for me to return to my seat, with a smile of course. We bob down behind a spot near the main street, which turns out to be the racecourse. What they race there I have no idea. Penguins? Could be wildebeest for all I care. The rotors return to gentle whooshing and we spill out. I'm actually in Stanley.

I don't know where I'm going, but Sticky seems to have an idea. We amble down the main street, which is littered with bullets and shell casings. Uniforms are piled up. Helmets lie like upturned turtles in the middle of the road. Thankfully, there are no dead bodies lying around. The convoy of trucks is silent. From the main street, I look across the bay. I spot a few merchant ships and the wreck of a galleon* at the end of a pier. I didn't think the Argy Navy was that poor.

I think back to the sinking of Belgrano on my sister's birthday. Those poor sailors didn't stand a chance when the submarine's torpedoes struck. At the time, we all cheered when we heard that such a large battleship had been taken out, but the more I think about it, the more pointless it seems. She had been sailing away from the exclusion zone when she was sunk and didn't seem to pose a significant threat to the task force. It had happened when diplomacy was still an option but it looked as though someone had a hidden agenda.

'Thank you, son, thank you!' I spin round and I'm being grabbed and hugged by two middle-aged women insulated with thick pastel-coloured scarves and dark, woollen winter coats. They're the first civvies I've seen in over three months, crying and smiling at the same time. Standing before them is a skinny, spotty, boiler-suited boy being

---

* a 19th century three-masted ship

given the freedom of Stanley. They're probably desperate to hug a marine or a para but are too scared, so they've psyched themselves up and targeted me instead. Sticky is getting it too, but he's lapping it up. They're a bit too old for him though, and he does have a reputation to keep up.

They hold our hands, stammer a few more embarrassed words, then with nothing else in common, they let us go and set off on their hugging and kissing expedition. Once they're gone, I regret not taking a snap. It would have been nice to have something that isn't gurning behind a captured helicopter or posing beside a gun. I look back at the galleon and click my camera. Sticky then leads Phil and I towards a wrecked Puma helicopter for a photo sesh. We do the necessary, standing in front of the cab door, arms folded, posing like maniacs.

'Right!' Sticky says after our war hero photo shoot. 'Let's ave a wander.'

We set off across fields of mud peppered with ammunition, clothing and abandoned weapons. The fresh air feels good. The sun is fighting for a gap in the clouds and the wind is picking up, making me wish I had put a vest on. We trudge through the mud, swinging our tool rolls. This is feeling like a real adventure. You can stuff the Navy's recruitment picture of three sailors in pristine tropical rig* looking at a map with the ruins of Athens in the background. They should replace it with us three posing beside a battered Argy helicopter, ankle-deep in mud, but grinning for Britain.

'C'mon Jock, let's get back,' Sticky moans.

'Just one more picture,' I say, not looking at him.

'Oi! You three! Stay exactly where you are.'

---

* uniform

A para had popped up from nowhere, about 50 yards to our left, cradling his rifle.

'You are standing on a minefield.' There is no emotion in his voice, just years of supressing it. As far as rank is concerned, he looks equal to us, yet he knows that he has our undivided attention.

'You will have to turn around and carefully retrace your steps,' he says, consistent with his tone. This was like telling an angler to put a worm on the hook, but we deferentially acknowledge him and turn around, laughing nervously. It could be a wind up. In fact, we take it all so casually, the para must think we're nuts. Then Sticky breaks into an old, warbling war tune, 'Tiptoe through the Tulips', and we nearly shit ourselves laughing. We make it back across the field to the burnt out helicopter, sore with laughing, but otherwise unscathed. We look around to thank the para, but he's gone.

'I say, let's get back to the chopper, chaps,' Sticky says in a mock Battle of Britain voice.

'Roger that,' chips in Brooksy.

We wander back through the side streets, the only sailors in a sea of troops. It feels good to stick out. As we round a corner, we encounter some booted feet sticking out of a piece of tarpaulin. We don't hang around. It could have been one of ours or one of theirs. I'm sure a train spotter or some army bod could've told us from the soles of his boots, but we exit stage left. The town is going to need a major rebuild, but I sense that the locals will have it back to normal in double quick time just to show the cavalry that they've been worth saving.

Our cab hovers overhead and the tight grass vibrates once more as the chopper's wheels get closer to ground. The pilot sets it down and the smiling crewman opens the door, while seemingly filming a toothpaste advert. We lug our toolrolls onto the floor and do a hop/roll action to get on board. I pray that I'll get to land in Stanley again. I remember when Glenrothes was growing up along with me; it was one giant building site. After school, Alan White would head down to the construction site for the new police headquarters (the old one was a semi-detached council house in a street full of semi-detached council houses). We would play Japs and Commandos among the newly broken windows and half-made floors. There were millions of places to hide on these building sites and loads of materials to improvise with. We made machine guns from two bits of wood held together with a single nail. Right now, Stanley looked like one of those places.

As we take off, the crewman closes the sliding door, but the disappointment must be scrawled all over my face. He looks at me, swings the door open once more and takes my breath away. This time we're airborne for a few minutes before the pilot puts us down near the airfield. I spot the wreckage of a Pucara and fiddle with the lens on my camera. The crewman, perhaps the most obliging man on earth at this moment in time, beckons me forward, puts his hands up to his visored eyes and presses his right index finger down twice on an invisible camera shutter button.

I leap off my seat, but the buckle hauls me back. I can hear everyone's muffled laughter through the noise of the rotors. But at this very moment, I don't care if my face is as red as a beetroot with high blood pressure. I undo my buckle and bum-shuffle along the floor towards the exit. I snap a few pictures, framing some with the mounted GPMG. I feel like a kid who's been given the keys to a sweetie shop and has well and truly stuffed his face. I look left and catch the pilot and co-pilot having a natter. They seem happy enough. Then I look at the chopper's pedals and spot that both pilot and co-pilot have wellies on, plastered with mud. It's such a surreal image, but I don't even think about taking a picture.

The crewman starts jabbering into his mouthpiece and we are off again. I scramble back to my seat and we accelerate, climbing steeply and banking away from the airfield. The pilot knows he has a captive audience and decides to show off a bit. We swoop across the boulder-strewn open ground, dotted white by sheep. I imagine a game reserve in Kenya with thousands of migrating antelope stampeding all over the place as a low flying aircraft swoops down to give the tourists a better look.

Back in my own landscape, we've picked up speed and the crewman partially closes the door to save us from hypothermia. I strain around and catch a glimpse of the rugged terrain through a small square window behind me. It isn't as much fun, but I'm able to match the landscape to a map I'd managed to yaffle* on board *Fearless*. Most of the grass below is yellow, peppered with boulders and hostile to settlers. There's no cover from the elements and I make out several Argentine trenches on the ground below the mountains. The helicopter arcs around and the mountains immediately disappear. We cross large areas of water and, twenty minutes later, I flinch as I make out the bombed-out shells of *Sir Galahad* and *Sir Tristram*. Apprehension wells up inside me and I remember the rumour of dead bodies still on board, but I can't remember now if the rumours were about *Galahad* or *Tristram*. The ships loom bigger, only a few hundred yards apart. A week after the bombing, *Sir Galahad* is still smouldering.

---

* steal

There's no room for the chopper to land on the deck. Both flight decks have been destroyed in the bombing, so the crewman winches us down onto the focsle of *Sir Tristram*. The deafening whooshing of the giant rotors bends to an eerie silence as the chopper rises then sweeps across the water and disappears. We all stand there for a minute, like a landing party from the Starship Enterprise. Sticky is first to move. He must fancy himself as Captain Kirk.

'We ave to go down the engine room and salvage a couple of pumps,' Sticky says, taking charge. 'They're still bolted to the bilge and I bet they're as rusty as fuck, so we'll probably need stacks of elbow grease.'

I immediately wonder what I am doing here.

'Can we have a wee look around first, Sticky?' I ask, tentatively.

'Don't see why not, Wee Jock. We've got stacks of time and the chopper is comin back at four so we should be sorted.' Sticky adds, confidently. 'Anyway, if it takes longer, we can always come back tomorrow.'

We wander around on the upper decks. I snap some pics of Brooksy and Sticky posing up by the Bofors guns. Then I take some shots of the damage to the superstructure.

The bombs were right on the button.

Sticky and Brooksy wander off in different directions so I take this as a cue for my own exploration. I open a couple of watertight doors. They creak a little and aren't as thick as the ones on *Fearless*. Inside, I discover cabins that are in a shit state. There's bedding lying everywhere; no time to make the bed while you're trying to save your skin, I suppose. I shiver at the images going through my mind of total chaos after a direct hit. I don't hang about and don't take any pictures.

Thank God it's not pitch black inside the ship; experiencing this in darkness would freak me out. The Argentine bombs have left giant skylights, opening the engine room up to the outside world. The ladders down to the engine room are still intact though. In fact, most of the ship looks normal.

It's hard to imagine the carnage and confusion as the bombs struck.

Now the place is quiet, peaceful almost. The engine room is virtually unscathed and somehow you just accept the twisted metal above as your new environment.

I know that *Galahad* suffered more than *Tristram*, but I start to wonder if men had died in the same spot I'm walking in. Thankfully, the ship had been given the once over long before we arrived. What if I'd been drafted to this ship instead of *Fearless*? My action station would have been around this area. I look around for a switchboard but can't find one. Maybe it was ripped apart in the explosions, the engineers burnt to death, fatally wounded or blinded by white hot shrapnel.

'Jock!'

'Fuck, Brooksy, Ah nearly shit masel,' I cry out.

'Sorry mate, but we have to make a start on these pumps.'

My heart is pounding against my ovies. I tell myself to stop thinking about the post-blast clatter of boots on the deck, the inevitable silence after the bomb hits and the subsequent screams of the unsaveable. I follow Brooksy down the ladder towards the bilge and we set about removing the securing bolts to the two bilge pumps.

Brooksy, to me, is Mr Sensible: polite, knowledgeable (without being a smart arse), and he's good looking. I don't mean that I fancy him or anything. What I'm trying to say is – what the fuck is he doing as a greenie in the Navy?

'The bilge is flooded with sea water from the firefighting hoses, so we're going to salvage what we can, beginning with these two forward transfer pumps. We really just have to strip them, clean them and put them back together again.'

Brooksy had spoken in his mid-counties voice. He made working sound like the most enjoyable task imaginable. What a gift.

It occurs to me just how cold it is. The spanner in my hand feels like it's been in a fridge for a couple of hours. The adrenaline from being in Stanley and exploring around *Sir Tristram* has dissipated, along with my appetite for work. I lever hard on the shifting spanner that is fused to its securing bolt. The spanner shears off the bolt, rapping my freezing cold knuckles against the metal cover of the ventilation intake.

'Bastard!' I yelp, while making sure all of my fingers are still present. Brooksy smiles and Sticky stifles a giggle.

'That fuckin hurt, Sticky!'

'Sorry mate, it was a nervous laugh. I was thinking about being down here when all the shit was flyin and when you screamed I thought it was, well, you know, a ghost.'

I rub my hands together, blocking out the pain and the cold. My knuckles are grazed, but it's hardly a war wound.

Once the pumps are out, they're small enough to be man-handled up to the workshop, which is at the for'ard end of the ship and has escaped bomb damage. I was half way through dismantling mine when I heard the dull thud of rotor blades. Time to clock off. More exploring tomorrow though.

We head for the upper scupper just as the chopper positions itself to hover. The winch lowers down and I look around at the sad skeleton of *Sir Tristram* one more time before ascending. The crewman gives me the thumbs up. I feel like calling him my new dad. Safely tucked inside, the chopper banks a sharp right and I slide forward on my seat, frantically strapping myself, again to the sound of muffled laughter once more. Sometimes I think Sticky has just brought me along for comedy value.

The weak southern hemisphere winter sun is bedding down for the night as we land a mile from *Sir Tristram* at Bluff Cove settlement. I have no idea why we've stopped; maybe the pilot has been caught short or something. There are green Snow Cats everywhere as well as the usual artillery and shells. Soldiers hop around makeshift fires trying to keep warm. God knows how long it will be before they're given the order to pack up and head home for their 15 minutes on the news. They fade away to tiny dots of camouflage as we become airborne once more. That kid in *The Snowman* doesn't have a look in. As we climb, I can see the water around *Sir Tristram* and *Sir Galahad* glistening in the last rays of the day. The crewman wedges the door open fully as the sun sets over Bluff Cove. As we approach Stanley, the town glows like the embers of a dying fire.

The pilot swings hard left. *Fearless* is framed in the winchman's door like a photograph. The chopper decides not to land, so the crewman prepares the winch for us, which is more fun by a mile. As he puts the loop through my legs, I pluck up some courage and give him the thumbs up. He smiles one last time, eyes still masked by the visor, but I imagine them smiling too. Down below, an airman conducts the motion of the helicopter as we are winched down one by one onto the flight deck. Another airman helps me step out of the loop and I crouch before sprinting towards the hangar. Then it's Sticky's turn and Brooksy is last. We stand with our backs to the hangar as the pilot turns on the gas and whooshes off to somewhere else. The crewman looks at his rapidly shrinking passengers and waves, then he closes the cabin door one last time, with a smile of course.

Reality takes some time to kick in. I check the frame counter on my camera, 26 shots used. I can't wait to get the films processed.

I slide open the door to the mess. The bottom part is submerged in darkness. Just think, some people have slept through my entire adventure. Wee George is sitting on the bunk opposite me with his ovies on, watching the telly. A fag clings to the corner of his mouth like a reluctant lemming.

'George, Jess'll kill you if he sees you on his bunk with yer ovies on,' I say.

'Don't fuckin care, Jock,' comes the lethargic reply.

'What are ye watchin?' I ask, changing tack, seeing he's not in the mood for a wind up.

'Don't know, some shite about Galtieri gettin kicked oot.'

Sure enough, on the screen images flash up of the new Argentine government replacing Galtieri.

'Ah bet,' Wee George says, 'that in 20 yeeahs' time, we'll be selling the Argies weapons, all over again.'

'Don't be daft, George, that'll never happen,' I snap back.

'Suit yerself.' Wee George glues his eyes back to the screen, his fag ash defying gravity.

'Keep the noise down, boys,' Phil Carter grumbles. 'Some of us watch-keepers need some zeds, eh?'

'Sorry, Phil,' I reply into the black, smelly recess.

I'm dying to tell everyone about my day in Stanley, but nobody gives a shit.

'Mind yer ed, Jock.' Wee George motions for me to get out of the way of the goggle box.

'Ye're no even watchin it!' I point out. 'Anyway, Ah've got tae get intae ma locker, Ah'm off fur a dhoby.'

Wee George is shooing me out of the way of the telly with his spare hand, his other holding fag number 20 of the day most likely, but I take my time getting my dhoby bag and towel out before heading for a shower.

'Oh, by the way, Jock, Scotland are oot the World Cup.' I detect a hint of delight in Wee George's voice as he relays the news.

'Ah hate football anyway,' I reply, nonchalantly, while thinking *pock-marked wee shite*. I later find out that we hadn't even lost a game, but we are still out before the second round. Fuck's sake Scotland, why can ye no jist do the business once and win the World Cup?

I remember when my mum worked at the Co-op in 1978, the year the World Cup was held in, of all places, Argentina. The Scotland manager, Ally McLeod, had uttered the immortal words "Ah think we'll get a medal". That was the catalyst for World Cup fever in Scotland. We already thought it was ours before the teams had even finished getting their hair permed. Then we were bombarded with adverts featuring the squad, hanging out of cars with perfect hairdos.

Poor Alan Rough, our goalie – what stick he would get after our miserable campaign and all because of a bad day at the office. Every Saturday for weeks before the World Cup started, I would see my mum and her pals at the Co-op. Her big pal, also called Margaret, would buy me the latest souvenir pendant for Argentina '78. I had bucket-loads of nick-nacks and my bedroom walls were plastered with the smiling faces of kneeling football stars. I strategically positioned the ones who played for Rangers where I could best see them. The Celtic players who played for Scotland could fight it out for a spot under the bed.

After weeks of frenzied speculation and anticipation, the night of our first game arrived, against Peru. Ha, what a walk over; we would murder them. We had never seen Peru play and as the minutes ticked on, it was obvious that Ally McLeod hadn't seen Peru play either. In fact, it was doubtful if Ally McLeod knew where Peru was. To add insult to injury, Alan's dad, Baz, was home on leave from the Navy and he watched it with us. As an Englishman, God knows what he thought of the team, but he diplomatically said that Scotland should lie in their ain pish, although the words he used were: "It's early days yet lads, and let's face it, nobody's even heard of Iran". Ninety minutes later, Scotland had lost their first game 3-1. What a disaster!

As the hot water rains down from the shower head onto my face, I decide to put Scotland's World Cup defeats in a file marked "Great teams, who are we kidding?" and carry on scrubbing the grime from my finger nails, intermittently checking that my knuckles aren't swelling up from the bilge pump incident. My shoulders ache with the lifting and shifting of the pumps on *Sir Tristram* but the hot water feels great.

'What was it like in Stanley?'

I nearly jump out of my skin and my eyes sting with shampoo as I leap out of the shower, instinctively protecting my nuts while ejecting the water swilling in my ears. 'Scouse, Fuck's sake!' I shriek.

'Give you a fright, Jock?' Scouse mocks. 'Sorry, mate . . . Hey, your eyes are a bit red, ave you been crying or something?'

'No way, it's the shampoo,' I reply, searching for my towel, which I'm convinced was hanging on the shower curtain rail.

'It's awright to cry, Jock, ye're not a sap or anything,' he says, his tone suggesting the polar opposite. 'Scotland, well they were just unlucky.'

'Fuck off,' I reply, instinctively putting my hand up to my eyes to check for tears. Then, as my vision clears, I notice a tightly wound towel in his outstretched hands and I duck back into the shower for protection, turning my back to him as he tries to sting my bollocks with the towel.

'Ah, ya bastard, Scouse, fuck off, eh?' I scream as he flicks and whips the towel again and again at my vulnerable, unprotected body. 'Ah, ya bastard! Oya! Oya, fuck!'

Scouse is really pissing himself laughing now. I look over my shoulder, but he flicks the towel again, catching me square in the arse, the sound like a whip in a cowboy film. I yelp in agony as he turns on his heels.

'Sorry, Jock,' he says, legging it from the heads.

I'm relieved the attack is over, but the last 12 hours is the most alive I've felt in ages.

***

The next day is a disappointment. We steam back from Stanley to San Carlos so I don't get my wish to fly on the chopper again. Most of the guys are bored sitting around and I guess that Scouse took his frustrations out on me in the shower after he had sat around all day yesterday while I was strutting about Stanley. I find out later that Scouse had spent all of that day trying to prise some rusty nuts from an extractor fan and had the bruised knuckles to prove it. I had done the same but had witnessed a dead body, survived a minefield, been hugged by two grateful Falkland Islanders, been taxied about in a helicopter and winched back in time for tea.

Walking in
Heaven's Sunshine

1982

The helicopter activity is fearsome. If you want fresh air, the whirring and whooping of rotor blades comes with it. Then the rumour snakes down the mess that a helicopter is heading our way carrying mail. I love mail. I love the feel of letters, especially if you get a pile and the handwriting is different on each one. The posh ones would often have smudged ink from a fountain pen, generating a frisson of excitement at the possibility of getting to meet them and their dad giving me a castle. I love sniffing them for clues as to who has bothered to write to me. The non-perfumed ones are from your mum, unless there's an Oedipus complex at work. I've collected stamps from the year dot so I get off on the postmarks and stuff.

When we were at Ascension Island, which seems light years ago, the newspapers back home had appealed on our behalf for penfriends and I had managed to blag about four different ones. I was definitely on the lookout for sex from one of them when I got back to Pompey, but the born again Christian was probably out of the equation, even though she was by far the prettiest. They all had to send pics of themselves in their first letters, so we had plenty of fun comparing their mugs. We pissed ourselves laughing at some of the characters who wrote to us, but it passed the time.

'Mail is now ready for collection!' announces the reggy[*] over the ship's intercom. He sounds happy; must have had some good news. I race up from the air conditioning space where I'm job carding, which, luckily, is on the starboard side close to the mail office. I haven't been here in ages and I have a massive adrenalin rush. As I get closer, I'm joined by other racing snakes eager for the first prize. It's shit being the second person from your mess to get to the mail office. Second spells last. You go from top dog to dog shit in a millisecond and end up padding along beside the collector in the hope he might drop a letter or a card and you've have a titbit to take back to the mess. This time I'm top dog though and there's a shit load of mail and parcels.

I smile at the reggy. He looks puzzled. *Shit.* You never smile at the reggy, so my guard was down. He makes me wait while he questions the very existence of 3H2 aft mess, the place I have lived and breathed for four whole months. That tiny lino-clad space, which has seen me drunk, sober, asleep, awake, fit and well, hungover, tense, happy, drunk again and scared stiff, registers as a question mark on his saggy, weathered face. Finally, he fishes out a pile for 3H2 aft. I take it and turn to go.

'Here, take for'ard's with you!' he orders.

Bimbling along the passageway with for'ard's mail under my arm, I dig into the pile of letters and packages belonging to my own mess. Bingo! Packets of slides with my name on them, a few letters from mum, one from Hilary (interesting) and one of my other pen friends Melanie (a bit freaky). The born again Christian, Debbie (blonde), is there too. Plenty of reading and imagining to

---

[*] a regulator in charge of naval discipline

be done tonight. I break into a run as I look for any interesting postmarks.

'Fuuuck!' I feel a skull-splitting pain in my forehead and I'm forced backwards as letters go flying everywhere. I make out a fuzzy image of a balding, bearded angry man, which turns out to be Netley Nick rubbing his head. As letters fan out across the deck, he mirrors me as I try to soothe the slow-forming bump on my forehead.

'Give us them letters, Jock, and the next time I want a Glesca kiss, I'll ask for it,' he says with a sliver of warmth.

I help him pick up the letters for his mess and apologise, the way you do when it's not your fault but you defer to rank. I nurse my skull with occasional rubs while trying not to surrender the letters to the deck again. My head is aching, but a bit of erotic reading will hopefully sort that out.

Soon the messdeck ladders shudder with excited sailors, eager for news. Some have a slightly pissed off look, Scouse being one of them, because I have the keys to the kingdom. It makes up a little for the towel whipping he gave my arse. Scouse lunges, but I turn sideways to him, hold the letters above my head and spin like a music box ballerina.

He tries to grab me, then stops suddenly and steps back. 'Whar happened to yer ed, Joch, it's bleedin,' he simpers.

I put my free hand up to check for blood. Scouse seizes his chance, wrenches the mail from me and runs off.

'Prick!' I call after him.

The atmosphere reminds me of when we used to begin the summer exodus from school with a film in the assembly hall. One year it was *Paper Tiger*, starring David Niven. You were so happy that in less than two hours you would be let loose for seven whole weeks. You were so happy that you nearly shit yourself controlling the volcano of laughter inside you. You burbled nonsense to your mates while the sharp wooden chairs in the assembly hall attempted to shave your arse. You knew that after this film you were free for seven whole weeks, yes I know I've said this already, but Christ! Seven whole weeks! The excited chatter rose to a crescendo and died instantly as the headmaster got up to tell us how to have a wonderful yet responsible summer holiday. 'Fuck off, Heidy!' replied 2,000 kids, telepathically of course.

Everyone is chirruping away while skimming their letters. The frantic ripping of paper reminds me of pass the parcel. Then the noise subsides as the seriousness of reading gathers momentum. I look up from a note from my mum and clock sailors immersed in their own private worlds. Occasionally, news is shared, but its flippancy reveals nothing about the writer or reader. The secret loves and passions within the letters are mostly kept hidden. Some of the married men read in their bunks away from prying eyes. Others physically retreat into nooks, forging an intimate exchange between ink and paper.

Scouse is smiling to himself. He's off guard but I'm too wrapped up in my own thoughts to care about payback. I've half forgiven him for the arse whipping, but the other half will have to come in the form of retribution, just not today. He looks up as if reading my mind but merely smiles gormlessly and returns to the page. Big George seems to shrink with each letter he reads. I've never seen him so contented; he looks ready to climb back into the womb. There are a few photographs that had been carefully laid on the bunks. I crane my neck to get a look; not bad, but not brilliant.

I think of a new military strategy and it is my intention to convey this to the military might of Whitehall. I imagine it thus:

"Come in, Cruickshanks!"

"Sir!" I yell, but my nerves throttle my answer on the way in and what is left of it squeaks towards the staff sergeant. Thankfully, it never reaches the admiral, who sits behind a desk so wide that planning permission for an adjoining car park is a distinct possibility. I salute and the boss man beckons me to sit on a leather chair.

All around me are framed photographs of heroic admirals and their painted ancestors. It's strange how they all look the same: the same cap, the same hand touching the same point of the same sword. Piss easy work for painter or photographer. I smell the newness of the deep pile carpet, blue of course, to represent the sea, or perhaps the First Admiral's love of Picasso's blue period.

"Now, Cruickshanks, tell me about this new military strategy," booms the admiral, arms crossed in a pose of domination.

Unaccustomed to speaking to the top dog in the Navy, I fidget in my large leather armchair, although it's not as large as his. "Well, sir," I croak, an attack of phlegm attempting to sabotage my audience with the Navy's number one. I clear my throat in a heroic attempt to regain lost ground.

"Take your time, young man," the now less boomy admiral says, reassuringly.

"Thank you, sir. Well, sir, during my time at Her Majesty's Service in the Falklands conflict, we received mail. Well, we always do, I know that sir, but when the war ended, we received mail and I used to take it down to the mess, and when the lads read it, sir, well they were of no use to man nor beast. They became so absorbed in the writings of their loved ones that they were reduced to a semi-catatonic state."

"And what is your recommendation?" the admiral asks, leaning forward, sensing that he may need to order sun cream to bask in my reflected glory.

"Sir, my recommendation, contained in my report, is that in future areas of conflict involving Her Majesty's forces, we subject the enemy to bombardments of mail, and while they are reading we sneak up on them and Bob's your uncle."

"Bob who?" the admiral queries. This last bit throws him completely, but then a light switches on in the middle of his balding crown and he smiles, the kind of smile that says *If it works I'll claim full credit, and if it fails I'll blame this little Jock runt.* He leans back and sighs before turning to his subordinate, who looms over me as I squiget* in my chair.

"Staff sergeant?"

"Sur!" the staff sergeant thunders. It's his time to be loud and boy is he milking it.

"Have the Navy's rules of engagement drawn up accordingly and we'll present it to the Prime Minister."

"Oh, sir, I took the liberty of informing Mrs Thatcher and she loves it," I add, not wishing to be left out of the loop and sent back with nothing but a commendation and a coupon for double beer rations.

"There's a commission in this for you, young man," says the admiral. Finally, someone has realised my potential.

"Thank you, sir!" I reply, my face beaming with pride.

---

* hybrid of squirm and fidget

I salute and push back the chair, which takes out a bit of the blue carpet, but the admiral doesn't take any notice. He's probably too busy thinking of a knighthood . . .

'Hey, Jock?'

'What?'

Wee George pulls at my mum's letter. 'Earth to Jock'. His face has crossed the paper border and I instinctively back away.

'What now, Georgie boy? Have the entire Scotland team defected to Russia?'

'I'm gettin a motahbike when I git ome,' he gleams.

'Ye canna fuckin ride a motah bike, ye daft shite!' comes the mocking tone of Big George. Some of the guys look up and laugh, then duck back down among the array of letters. The motorbike subject is closed. I wonder what a letter from Motorcycle Girl would smell like. Wee George deflates and heads for his pit.

After reading Mum's letters, which are mostly about making sure I'm not eating too many sweeties and have enough clothes on, I start on the remainder. Debbie the Christian has sent another photo, full length this time. She looks a bit like a page three model with clothes on. Perhaps our first date could be church on Sunday followed by copious shagging in the graveyard. Choosing not to let anyone see the picture, Debbie is carefully tucked away in the top drawer of my locker, nestling between my socks and skids*.

The orgasm of mail day subsides and we spend the rest of the week storing ship back in Port William. Unlike Portsmouth, where most of the stuff had to be humped up the gangway (except for the odd box of fluorescent tubes),

---

* underwear

stores arrive by helicopter. As usual, beer arrives first; crates and crates of the stuff. It reminds me to buy shares in Carlsberg and Newcastle Brown Ale when I get home. The unsteady choppers, with their underslung nets bulging with booty, dance a drunken waltz before dumping their loads onto the flight deck.

The duty fairy uncouples the skyhook and lugging stores begins in earnest. My arms ache as the jaggy cardboard boxes dig into the soft flesh that should be my biceps. The one consolation of all this lugging is that I'm excused from doing job cards in some noisy air conditioning plant.

As the crates are passed along the line, some of the macho guys want to double up the loads, but I protest. Miraculously, they relent, satisfied by my suggested alternative to shift them twice as fast. It isn't as if we all have a date at the pictures, so what's the point in finishing the job quickly? After about an hour of solid lugging though, I'm totally shattered.

The sky is darkening and the wind's getting up, blowing at the ankles of my trousers. My shirt swells like a tethered balloon. I'm shivering, but my back is wringing with sweat due to the relentless exertion. The wind threatens to freeze the droplets on my forehead and it looks like it might even snow. Praying for a rest from this Neanderthal activity, I look over to Sharkey Ward, who I've passed what feels like a thousand crates to, and raise my eyes to heaven. Unaffected by the weight of the boxes of beer, he starts singing Michael Jackson's 'Billie Jean' in his high-pitched voice. Sharkey doesn't look fit, but even butchers' dogs are in awe of him. He's strong as fuck, despite having the beginnings of what looks like cellulite around his waist and tits that would give Sam Fox a run for her money. His face looks like it's been attacked by a frenzied cheese grater, his eyes are sunk back, shark-like into his pocky forehead. A shock of blond hair insulates his freckly napper.

Sharkey adds dance steps to his Michael Jackson impersonation, causing some of the lugging party to down tools, delighted to be distracted by his wind-assisted moonwalk. He grabs his crotch and *eee-heees* in mock appreciation of the disco king, but a flurry of sleet ends his routine prematurely and we all sprint towards the hangar for cover. Sharkey isn't up for singing in the sleet so he legs it after us. The choppers have now disappeared. A fairy descends from the ship's flight control centre and informs us that store ship has been deferred until better weather. There will be a pipe[*] for us to muster again when we are needed. Another prayer answered.

The snow flurry clears quicker than expected and soon enough the pipe, 'Hands turn to for store ship!' bounces down the mess. Sharkey, Jacko and I look at each other.

'Naaaah!' we say in unison, then piss ourselves at our universal declaration of defiance.

'My arms are fucked, look at the bruises coming up,' I moan.

'Come on, ya wee Scots git,' Sharkey gnarls, grabbing my arm.

'Fuck off, Sharkey!' I reply, piteously. There's no use getting angry with Sharkey cos he'll flatten you. I reckon he fancies his chances with anyone in our mess. As I'm thinking this, he puts me in a headlock and knuckles my scalp so hard it's like he's trying to make fire.

'Get tae fuck, ya ugly bam, ye!' I shout, trying to wriggle free. His grip around my neck tightens and I'm yelping like a squirrel gripped by a whippet. Sharkey is a bit self-

---

[*] call

228

conscious about his fizzog, but thankfully he eases up on my exploding neck veins. I hit a weak spot, but he knows he's delivered enough payback.

'Give over, Jock,' Jacko chips in, basking in my misfortune.

'How would you like it, Jacko?' I moan, not that I'm able to hand out any punishment to the wiry shagmeister. My pleas for clemency are answered from the darkest corner of the mess: 'Shut the fuck up all of yiz, or all bang all yer eds together.' Sensible Dave has spoken.

'Sorry, Dave,' Jacko says, oozing sarcasm. 'Time to go lads, stores here we come,' he quickly adds, keen to dodge further flak from Sensible Dave, who could put Jacko on his arse any day of the week. Jacko leads us up the ladders, but veers off as we approach the upper deck. 'See youse in a minute lads, just off to the battery shop to see a dog about a tree.'

'Aye right,' I protest, but Jacko's off, leaving the rest of us to the delights of assault by cardboard. 'Fuck stores, Sharkey, Ah'm off tae find some job cards,' I announce.

'Lyin little bastard,' says Sharkey, his dark eyes narrowing to slits of accusation, but thankfully the abuse is just verbal this time.

The late afternoon sun parts the clouds but the sharpness of the wind is still skin-splitting. The helicopters return, bringing their relentless thudding with them. I've decided that helicopters are only fun if you're flying in them or if they're delivering mail. You can't use the flight deck to run or play deck hockey if the ship is at flying stations, which for *Fearless* is most of the time. They deposit a relentless supply of stores like seagull shit on a statue. *Fuck it.* I decide to skive a bit, so I head back down to the mess and get my tool roll out of my locker. I want to see what's going on around the ship, so I decide a trip to the bridge is my best course of action. I'll pretend to check the power on some of the watertight sockets around the bridge wings. They probably need testing anyway.

Fuck's sake! The wind is even stronger up here. I should have put on my woolly pully. The wind snags a stray snotter and drags it across my cheek. I pull my shirt cuff over my wrist and use it to prise it off. My eyes are stinging with tears as my shirt flaps around like a penguin attempting to fly. The deck is slippery after the sleet and I struggle to retain my balance. At this rate, I'm going to die of exposure in about five minutes. In pursuit of shelter and warmth, I totter off the bridge, the wind still bullying at my back, and gingerly make my way aft. The weather is truly depressing. The milky sun is taking a pasting from the clouds and relinquishes its grip on the sky. Down it goes like a beaten boxer. Eight! Nine! Ten! Ouuu...t'ah! But somehow, it stumbles to its feet, until boom! Another cloud. Eight! Nine! Ten! Ouuu...t'ah! The clouds win, but maybe there will be a rematch tomorrow with a brighter outcome. The helicopter traffic finally thins out and now that I know it's safe to return to the rancid but cosy mess, I'm looking forward to it. Funny how when you're out, you want to be in.

The following morning, I wake up sober and refreshed. The first of the fluorescent tubes flickers, its plastic-entombed light a poor substitute for the real thing. I cough as newly exhaled cigarette smoke invades the stench of bodies in sleeping bags that had last seen a washing machine 8,000 miles ago. The dregs of last night's beer, which has wept from discarded tins, has fused with floor polish and cooked into mottled melanoma. Sailors do unusual things with cigarettes when they're pissed, so last night's fag ends – and sometimes full cigarettes – are twisted, snapped in two or drowned in beer-sodden ashtrays. I hear the stirrings of human life; the gargling of phlegm, the intermittent farting – which starts slowly but quickly becomes an Olympic sport – before coughing and scratching join the mix as sleep retreats with the flickering of the last fluorescent tube. Welcome to another morning in my half nightclub, half prison.

Scouse and I head for breakfast. There's a tiny queue but it recedes rapidly as sailors are always in a hurry to eat. In half an hour's time there will be 30 or 40 ratings lining up for breakfast. I have a smug feeling, brought on by getting up early and being sober.

The scran is dished out: sausage, bacon, eggs, beans, two slices of toast, accompanied by the obligatory mug of tea. We no longer lug our anti-flash hoods or gas masks, so our scran trays are easily carried across to the tables, though why we carried gas masks in the first place is anyone's guess.

'Ah've got a good feelin about today, Joch,' Scouse ventures sagely, between mouthfuls of toast and runny egg. Ten seconds expire as I struggle to remove some bacon fat from my throat without turning blue.

'Ah said . . .'

I instinctively breathe into my hand, like I did when I was a kid, to check that I'm still alive.

'Ah know whit ye said, Scouse,' I splutter, 'Ah wiz tryin tae answer ye but chokin tae death got in the way. Sorry, mate, you carry on.'

'We are goin ome today, Joch, Ah can feel it.' Scouse's smile is irrepressible. Sometimes his smile can tell you a

231

different story from what he's thinking, but his eyes . . . his eyes always tell the truth.

The pain in my lungs subsides as my breathing approaches normal again.

'D'ye want that sausage, Joch?' Scouse asks, his eyes wide with anticipation.

'Fuckin take it,' I rasp. My appetite has disappeared thanks to the stringy pig fat. Imagine surviving a war only to choke to death on a rasher of bacon. I gulp down a few mouthfuls of tea. The mess hall is filling up. The odour of a thousand sleeping bags makes its way through the ship on the backs of unwashed sailors. Maybe that's why we were issued with gas masks. Scran trays bang and crash on tables, making me flinch.

Time to escape.

'Ah'll see ye back doon the mess, Scouse.'

'Okay mate,' Scouse replies, up to his neck in a sausage butty.

The dining hall din is snuffed out with a rush of air as I close the heavy cross passageway door and secure it with two clips. Out on deck, things become clearer. The sun is up and thriving, no discernible damage from the pasting it took yesterday. The air is crisp and clear but bearable once more as the wind declines to make an appearance. For once, there is no helicopter activity. There are a few more ships at anchor in Port William. The hospital ship, *SS Uganda*, squats in the swell, sluggishly displacing 8,000 tons of water, a giant red cross on its belly that says *Do not shoot!* The newly christened white paint snuggles the ship like a matronly apron, replacing the sickly pallor of yellow and rust from the ship's less salubrious days.

A few hundred yards away sits the *Baya Paraiso*, the Argentinian equivalent of a hospital ship. It is a shitty brown colour. To think, just a few years ago I nearly went on a school trip to Russia on board the *SS Uganda* but my dad refused to shell out the couple of hundred pounds to make it happen. Now, here she is, still out of reach, but this time I'm delighted not to be a passenger, although I'm sure some of the nurses will be fit.

Suddenly, I'm hungry again. Too late, time to work.

I head down to the workshop more out of curiosity than any desire to do any graft. I find a fan motor on the workbench and begin fiddling about with it. Like a jobsworth traffic warden, Jock Blair materialises from nowhere in his gleaming dress uniform and peak cap. The man must be psychic. 'Jocky?'

'Aye, Chief,' I respond, flinching to attention.

'Nip up the bridge and test the bridge watertight sockets,' he orders, tilting his head in the direction of the bridge.

Jock Blair and I know perfectly well that there's fuck all wrong with the watertight sockets and he's just caught me daydreaming. I've learned a bit since my early days on board *Fearless*, so I manage to mask my contempt. 'Yes, Chief,' I gush.

I look around the workshop as Jock Blair starts dishing out the jobs with his customary brevity. Sharkey insists on wearing his anti-flash hood; standing out from the rest of us is something he aspires to. The other ten or so greenies lean against the workshop cupboards, awaiting their fates. I have escaped lightly. The less fortunate are despatched to the giant fridges in the ship's bowels for job card frolics.

'Oh, before you all go, there's a wee thing you'll all be interested in,' Jock Blair adds. I swear I see one of his eyebrows rise. There's a collective intake of breath and tensing of shoulders. 'The ship has received orders to sail home.'

'Yessss!' we shout in unison. Sticky grabs me and kisses me smack on the lips. I instinctively pull away and drag the back of my hand over my lips – even though it's the first real kiss I've had for five months. 'Yes, Jock!' he bellows. 'Goin fuckin home, mate!' Some of the guys are banging on the benches with hands and fists, yet Sharkey is still clad in anti-flash.

'Shhhhhh, fuck's sake, be quiet,' Jock Blair hisses, 'you ain't supposed to know yet. The skipper will be making a pipe at 0900hrs, so look really fuckin surprised when you hear it.'

I already looked surprised because I've just heard Jock Blair swear . . . twice in the one sentence!

Jock Blair leaves us to our celebratory hugs and handshakes. Everyone is grinning, fists clenched in sheer joy. Sharkey finally removes his anti-flash and I grimace as I think of tomorrow's hangover, or is it just the sight of Sharkey's face?

'Come on, Sharkey,' Scouse cajoles, ruffling his hair, but Sharkey flicks his hand away like it's an errant fly. Undeterred, Scouse grabs his chin and forces a smile out of old crinkle-face. There's a hint of mischief in Sharkey's eyes and I hope I'm not on the receiving end. I bound away from the workshop clutching my tool roll, delighted that I really am going to get out of this alive.

The captain's pipe is duly made. Whoops and cheers can be heard in the distance, but the evidence of so many smiling sailors nodding to each other throughout the ship suggests that everyone already knows. Up on the bridge, I toy with the idea of testing the sockets, but the excitement is overwhelming.

I'm going home.

But it's hard to let it sink in. I'm terrified that news will come through that we're not going anywhere. Maybe it's because my dad always promised he'd take me somewhere and then take the promise away in the same breath.

Fuck me, I've saved a fortune though! A new camera, that's first on the shopping list. A holiday for Mum and the ungrateful, evil, mad bastard who is my dad. A video recorder and fuck knows what else. Then I think of the kind of reception we might get when we sail into Portsmouth. Hopefully, girls will be throwing ropes onto the ship and climbing up them to grab my bones. The rest of the day passes in blissful oblivion.

Next stop, Ascension Island. Up at 0700hrs for Yankee hatch party. I can't even remember what the fuck a Yankee hatch party is, but I think it has something to do with closing watertight doors and hatches below the water line in case we hit something. I get my head down after breakfast and no-one comes looking for me. I land the dogwatch/morning watch* later, which is a real pisser. It is hard to believe that we really are on our way home. I decide to keep away from bacon from now on, just in case.

We sail at noon. I awake to the familiar shuddering of *Fearless* under way. I get dressed quickly and leg it onto the upper deck. The bracing wind robs me of breath, forcing me to turn away, gasping. The ship is once more at flying stations and the duty fairy is in danger of going overboard as he struggles to catch a fire extinguisher, which has gone rogue and threatens to roll over the side. The coastline has receded out of sight and a tinge of regret pinches my stomach as I realise I'm never going to see this place again.

---

* dogwatch: 1600-2000hrs after a full day's work; morning watch: 0400-0800hrs, followed by a 0800-1200hrs regular working day

The sharp, hostile outcrops become hazy, irregular shapes. I had missed a last look at Stanley and, for a moment, I feel cheated.

For days I had thought of little else but escaping these islands, their barren plains pocked with rugged mountains and now cratered with British Army shells. The landscape reminds me of the moon, but with grass and less atmosphere. I struggle to think of any redeeming feature; even the sheep look thoroughly miserable. I could see masochists the world over booking up for a fortnight once word got out. I truly knew that I never wanted to come back and certainly not for a holiday. I imagine a sign above the local shop in Stanley. *You don't have to be mad to live here, but it helps.*

But now I pang to have a last look at something resembling civilisation, confirmation that I had actually sailed here for a purpose or was I just going to wake up in the shower like Bobby Ewing* from *Dallas?*

Fearless bangs and crashes against the waves as she gathers speed. I leave the upper deck feeling a little sick.

---

* If you're not familiar with the Bobby Ewing story in Dallas, ask your mum (or your gran)!

Sticky Green leaning against a crashed Argentine helicopter at Stanley Racecourse, shortly before a paratrooper tells us we're on a minefield

Posing like a plonker on a Bofors gun aboard *LSL Sir Tristram*

Damage done to *LSL Sir Tristram* by Argentine bombs

An airborne Sea King and Wessex helicopter at Bluff Cove settlement, five days after the Argentine surrender

Having a post-war carry on in the mess with Yorkie Keeling and Paul Calcutt

The view from the Sea King helicopter, looking down on *LSL Sir Galahad* in Bluff Cove

A Royal Naval Lieutenant plays violin on the bridge of a landing craft in Bomb Alley

Standing on Tumbledown in 2013, looking down on Stanley.

As a local photographer, demonstrating my acting abilities to the local dramatic society

Life is a rollercoaster: Me with journalist and novelist, Matt Bendoris

Looking serious and proud in my number ones

In the Midnight Hour

1982

It's a few days into our voyage back to Portsmouth and we're all in danger of dying of boredom. Another Saturday looms and there is bugger all to do. I re-read a locker-full of old letters. The telly is nothing but repeats and I develop a pathological hatred of the film *The Blues Brothers,* which has been shown at least four times since we sailed from Portsmouth on April 8th. I alternate between the upper deck, the mess and the canteen, all of which inspire nothing but contempt. I meet up with other bored mates . . . The going home euphoria is smitten with catalepsy . . . The ship is in danger of succumbing to an epidemic of boredom . . . I wonder if the sailors on the *Marie Celeste* had become so bored that they invented an invisibility ray and laughed silently at the mariners who boarded her only to encounter a seemingly empty vessel. This is how bored I've become.

Grey, grey Sunday. There are no ships with us to share our fate and any fun-loving whales are giving us a wide berth. The monotonous waves belch their white foam sluggishly against the lolling hull. Most of the ship's company has caught up on sleep, crossing the barrier from refreshed to zombie. The officers also seem to be feeling the pace. Announcements are languid and infrequent. I begin to wonder if they've done a runner. Only the watch-keepers have any sort of routine, the rest of us drifting in and out of consciousness between eating and taking a shit.

The passageways creak and groan in tune with the swell of the sea. Emergency cables, which thankfully had remained dormant throughout the conflict, bump against the bulkheads unhindered. The minutiae of firefighting equipment lazes in unfettered cupboards, swaying like kelp in a sub-sea storm. Stretchers strain against their straps, chaffing the once shiny leather. The passageways are the sole domain of inanimate objects. The white lights glare down at the barren lino decks, reflecting a bluish tinge, a transfer of useless energy. Occasionally the comforting noise of machinery can be heard from an air conditioning plant or machine room below. The ship's company has retreated to their living quarters, leaving the hard core of watch-keepers to get on with it. We've been back at sea one week, but it feels like years.

***

'Ger it up er, man!'

We all laugh.

'Stockings and sussies, a bit o class.'

'Ah'm joinin the mile high club when a get off this rusty piece o shite.'

'Yid never get in the toilet, ye fat bastard!'

Nervous laughter fills the mess.

'You cheeky cunt.'

Big George laughs, so we all laugh, less nervously this time. It helps that the last joke came from Sensible Dave, who could abuse Big George and get away with it, coupled with the fact we were all watching Sylvia Kristel as Emmanuelle getting shagged in an aeroplane.

The sap is definitely rising. It's an hour into the film and no-one dares go to the heads. Anyone who does will immediately be accused of going for a wank and the last taboo on board a ship is to be caught in the act of choking the chicken. I have an erection that any 18-year-old would be proud of, but I'm lying belly down in my pit with my penis neatly stowed in a groove that I've fashioned out of my sleeping bag. We're all mesmerised by the arty shots of Sylvia getting banged in Bangkok and being taught how to love properly, as if she needed any training.

'Stop playin with yerself, Jess,' Big George teases.

'Shut up, George,' replies the battleship grey one without any trace of meaning it. Even after all we've been through, Jess is still the mess doormat.

'Hey! Wee Jock, are ye avin a quiet tug up there?' Big George says, continuing his attempts at banter.

'Aye, George, Ah'm nearly on the vinegar stroke,' I reply, trying to mask my sarcasm.

'Ha ha, ya wee shite,' he laughs back.

God! Have Big George and I become friends? Doubtful.

Emmanuelle sits back in her oversized wicker chair, completely shagged out, and the credits start rolling. No-one dares move.

'Right, who's first for a hand shandy then?' Jacko chuckles.

'Are you offerin?' says Pete Higgins from the bowels of the mess.

'Yeah, right, ave seen the mould on the end of yours! You wanna get the doc to ave a look at that before it comes off in yer ands.'

More laughter, but things are getting tense. Even if someone genuinely has to go for a piss, they'll be ridiculed.

'Right enough of this bollocks, Ah'm goin for a slash,' says Sensible Dave, the god of authority and wisdom.

'Watch you don't pass out up there,' Jacko snipes.

'D'ye wanna come with us, Jacko, just to see if I'm doin it right?' Sensible Dave replies, caustically, rising from his pit, scratching his bollocks.

'No thanks, Dave, yer wife says you're a right wanker, and who am I to disagree?' Jacko says, still entombed in his sleeping bag, chin propped up by a scrawny elbow.

As soon as Sensible Dave makes his move, I feel the tension lift. A trip to the heads no longer leaves me open to ridicule. However, I don't want to risk getting caught like the cheeky cockney chap Nigel who got photographed having a wank and his picture was put up in the galley.

Suddenly, I feel a strange attraction to the place that I like least: November switchboard. I'll have to leave it half an hour or so, but that just intensifies the tingling sensation in my cock. I look around the mess, laughing when others laugh, silent when there's no need to join in with the frolics. Cockney Nigel, the wee fucker, is mute. He's only recently survived the barrage of jokes about sitting in the bogs with a coat hanger squashed onto his head and a scuddy picture stabbed onto the hook, so both hands were free, one to wank and one to hold the door closed. Sadly for Cockney Nigel, he forgot the over-the-top method of exposure. To be caught was a disaster, but to be photographed suggested suicide as the only way of preserving what dignity you had left.

It's nearly midnight and the buzz about *Emmanuelle* gradually dies down and going to the heads is no longer greeted by snide remarks, as, gradually, we troop up the ladder to piss before turning in. I wait till the last man returns before I make my move. Still wearing my number eights, I rattle up the ladder, carrying my towel and toothbrush. The heads are empty, so there'll be no witnesses to my slight detour. I consider running across the cross passage but decide to calm myself down and take my time. My heart is pounding. The adrenaline stabs me in the chest. I giggle to myself in guilty anticipation. The red passageway lights lead me down towards November switchboard. Thankfully, I meet no-one on the way.

My brain plays back the best bits. The scenes on the plane where Emmanuelle is shagged, once in her seat and a second time in the toilet, are without doubt the most erotic images I've seen in my 18 years on this planet. Hardcore porn comes a poor second. Cucumbers in gaping orifices pale in comparison with the notion that you could get laid on a plane by a total stranger while everyone else is asleep, excluding the pilot I hope.

The mess adjacent to the switchboard has remained empty since the troops landed in San Carlos. There is one bunk light on, just enough to see down the ladder. The metal door to November is ajar, beckoning me in like a punter to the red light district. The fluorescent lights illuminate the interior, reflecting off the dials and switches; there are no whining noises from the generator this time, only the sound of heavy breathing and my heart thudding in my chest for company. I look around the switchboard and check that no-one has followed me down. Scouse is the most likely candidate for a stitch-up job. I tug at the watertight door and, with the clunk of two clips, entomb myself in the one-metre-wide space.

I'm alone. My pulsing cock is champing at the bit. I unbutton the flies on my number eight trousers and pull it out. I'd love to say it's huge, but who am I kidding? The room still smells of rubber. I don't risk pulling my trousers down in case one of the duty watch-keepers makes a detour on his rounds. My cock is tingling and I haven't even started stroking it yet. My right thumb is wet with smeg. I don't want it to happen too quickly but I'm greedy for the sensation. I begin to caress the foreskin back and forth. The engorged blue vein swells almost to bursting point and I wonder if it could actually burst while having a wank, with blood and spunk shooting all over the walls – but I quickly snuff out the image.

I'm nervous about being caught, but the heady euphoria of a brilliant orgasm forces me beyond the point of not giving a shit. I tense up, compressing the pectoral muscles in my chest inwards, constricting my breathing. I look at the archaic phone system with its yellow flags, remembering the farce of trying to talk to someone while wearing a gas mask. I replace Jock Blair's gas-masked face with Emmanuelle's, her eyes rolling back in fake orgasmic delight. I picture myself as the lucky French bastard who shimmies next to her on the plane, unbuttons her blouse and rubs her milky-white tits, while the subdued light filters through the window . . .

I'm now in the devil's advocate role, desperate for the orgasm – which I know will be brilliant – yet I greedily hold on to that pre-orgasm tingling sensation, the spunk rising to the head of my cock, only to be stifled for fear of being caught in the act. It's like I want the tingle to last forever, but I'm desperate to come at the same time, exhilarated by how enjoyable the sensation will be once I reach the point of no return. I picture Emmanuelle sitting on the lucky bastard's cock. He muffles her squeal with his hand and some interested passenger looks round and gets an eyeful of suspender belt.

I can hold it no longer.

I jerk the foreskin hard. My breathing has stopped. The spunk surges to the head of my cock unchecked and is let loose onto the grubby rubber matting in thick blobs. It's heaven to see the amount that spurts out onto the deck, splatting in dollops on the lino tiles around the rubber. I hold back a cry of pure ecstasy as my rock hard cock shoots out the contents of my balls like a flame thrower. At this very moment, I couldn't give a fuck if the captain and his missus appeared on the scene.

My balls tighten as they give up the last of their precious seed, the remnants trickling over my thumb into my palm, losing its thickness as it cools. As my breathing returns to normal, I look down at the five large pools of spunk as droplets of sweat land next to them. I button up my trousers and push back the clips on the watertight door. As the vacuum seal releases with a hiss, I let out a full-throated laugh, a mixture of relief and ecstasy.

Thank you, Sylvia.

When You're Young

1982

'It's fuckin sunny up top, you lot should ger out there and get the rays, man.'

Jacko has spoken, a fag dangling from his bottom lip, which looks like a trick that has taken years to perfect in front of the mirror before trying it out down the pub. Jacko the dancer, the cool smoker, the wise cracker and Shaggy lookalike, owes a lot to the art of smoke and mirrors.

Wee George sits glued to the goggle box, carefully rolling a ciggie. Never once looking down, he presses the baccy between his nicotine-stained forefingers and thumbs and stretches it along the length of the Rizla, before expertly rolling it over the tobacco. That man is an artist with a cigarette.

'Good idea, Jacko, time for some bathin,' Scouse replies, rising from his pit. 'Comin, Jock?'

'Yeah, why not,' I say, unzipping my sleeping bag. 'Let me get my camera.'

Up top, the sun duly shines. The colour blue has a monopoly overhead, the clouds having once again succumbed to the sun's brilliant rays, magnified by our proximity to the equator. I screw up my eyes to look down at the shimmering sea. The sun slaps the back of my neck and my shoulders loosen as the heat burns through my hair onto my skin. It'll soon be time for a haircut. There are still no other ships in sight. Not a thing on the horizon.

Am I dreaming this? I haven't seen another ship in almost a week.

'Photie time, Jock.'

'Eh? What?' I spring out of my dream state.

'Come on, ye dozy get,' says Scouse, with a playful punch to the kidneys.

'Right, over there . . . no, turn around,' I say, shielding my eyes. 'The sun's in the wrong place.'

'Hang on, Jock, Ah'll move it for ye if ye like,' comes Jacko's sarky reply.

'And risk a hernia for goin ome wiv,' Scouse quips.

I take some pics of Scouse and Jacko in various stages of madness before they get bored: tongues out; eyes crossed; tongues out *and* eyes crossed, followed by cheek pinching, headlocks and dead-arming.

Thankfully, Jacko breaks out of Scouse's headlock. 'Hey. Jock, are you gonna see any of them pen pals you've been writing to?' he sniffs.

'Don't know, really.' I swallow, taking my hands off the camera and letting it dangle from my neck.

'Are you gonna try and get yer leg over with that Debbie bird?' Scouse chips in, like the cheeky one in a double act.

'How the fuck dae you know aboot Debbie?' I say, my face reddening, but not from the sun this time.

'We know everything, Jocky boy,' Jacko proclaims.

'Is that right?' I say, hands on hips and chin jutting out, the back of the camera bouncing off my belly. 'Well, huv ye seen her photie then?'

'Yeah,' says Jacko, preening. 'Scouse wants to know: if ye shag er, can e ave sloppy seconds?'

'Dirty bastards, the pair o yiz.'

Scouse walks towards me, cups the base of my camera and looks me straight in the eyes. 'Are you a virgin, Jock?'

'Fuck off, Scouse, nae way!' I blast back, feeling the adrenalin stabbing my gut into fight mode. I try to move away but Scouse still has hold of my camera. I feel like a dog on a leash.

Jacko sidles up and thumbs my shirt collar. Suddenly, memory of Darren Haldane and a poofy pink shirt invades my consciousness.

'Come on, Jock,' he needles, pointing back and forth between himself and Scouse. 'Ye can tell us . . . we're yer mates.'

'Get tae fuck, the pair o yiz,' I say limply, mouth drying up.

'Awright, awright, Jock,' Scouse says, letting go of my camera, but still invading my space.

My face must be beaming bright red. It's getting harder to breathe, so I take my chance and break free. Scouse and Jacko look at each other and burst out laughing. 'Fuckin perverts,' I say, trying to claw back some dignity. I turn and walk away, a familiar sting in the bridge of my nose.

Fuck! Whit am Ah gonnae dae noo? It'll be all around the mess and when Ah get doon, Ah'll get pelters. Fuck, why did Ah huv tae crack? Why could Ah no jist have made a big joke ootae it? Everythin wis goin fine. The sun had brightened ma spirits, urgin me tae think o the thrill of getting hame, three weeks leave tae dae whit Ah like with, and noo Ah wiz gonnae huv tae take loads o stick until someone else becomes a scapegoat. Fuck, Ah'm in deep. Better keep ma heid doon fae now on.

Exhausted by my own thoughts, I collapse onto my pit, turn my back on the noisy messdeck and succumb to sleep . . .

I look up at the sky. It's dirty, white and thick, almost buzzing with tension. The silence scares me. All around there is violence and mayhem, but it's carried out under a thick blanket of silence. Objects fall from planes: bombs? No, not bombs, rolls of pink toilet paper slipping from the undercarriage of a warplane. The rolls unravel and pick up speed, spiralling towards their targets. I look away before impact. Close to me, a tin-hatted sailor is firing a machine gun into the sky. The gunner shakes uncontrollably, his face alternating between terror and orgasm, barely controlling the silently vibrating weapon. He seems to be shouting but no words come out. The noise from the gun should have been deafening but there is no noise. The smoke from the barrel coils up into the air. Overhead, more silent warplanes ejaculate their payloads over the ships. Each one takes a hit, the toilet rolls finding their targets and engulfing them in flames. Sailors jump into the water. Their splashes go unrecorded, their cries unheard, a muted war film in the making, then someone cries out, piercing the now thick blackened sky. 'Fuck's sake, what the fuck's goin on? Here it comes! It's gonnae hit us!' The object plummets towards me, eclipsing everything. I look over my shoulder. The gunner has gone, the ship abandoned but undamaged. The toilet roll threatens to smother me. I look over the side and then climb onto the railings. I wobble and flail at the top railing, failing to grip it. I look over my other shoulder. This time, the whole ship's company are in their white tropical uniforms with matching shoes and the Royal Marines Band is marching in slow motion up and down the flight deck, first upright then upside down, the trombone slides turning cartwheels as they flip, but still no sound. A trombone slide narrowly misses my face and I jerk backwards, my throat grabbing my heart as I plunge backwards into the freezing water . . .

'Fuck's sake, Jock, wake up!'

'What? Get aff me, ya bastard, get aff me!' My arms flail as I fight the intruder, head fuzzy, eyes struggling to focus.

After a few seconds, the voice becomes recognisable as Sensible Dave's. 'It's alright, mate, loosen up, you were dreamin, that's all.'

I cease wriggling like a rabbit in a bag about to be drowned.

'Just a dream, mate,' he soothes.

'Sorry, Dave,' I mumble, mouth like it's full of cotton wool. 'Whit time is it?'

'It's about three,' he replies, in a manner that suggests he should be taking my pulse and checking my blood pressure.

'Hey, Jock, get yer fuckin ed down, man!' Big George's voice booms from the gloom. There's no way he's ever going to be a nurse.

'Hey, Joch?' Scouse looms in.

'Whit, Scouse?'

'You dreamin of gerrin yer end away?'

'Fuck off,' I snap, wrapping the sleeping bag over my head, praying that I can block out the monsters next time.

The next few days pass painfully. I'm obsessing about my virginity and taking lots of flak from the usual suspects. One upside is that it's getting hotter and I can spend less time in the messdeck. The telly is shit anyway; fuckin *Blues Brothers!* If I ever see someone dressed in a stupid black suit, white shirt and porkpie hat, I swear I will fucking kill them. I seek solace on a bollard close to the ship's stern. The vibration from the propellers stops me listening to myself too hard. It's good to see the ship's wake shrinking, marking our progress. Every hour we get 20 miles closer to home. We're due at Ascension Island tomorrow; hopefully we won't hang around. I've given up on Tolstoy's *War and Peace*.

The sun's worrying a patch on the back of my neck. I think about my mum's visit to the doctor about her moles and decide I've probably had enough rays for one day. When I stand up, some grease from the bollards has stained my number eights, but I shrug it off and head back to the mess for a kip.

***

'Jock?'

I wake to find Jacko sitting on my bed, a fag in one hand and the other half way to scratching his grizzled chin.

'Whit?' I snarl.

'The mail pipe,' Jacko barks back, a finger pointing towards the mess ladders in the direction of the mail office.

'So?' I dismiss, with a shrug and a rub at my eyes.

'Aren't you goin, bonnie lad?' he mocks, another hopeless attempt at a Scots accent.

'Naw,' I sniff.

'Why not?' he quizzes, his voice softer now. I wait for the punchline.

'Cannae be arsed,' I whinge.

'Come on, Jock, get yer skinny wee arse doon that mail office,' chips in Big George.

'It's too late now, someone from the other mess will already be there, George,' I plead, my tone softening in subordination.

'Away, man. Off ye go,' Big George counters, and I realise I'm boxed in a corner.

I sluggishly slip from my pit and slide on my flip-flops. Letters have lost the appeal of just a week ago. I traipse up the ladders towards the upper decks, but I'm too late. Bomber bounds down from the cross passage, his arms brimming with letters and parcels. 'Hey, Jocky, you're a bit tardy, wing nut,' he says.

'Ah'm no really fussed aboot mail today, Bomber,' I mumble, trying to avoid looking at him.

'Well, ye'll ave to be, cos this little lot's all ours.' He smiles, does a bicep curl with the mail, then he's off.

'Right then, see ye,' I say to no-one in particular.

In the next few days, the conversation miraculously shifts away from my virginity and focusses on the remaining week left at sea. I count my lucky stars that no-one has thought to put my picture up in the galley with the word 'virgin' underneath. There is a vote to see if we want a run ashore in Gibraltar before we dock in Portsmouth. The pissheads lose out to the married men, but retaliate by organising a mighty on board piss-up, which nobody objects to. We start to stow our beer ration, which the top brass turns a blind eye to. It's planned for the night before our arrival in Plymouth. Suddenly, I can't wait for the grey, angry seas around the Bay of Biscay.

Jock Blair decides I should change sections and moves me to Domestics, working on lighting, kettles and mess fridges. It turns out to be a great section for hiding. I think he realises that Bomber and I don't really get on and I'm not 'switched on' enough to do fans and starters on my own yet. Bomber had tried to teach me what he calls "stans and farters", but when he got frustrated, he cuffed me round the ear. Everyone turned a blind eye to this in the hope they didn't become the next target.

The petty officer in charge of Domestics is much more laid back. Sharkey works for him and he seems to have an easy time of it. I start off skiving, but the days drag so I throw myself into doing job cards and the clock moves faster. I even start working on my task book, which has to be completed for promotion purposes. Gradually, I spend less time fucking about and more time studying. I even study when switchboard watch-keeping. Wonders will never cease.

It's three days to go. We have a deck hockey tournament, which the greenies and stokers lose in the final to the wardroom, who are confirmed by visits to the sick bay by the losing finalists as a shower of dirty hackin officer bastards. My knee blows up like a helium balloon after some scabby lieutenant cracks me on the kneecap with his stick. To lose to the officers is a major embarrassment but our defeat is softened by the thought of the night's impending hooley.

David Watts

1982

Pfffft!

'Mind me kechs, Jock!' Scouse says, jerking back to avoid my exploding tinny.

'Sorry, Scouse,' I laugh, 'Jacko must have shookin it.'

'You lyin twat, ye shook it yourself,' Jacko protests.

I cast him a look that says *You know ye're lyin through your fuckin teeth. Why don't ye tell the truth for once in yer life?*

'Jock, drink yer beer, mate, and shut the fuck up!' he gripes. 'Awright?'

Yeeha! He's riled, but I decide a riled Jacko means a scrap, so I comply and keep quiet for a whole five minutes while Cockney Nigel gibbers some nonsensical pish.

We all get stuck into our hoarded beer ration as the radio blares out some Motown.

'Old on a minute, Nige,' Jacko interjects, stopping Cockney Nigel mid-sentence. 'Turn that up, George, Ah love this song!'

Jacko whirls and glides around the narrow mess, fag in one hand, tin of beer in the other. He's doing a northern soul style shuffle, punctuated by the tightest of spins, constricted by the width of our tiny living space. His strawberry blond mop tilts towards the fluorescent lamps, eyes closed, lips perfectly in synch with the words of The Isley Brothers' 'This Old Heart of Mine (Is Weak for You)'.

'Jacko, man, ye're fuckin unique,' Big George whoops, without a hint of sarcasm. The big Geordie plants his ample arse on Jess' pit commanding the best view of Jacko's antics like a Roman emperor at the Colosseum.

'You're a eunuch alright,' Sensible Dave adds.

We all laugh our heads off, not because it's that funny, but because it has come from the mouth of the only sensible man in the entire Royal Navy. Jacko almost topples mid-spin, but manages to correct himself and continues to glide, albeit with less conviction, before stopping and reaching down to the floor for his beer. Sensible Dave clearly hadn't forgotten his earlier altercation with Jacko and had timed his revenge perfectly. Snubbing him, Jacko swills from his can, crushes it and flings it towards the spittoon[*]. There's a big cheer as it misses its target, bounces onto the deck and lands at the feet of Big George.

I'm enjoying Jacko's humiliation as much as everyone else. I think back to the boozy carnage of my 18th birthday, smile and crack open another tin of beer, which is weird, cos I'm sure I'd just cracked a fresh one only a few seconds ago. Jacko swivels one more time, but the song stops and his momentum is gone. He's reduced to ferreting in his pocket for a cigarette. He brings the packet out but they're all crushed. He tries to light one anyway in a last act of bravado, but it's useless.

'Touché´,' Jacko mutters, removing the fag from his lips and crushing it tight.

Big George kicks the empty beer can towards Jacko's feet. 'Ah think that's yours, hinny[**].'

---

[*] a large, circular, silver-coloured ashtray that sits on the floor
[**] Geordie term for honey, used sarcastically in this context

Jacko flops down on the nearest pit, directly opposite Big George, and sucks in recycled air, the sweat from his forehead trickling down his nose. He claws away limp strands of hair from his reddened face and looks directly at Big George. Then there's a moment's hesitation as he looks away, and in that very moment it feels like all the air is being sucked out of the mess. Then he turns his attention back to the smug Buddha opposite. 'Who rattled your cage, big man?'

The words act like a needle being dragged across a record.

Big George lunges at Jacko, but Sensible Dave, Pete Higgins and Smudge get between them before any damage is done. Wee George slips on some beer and bangs his knee on a bed bar. His scream is so high-pitched that the crowd formed at the bottom of the mess hoping to watch a fight now dissolves into laughter. Wee George grimaces while doing a theatrical bow, before rolling up the leg of his ovies to check for collateral.

'Relax, George,' Sensible Dave cajoles, a palm across Big George's sternum. 'And Jacko, button it!' he commands, his voice switching from nurse to sergeant major.

Jacko is only too happy to back off. Big George swats away Sensible Dave's hand and backs off on his own terms.

'It's a good job you can dance, cos you'd be fuck all use in a fight,' Wee George chips, and the subsequent eruption of laughter is Jacko's get out of jail free card.

'Sorry, George,' Jacko says to Big George, avoiding eye contact. He stretches over and opens the fridge without leaving his seat. 'Let me get you one of Jock's tinnies.'

'Better make it two,' Big George orders. 'That wee gobshite looks like he's had enough.'

I look at Big George, then at the fridge, and then at Jacko, who winks at me. He knows he's dodged a 15 stone bullet.

'Giz anither beer outae the fridge anaw, wid ye, Jacko?' I slur.

One of my tinnies was caught in the crossfire and is mortally wounded, the contents pooling on the messdeck.

Jacko holds up something that looks like beer, but I'm struggling to focus. 'Naw! No wan ae thae Courage ones,' I protest. 'Gies a Red Devil. Scottish beer is the best.'

'Jock, just take it, ye're too drunk to notice the difference,' says . . . someone. If I said I knew who, I'd be lying.

'Ah'm no drunk, but Ah will be soon,' I mutter. 'In a week's time, I'll huv lost ma cherry.'

I vaguely remember peace breaking out again in 3H2 aft. More music, lots of smoking, dancing, laughing, bumping into each other trying to go for a piss. No more aggro.

Strangely, I find myself in the for'ard mess and I've no idea how I got here. I squint at the shapes of men all over the place; some lying on the floor, some slumped against lockers and a few swaying upright, or maybe they're standing still and I'm the one swaying about. I try to focus, closing one eye, but I can't make anyone out. An idea enters my head that if I was this drunk and I fell off the school roof, I would just bounce.

I try to concentrate through the boozy fog. There's the smell of something illegal and they've been at the spirits.

Someone is boasting about an Argentine machine gun, which is stowed in the air conditioning plant apparently. I stumble as I lean against the sliding door that separates their mess from ours.

'Jocky! In ye come, wingnut,' beckons Bomber Wells. There's a rasp in his voice that suggests he's smoked his entire ciggie ration in a oner. He seesaws towards me and I instinctively take a step back and bounce off something that I know will be a bruise tomorrow.

'Ah'm no pissed, Ah jist slipped against the door,' I hear myself say.

'Not pissed!' Bomber booms, his arms wide, face surveying the mess like an actor expecting applause. 'Not pissed!' He's now in full panto dame mode.

There's a mix of boos and cheers at my arrival, making me think I've stumbled into a Grimm's fairy tale where I'm playing the part of Pinocchio and, despite their laughter, I'm worried about being planed to death. Bomber grabs a bottle from the top of the fridge and I'm thinking *at least they're going to give me an anaesthetic before they tear me apart.*

I look up and see Netley Nick on his top bunk, a huge roll-up sticking out of his gob. He smiles down at me, demon like, before blowing out a giant smoke ring. The smoke stings my eyes and I get a fuzzy feeling deep in my stomach, like when Motorcycle Girl calls me David.

Bomber is now cradling a bottle of beer and shot glass with some clear liquid in it. 'Tell me, Jock, are you a girl?' he asks, his voice softer now, stooping so his face is level with mine, as if he's comforting a toddler with a skint knee.

'No, Bomber.'

'Are you sure?' he prods.

'Positive!' I insist.

'Then why, me old son, are you not legless by now?'

'Jacko keeps knockin over ma tinnies.'

The room starts spinning. I survey the carousel of beds in front of me and stretch out a hand to grab one, but miss and land on the blue polished lino.

The mess howls with laughter as I warily get back on my feet and bash myself against the sliding door again on my way out.

Back in 3H2 aft, beer is rivering along the lino, picking up dust and fag ash, wetting it like a newly formed spring after a burst of rain. The manic singing and dancing has morphed into smoke-enveloped philosophical discussions that seem to be happening in slow motion. I think I'm sitting but I could easily be slumped against the fridge or leaning on somebody's bunk.

Jacko gazes up through the smoky haze and smiles. My shirt is soaked in beer, but I've no idea how it happened. Jacko saves my tinny as I take it off. I resist at first but then I realise he's just trying to help. He's alright really.

'Ye're awright really, Jacko!' I tell him.

'So are you, Jock, me old mucker. Who spilled beer on ye any road?' he asks.

'Ye're a fuckin good dancer, Jacko, Ah'll say that fur ye.'

'Jock?'

'What?'

'Shut up an drink yer beer,' he says, handing back my tinny.

'Are you pissed or something?'

'Not me, Jock, that should be a rhetorical question,' he snorts.

'A rhetorical question? Whit's that?'

'It means you're too stupid to know and too drunk to care.'

'Up yours, Shaggy, but I love you, mate.'

Jacko jerks his head back laughing. During that moment, it feels like there isn't anyone else in the mess, but when I look around, I can make out loads of happy faces. They're all looking back and laughing or smiling. It feels great. My head is getting cloudier, but the sensation of being slightly out of touch with my central nervous system only encourages me.

'Hey, Jacko?'

'What is it, Jock?' he sighs.

'Any chance of a fag?' I ask.

'You, Jock? Ah thought you hated the fuckin things,' Jacko says, screwing up his face.

'Naw, no really,' I reply, shaking my head slightly. 'Go on, jist one.'

He flicks open the golden top of his fag packet and slides out a cigarette, motioning me forward with his yellow index finger. The smell of fresh tobacco excites me in my booze-fuelled haze. He pulls out another, taps it on the edge of the box and slips his shiny Zippo lighter out of his pocket. With one well-practised flick, he unhinges the lid and flares the gas, causing the tip of his cigarette to hiss into life. The bold yellow flame dancing in Jacko's fingers mesmerises me.

I lift my cigarette to my lips, the fresh tobacco smell beckoning me closer to the flame. It dances around the fuzzy tip of the cigarette until what seems like an age has passed. Then flame and tip dock. I draw in the cool smoke and immediately feel my head tingle. I have no idea what drugs feel like, but the buzz I get from the cigarette seems just as potent. I take another long drag and throw my head back as I eject the smoke, stifling a laugh that morphs into a cough. This is the fucking business.

'Ye know, Jacko, Ah forgive yiz all aboot that virgin thing, but Ah jist want ye tae know that there's nae hard feelins an that Ah hope whitever you an Scouse dae in the future, Ah'll be right behind ye . . . yiz.'

Jacko looks at Scouse, then at me, and smiles. 'Jock, bonny lad?' he says softly, resting a hand on my shoulder.

'Whit, Jacko? Tell me,' I urge, realising that Jacko's hand on my shoulder hasn't made me flinch and I thank God for the gift of booze and fags.

'You'll get laid, defo, now fuck off to bed or you'll be mingin in the morning.' Jacko says, knuckling my hair and breaking the spell of intimacy. He gets up and nods to Scouse as if they've tried to save a condemned man from the executioner.

'Laid, aye. Bed, naw.' I bite back, before trying to take another slug of beer, but I miss and the liquid runs down my bare chest and onto my trousers.

'He's a bloody mess,' says someone, but I'm fucked if I know who – could be Scouse or Jacko, or, God forbid, Jock Blair.

Pretty Green

1982

I awake feeling like someone is prising my eyes out of their sockets with a rusty hammer drill, which is not as bad as I thought I would feel. Fortunately, I had succumbed to only one ciggie, even though Scouse and Jacko had seen the potential for me to smoke a whole packet. I also know that I wasn't the last to fall asleep, meaning a hardcore had stayed up bevvying, knowing we all had to be up for harbour stations in Plymouth. Fuck the hangover though, we're nearly home. I slither out over the edge of my second storey pit and view the debris below. Crumpled cans remind me of the twisted wreckage of *Sir Tristram*.

Bodies stir and coughing penetrates the acrid air, followed by an anonymous fart that provokes a dive to the heads. The unzipping of sleeping bags suggests that even those with a hangover are hungry or bursting for a slash. Sensible Dave frees himself from his pit. He sits up, swings his legs round and lands between an overcrowded ashtray and a pile of dead tinnies. He catches my eye and casts a judgemental grin.

'Smoking last night, were we?' he quizzes.

That's what I mean about him being a good nurse, he even uses that "we" thing.

'Honest, Dave, it was just the one. You know me, Ah hate the things,' I croak, unconvincingly. Funny how Sensible Dave could easily wheedle you into a confession.

Deep down, I hope when he gets home, Sensible Dave is his wife's gimp, complete with PVC jumpsuit. Smudge, the sleep addict, has miraculously wakened third and automatically sticks a fag in his gob. I wonder what Smudge would do if he had no fags in the morning, and imagine the headline: *Cig-starved morning drove me to kill.*

The ship rocks and uncrushed tinnies roll, waking up the heavier sleepers. I look under my pillow and pull out my watch. Five to seven. Five minutes to go before harbour stations. Underneath my bunk, Wee George is emerging from his sleeping bag like a maggot from a dead cow's swollen belly. Predictably, he's deliberately bumping his knees off the underside of my bunk. And if the roles were reversed, I'd be doing the exact same.

'Alright, George?' I say, leaning over my bunk and inhaling a whiff of his body odour. He frowns, obviously pissed off that my eyes are fully focussed. No way am I going to spoil the glory of arriving in Plymouth by chucking up over the side. I duck my head back in, slide the sleeping bag down over my body, lift my legs and release myself from the polyester cocoon. I double-check the lie of the land so that when I crouch and stretch out my legs towards the deck, they won't land anywhere near a ciggie minefield or a tin can depth charge. I know it wouldn't be the same as nearly stepping on a land mine in Stanley, but I'm not taking any chances.

The pleasing sensation of warm flesh on cold, beer-stained lino registers a *One small step for man . . .* kind of feeling in my brain. Also, unlike many a previous piss-up, my brain and the contents of my stomach have followed the rest of my body onto terra firma. The stragglers of the mess follow reluctantly, which means no loitering; time to get dhobied* and find out if the locals are friendly, but not before another fun-filled couple of hours with Jock Blair in November switchboard as we anchor in Plymouth Sound.

I think back to the time I won the cross-country race at *Raleigh* and my longing to have a good piss up in Plymouth. There'll be no chance of getting off the ship here, but at least I know that in less than 24 hours, I'll be on UK soil.

'I hope your number ones are clean and pressed for tomorrow's Procedure Alpha, Jock?' Jock Blair says, looking at me accusingly. *Burst my party bubble, why don't you?*

'Oh, aye, Chief, I was polishin ma boots all last night,' I say, doing my best to mask my sarcasm.

'Are yer mum and dad comin down tae see ye?' he asks, wrong-footing me, as I expected his response to be something like "Shite, ye were pissin it up like everyone else on board."

'Naw, Chief, they cannae afford it, but Ah think Ah'll fly up anyway, jist fur quickness,' I surprise myself saying.

'Ah'm sure they'll be pleased tae see ye.' His voice betrays a hint of emotion, which catches me off-guard.

'Aye.'

The intercom interrupts us. 'Hands fall out of harbour stations.'

'Right, Jocky, off you go and find somewhere to skive,' Jock Blair says, recovering his stiff upper lip.

I swear I see the flicker of a smile on Jock Blair's face. We had survived 100 days cooped up together, bombed together, won and lost at Othello together, and almost laughed together. This day draws a line in our buddy movie adventure, but there won't be any celluloid hugs or walking off into the sunset moments.

---

* washed

'Right,' I say, almost smiling back as I open the clips on the switchboard door. 'See ye.'

'It's see *you . . . Chief.*'

'You, Chief,' I enunciate, clearly, and then leave him to pack up his cassette recorder and exit the watertight door to November switchboard one last time.

Shit! Up top, the weather is lousy; visibility ranges from hand in front of your face to hand inside your eyeball. There's a steady drizzle. I hear the klaxon of another ship at regular intervals, but I have no idea what kind. It could be a kid in a rowing boat playing with a foghorn for all I know.

Hopefully tomorrow, we'll be greeted by screaming, cheering crowds waving flags and bunting, swearing undying love to every member of the ship's company – but today I'm going to have to make do with a soggy welcome from a bank of fog.

The drizzle thickens to droplets, nipping my face as it conspires with the wind. I look up and down the deck but no-one's about.

***

Pommy* Smith from Domestics goes easy on us. I think he has a bit of a hangover from last night anyway, so after turning up at the battery shop and looking around at the carnage caused by last night's binge, he's given Sharkey the task of making sure the sea boats' batteries are fully charged. He punts me off to test navigation lights, which I actually do, because the switches are behind the bridge and I can glean loads of info from the officers on watch up there, plus I can have a good look around at the damage

---

* slang for petty officer

caused by the Argy aircraft. The rest of Domestics are told to keep out the road. Pommy Smith's eyes are bloodshot from the senior rates' piss-up, but his face suggests he can't wait to carry on bevvying in the nearest boozer.

Slowly, the drizzle surrenders to a cloud-ridden grey sky with patches of white, the sun limp and intermittent, like it's also nursing a hangover. The wind has eased off and it's bearable to walk on each wing of the bridge without a burberry. Off the starboard bow prowls the destroyer *HMS Brazen,* which must have provided the fog klaxon earlier. The ship is so close that commands could be shouted over, but the seamen persist with their signal lamps. Tradition and common sense are not linked in any shape or form in the senior service. These same sailors will be up to their elbows in grease and shite in their best rig tomorrow when they bring the ship alongside* in Pompey harbour, but hopefully they'll have an appreciative audience. I hope the indigenous Pompey population throw money. After all, it'll only come back to them in the pubs later.

As I fart about on the port wing, I catch sight of the damage done to the bridge windows by the Argentinian *Mirage's* 60mm cannon. Several of the two-inch thick windows have been completely taken out and are now replaced by timber. The third is scored in the top right corner, the bullet hole clearly visible in the centre of the spider's web shaped crack. It must have been a terrifying place when bullets were whizzing about, hitting off all sorts – including bodies – while officers barked orders at gunners and others barked orders down to the engine room to get us out of the way. Who knows what the

* adjacent to the quayside

others on the bridge did when they saw blood around the wounded gunners. I know I would have freaked.

I gaze again at the bridge windows. The havoc wreaked by one cannon shell is frightening, I mean really fucking frightening, and I know one of the gunners copped a shell into his calf muscle.

'What are you doing, Cruickshanks?' a spotty young lieutenant enquires, having spotted me daydreaming. I immediately think of my old Latin teacher belting me for looking out the window. I tense up and pull my shoulders back, hoping to look simultaneously interested and subordinate.

'Sir, just testing the nav lights, sir,' I reply, trying not to look as if I've just shit myself.

'And you do that by looking out of the bridge windows, do you, Cruickshanks?' he snorts.

At least he's getting my name right.

'No, sir,' I reply, trying not to sound cheeky but wanting to all the same. After all, fuck em – in one day, I'll be home and in civvies. 'Just doing a bench test on the starboard anti-gravity davit, sir.'

'Carry on, Cruickshanks,' the spotty lieutenant says, clearly not understanding a single word I said. Opting to let me off the hook, he flicks his wrist dismissively, like I'm a pesky fly.

The rest of the day is spent dodging work. There are reporters on board, anxious to speak to sailors. They seek out the youngest lad, a little wanker I remember, skinny as a streak of piss and twice as smelly. I'm jealous as fuck, but I console myself that I'm the youngest Jock sailor on board. How's that for desperation? No-one comes to interview me.

The grey sky now squats on top of us like a depressed Sumo wrestler. Down in the mess, there's bugger all to do except play cards or pack your kit bag and suitcase for going on leave. Some of my mates have started painting their suitcases: *Falklands '82. We came. We saw. We conquered, and fucked all the penguins.* I am reliably informed that this will be a 'fanny magnet' in Pompey.

I can't work myself up to pack any of my gear. *If the mist lifts, I'll get stuck in,* I tell myself. I make up my mind to travel home in my best rig: my number ones.

Big George utters the immortal words, 'Ye glory grabbin wee bastud', but Jacko assures me that if suitcase art doesn't do the trick, going home in uniform is the dog's bollocks.

Smudge burps in, 'Pure fuckin fanny magnets these suits, Jock,' before lighting up another fag.

Smudge's pulling mate, Smurf, who's busy putting an extra shine on his best boots, nods his head. Smurf, who seems to spend half his life in his best rig, always tells the best stories about women and his conquests. So that settles it – but not before Big George has the last word, 'Posin bastuds.'

On runs ashore, Smurf and Smudge are partners in crime. Smurf's rusty-brown wavy hair has incredible volume and his little upturned nose and deep brown eyes remind me of Bambi the cartoon deer. He's been bouncing excitedly around the mess as if the lino is on fire, his hair occasionally falling forward, forcing him to sweep it away to prevent him clattering into someone's bunk. After a while, he stops to help me despatch the fluff on my number ones.

I like Smurf, despite his success with women. He also has a lisp and as I've never been beaten up by anyone with a lisp before, I think I'm on safe ground. As to why he's called Smurf, I think Smudge would have the answer, but I'm too scared to ask. My guess, though, is it's because he's tiny and his voice is an octave higher than anyone else's in the mess.

'So, Jock, you signing up for the mile high club today, sunshine?' Smurf lisps, effeminately, fussing around me.

'Not sure yet, Smurf.' I reply, trying to focus on some part of him that isn't moving.

The only problem with flying to Scotland is that I've never flown in a plane before and I'll only have an hour to chat someone up, unlike the train where I'd have five hours to find the love of my life and maybe neck a few cans of beer.

I think back to that spurned chance when I had finished my six weeks' basic at *Raleigh* only 15 months ago and headed home from Cornwall on the train. This beautiful brunette, who reminded me of Motorcycle Girl but with darker hair, got on at Bristol and chatted away, commenting on my uniform, which I had narrowly avoided being sick over earlier that morning. The night before, we had celebrated our passing out parade by getting pissed with our training petty officer. I can't remember his name but he was a great bloke and I hope he's still alive. I was suffering badly on board the rickety, stop-everywhere, non-express that rumbled towards Scotland at what felt like 20 miles an hour.

I took no notice of the sexy signals she was sending me. I screw up my face at the thought of missing out on a shag on a train with someone good looking who was actually interested in me. I had seriously fucked up, thanks to the drink.

'What's the matter with you Jock, bad pint last night?' Smudge asks, vigorously shaking me out of my reverie.

'Naw, Smudge, I wiz jist thinkin aboot something,' I reply.

'Looks like yiv shit yerself,' he says, flicking the ash from his fag onto the lino.

'Worse, Smudge, a lot worse,' I add.

His limp, greasy hair frames his tanned, smoking face as he leans forward, his fag in danger of singeing my nose.

'Come up to Brum with me an we'll ave one big fuck-off party, all weekend.'

'Cheers, Smudge, but I huv tae see the family an that.'

Smudge turns away, seeming genuinely hurt that I'd reject a weekend of drunken debauchery in order to see my family, who half expected me to come back in a box.

'Sorry, mate,' I yell in the direction of his slumped shoulders.

As the darkness closes in on the heavy grey sky, we slip anchor* and head for the channel. Our Plymouth anti-climax over, the ship's power engages the giant propeller screws, leaving a trail of beige-coloured gash bags bobbing in our wake. *Brazen* escorts us some of the way before disappearing into the darkness.

I watch the arc from a lighthouse draw a semi-circle of white around the waves, before turning in on itself, rubbing out its previous attempt and then reappearing two seconds later to redraw; it reminds me of the radar on that first day in Bomb Alley.

It's too cold to stand on the upper scupper for long, but there's nothing happening down the mess apart from a few tinnies being drunk. It feels like one of those days between Boxing Day and Hogmanay, where the euphoria of one

---

* pulling up the anchor in readiness to sail

party is a long way from being replaced by the next. Time for a kip.

Private Hell

1982

My eyes flicker open. Dumbly, I stare up at the black bellies of helicopters, their giant blades scything the air, bloated with ominous thunderheads. The winchmen are perched on the edges of their cabs, charmless in their visor-clad faces, jaws chewing into mouthpieces, all other sound obliterated by the pounding of rotor blades. Their gloved hands steady the steel cable of the winch as they lower the attached hook to the ground.

I smell smoke and the stench of burning pig flesh. Below me, the cold, wet mud causes me to shiver. I squirm as my fingers make contact with something slimy in the wet filth. A giant worm maybe? My head and neck are paralysed, meaning I can't look left or right. I close my stiffening fingers around the mud at my right side, arm tense like a first time blood donor.

My eyes stream as the stench of burning pig intensifies.

Slowly, the winches draw upwards towards the mass of helicopters. Then I make out their cargo. Soldiers are being winched up by their bellies, their limp torsos arching upwards, heads slung back, eyes, noses and mouths facing downwards, pain etched on their contorted faces. Their uniforms and bodies are identical, right down to the stumps where their right legs used to be.

My belly jerks away from me and I begin to move upwards. I didn't spot the hook that's now attached to my belt. I struggle to lift my chin and my head lops backwards. The sound of the rotor blades becomes louder and louder. I vaguely make out the jabbering winchman matter-of-factly describing my condition. He looks familiar, but he's not smiling this time.

It was then that I realised the slimy thing had come with me. I gasp for breath like the last man to put on his gas mask. My chest grows tight as I fight to remain conscious. I frantically grab at my kneecap. *Thank fuck, it's still there.* I engage my stomach muscles to lift my head up, and I catch sight of the winchman. Nearly there; nearly safe; two more feet. Then I see the reflection in his visor as he lets slip a grimace. I blink hard and look again. Everything is there, apart from one foot. The grizzled jaw of the winchman widens to reveal rows of rotten teeth and that familiar reek of decay, my contorted face filling his visor.

'I told you you'd amount to nothing, son,' he snarls.

I gaze at the reflection of my contorted face as my belt snaps and I fall. This is it. This is definitely it.

***

The mess is dark and still when I wake. I check my pulse on my neck, which is returning to something close to normal, and I couldn't have been screaming because no-one else is awake. This must mean I'm beginning to cope better with the nightmares. I've even stopped myself from reaching down into my sleeping back to check that I still have two feet.

It feels like about four in the morning. I need a piss but I can't be bothered getting up in the dark, so my bladder will have to hold on for a bit. I wonder when we'll get our medals. I turn over onto my side and try to think of nice things, but I can't seem to shake the images. I reach down into the sleeping bag and check, just in case.

Thick as Thieves

1982

Breakfast is a disappointment. It seems even the cooks have got their minds on something else. I stick my head outside for some fresh air, but the sun still isn't shining. I suppose it's time to get into my number ones and pray that at least a few people are bothered enough to wave at a desperate sailor.

'Your suit smells of smoke, Smurf,' I point out.

'Put some aftershave on it, Jock, will ya?' Smurf replies, looking over his shoulder, nostrils twitching.

'Aftershave? Will that get rid of the smell?' pipes up Wee George.

'What do you think?' I add, sarcastically, wishing I hadn't.

I dab away with masking tape at Smurf's suit, the shiny golden propeller complete with star on his right arm denoting his rate as an MEM(L) First Class. The masking tape lifts the stray hair and dandruff from the rough black serge with varying degrees of success. I pat around his shoulders like a hairdresser finishing off a new client.

'Mirror for the back, sir?' I joke.

'What?' says a confused-sounding Smurf.

'Nothing,' I reply, continuing to dab away at his shoulders, even though the dandruff is long gone.

'Right, my turn,' orders Smurf, spinning on his heels and – suddenly – he's in my face. 'Stand still,' he rasps, like a camp drill sergeant.

'How can I stand still when the ship's like a fucking rocking horse?' I plead.

Smurf clamps his left hand around my right bicep and uses his other hand to pad away at my shoulders. Suddenly, I feel constricted and the muscles around my arms and chest stiffen. Smurf isn't helping; he should be filling the dead space with chatter but instead he's deadly quiet. I take a deep breath, but it only fills up half my lungs, so I try again but my lungs aren't playing.

Standing there, being prevented from moving, drags up memories of being frozen to the spot in a corner of the living room while my dad looms over me, his index finger so close to my face that I can see the fungus on his nail. I can hear the burbling of the oxygen pump in the fish tank and remember how I nearly killed myself by opening it up while electricity was still surging through the motor. Sometimes I think frying myself might have been a good idea, but I would really miss my mum – and her scones.

'Hang on a minute, Smurf,' I plead, wrenching myself away from his grasp.

I can hear him mumbling something about hairs and the word arsehole, but I'm halfway up the ladder in search of oxygen. A minute later, I discover it still isn't sunny.

The fresh air makes me laugh at myself. *Fuckin idiot, whit are ye panickin for?* I take a few more lungfuls of air and smile to myself. The breeze against my face reminds me how good it feels to be alive.

Back down in the mess, things are hotting up. Sailors in their best kit are frantically bulling[*] boots, straightening cap tallies and masking taping themselves into a frenzy. No-one else has run away from the masking tape treatment.

---

[*] polishing

At 1000hrs, the ship's intercom goes into overdrive, barking commands down every nook and cranny. The mess activity has died down. Everyone sits in their best rig, smoking or biting their nails, waiting for their specific orders. Jacko is biting his nails *and* smoking. Smudge sucks on his last fag at sea before blowing the smoke into Smurf's ear. We sit side by side on the bottom bunks looking like a row of well-dressed paratroopers waiting to jump.

'Arsehole,' Smurf sneers, jerking away from the smoke, coughing and waving his hands about.

'You love it,' Smudge slurs, through a smoke-filled haze. I'm convinced that Smudge has tried to blow smoke through Smurf's ear, hoping it'd emerge out the other side.

Then he clocks me sniggering, so now it's my turn. 'Look at Jock's little boots, aren't they the shiniest mother fuckers?' he says.

I look at Smudge's boots and decide that to comment would be to meet with the loss of a limb or at least 20 quid, depending on his mood, so I keep quiet.

Our best boots hurt like fuck. They are so stiff that your toes bash against them every time you march. They're also a liability; the slippery soles can send you to a watery grave in double quick time. The toecaps are so shiny that a few ugly fish would die of fright from their own reflections as they watch you sink to the sea bed.

The pipe breaks into my daydream. 'All hands for Procedure Alpha to muster on the flight deck.' Even when I know an announcement is coming, I still flinch when it's barked down the crackly tannoy. Procedure Alpha here we come. Time to milk it, as long as we can stay upright and attached to the deck.

We're laced around the upper decks like Christmas tree decorations. The ship slips anchor from Spithead, where we've been parked since the early hours of the morning, waiting for the right tide and, of course, the maximum amount of TV coverage. The blustery wind tugs on our caps, our chinstraps chafe against our freshly shaved skin. I think back to the lieutenant commander in charge of drilling us on the parade ground – nicknamed Bucket Face – just 18 months ago, and whisper *Fuck you* in recognition of my miserable six weeks at the hands of the drill officer. I whisper another *Fuck you* to the bastards who tried to turn me upside down in my bed. Then I think back to my cross-country win in the pissing wet soggy fields around *Raleigh* and burst out laughing.

As we make our way to the harbour entrance, a rush of excitement courses through my body, like thousands of spawning salmon heading upstream. Edging closer, the different coloured dots lining the sea wall grow into people's heads, gradually enlarging to reveal faces and then individual features. Some are cheering, some are crying, and some are cheering *and* crying. As we slow down at the entrance to the harbour, the wind dies down and our caps, which have threatened to break free since we stood on the upper deck, settle.

There are Union Jacks and banners hanging limply above the crowds as their arms grow heavy. The sky has remained leaden in defiance. In the blink of an eye, a flotilla of boats surrounds us. Horns go off and fireboats shoot water jets hundreds of feet into the air. The cheering gets louder. Hands wave faster, people laugh and cry harder, but the sky mopes down at us, refusing to join the party.

Scouse is at one side of me, Jacko the other. Scouse is smiling into space, eyes glazing over. Jacko stares straight ahead, until he catches me glancing at him.

'Stand still, eyes front,' he growls.

We giggle like school kids for the next five minutes. I try to suck in the atmosphere, telling myself to milk the glory for all it's worth. Tomorrow, there will be no crowds cheering. It'll be down the shops for a loaf of bread and a pint of milk.

The ship swans past *HMS Glasgow*, which is docked and tied up. I bet they're sick they have to stand and cheer us. 'Hip pip, hooray! Hip pip, hooray! Hip pip, hooray!' they cry, raising their caps, probably calling us glory-grabbing wankers under their breaths.

Just a few yards to go to the jetty, *Glasgow's* foghorn sounds and my heart jumps. The tugs and fire boats join in and the crowds on the jetty cheer. Some of the sailors break protocol and wave back. Scouse signals to me with a wink and Jacko and I do the same, waving frantically to no-one in particular. The bewildered spectators wave back and we giggle. It feels brighter, but the sky is doing its bad bastard routine and not clearing for anyone.

As the ship grinds to a halt, the seamen grab at the giant hawsers and sling them around the dockside bollards. The fenders creak and stretch as they get squashed between the harbour wall and the ship's side. The cacophony of klaxons and cheering crowds makes my nose tingle. My forehead tightens and I fight back a lump in my throat. A gangway thuds onto the harbour concrete. I take a deep breath and force the tears back.

I am home.

The gangway bounces in time to the footsteps of marauding civilians, hell bent on locking on to their loved ones. Some of the seamen find their wives and girlfriends. Women and children are scooped up in frenzies of hugging and kissing. Children cry, adults cry. You could cut the atmosphere with a rusty hacksaw. This is happening all around me, but I don't feel part of it.

'Hands fall out from Procedure Alpha!' the ship's tannoy crackles.

'Hey, Jacko, look, der's me girlfriend,' Scouse points down the gangway at his girl, but for some reason I can't look.

'Awright, Scouse, but let's get down the mess, these boots are fuckin' killin us,' Jacko says, rescuing me from embarrassment.

'Cup o tea, Jock?' Wee George asks. 'You alright?'

'Aye, fuckin fly, right intae ma eye it went,' I muster. I'm desperate to soak up the atmosphere, but I also want to be heading home to Scotland.

'I believe ye, Jock, but only cos me bullshit detector is off,' Jacko quips, sensing my awkwardness. He then hugs me, but quickly turns it into a headlock.

Scouse is away. 'Abandon mates, abandon mates!' Jacko shouts at him, but he doesn't turn around.

Then Jacko heads off too. I stay, leaning on the guardrail, mesmerised by the colours that make up the dockside people, their clothes, the blue, red and white of flags, all the waving and cheering, faces looking up at me and smiling. The adulation of strangers is a strange thing. I feel like a rock star on stage after a virtuoso performance, except I'm not sweating and there are no groupies waiting for me.

There's no-one waiting for me.

I climb down the ladders onto the flight deck. The gangway is safely across and civilians are still swarming the ship without so much as a salute when they get on board. Women wipe the running mascara from their cheeks. Sailors grin and children shriek with delight, probably looking for presents, but smuggled mortar shells aren't everyone's cup of tea.

Shore cables are already being craned on board, reminding me that I should be helping to connect them up. I swan off down the mess. *Fuck it, the shore cables can wait.*

Down below, the mess has been transformed into a riot of noise and colour. Sailors shamelessly kiss and cuddle their wives and girlfriends. Mercifully, kids haven't found their way down yet. Everyone is engaging in some kind of activity, apart from me. I feel like I've stumbled into the wrong wedding reception. I seek out Wee George; he'll have nobody either.

'Jock Blair wiz lookin fuh ya, Jock,' Big George pipes up, breaking off from a hug.

Christ on a bike! Big George is smiling! Well, at least his family love him.

'Ta, George,' I say, 'Ah'll jist go an get him.'

Jock Blair – of all people – is in charge of shore cable party[*] and he'll know where to find me.

I know that my mum wouldn't have been able to afford the journey down to meet me, and my dad would have a million and one excuses why it would be "a waste of time". Christ, I'll be flying home to meet them in a couple of hours. *Get a grip, David.*

The last time I felt like this was my passing out parade over a year ago when families came down to see what the Navy had made of their unruly teenagers and ended up crying buckets with pride. That day, there were only a few

---

[*] electrical engineers tasked with connecting shore electricity to the ship

of us without anyone. The worst thing was that those without families had to wait until the next day to go on leave. The lepers sat and watched the rest lug their kit bags and hand them to their dads. One of the lucky bastards was Gordon Pugh, or Pug H as he was nicknamed.

'Cheers then, Jock. See you at *HMS Sultan* in two weeks,' said Pug H, with just a hint of a smirk.

'Actually, I'm taking the whole fortnight,' I replied, using the default weapon of sarcasm to quash my feelings of loneliness.

'Well, anyway, don't get too pissed with the rest of the no-hopers,' Pug H quipped, walking off with his proud family in tow.

'Fat chance of that,' I shouted back, 'I'm still underage!'

At that very moment, one of the other no-hopers turned up – a guy from South Africa who refused to get a buzz cut during the first week of training, immediately marking him out as a target for bullying. 'Fancy a pint, Jock?' he asked, thumbing towards The Raleigh Club.

'Okay, but just one,' I nodded.

The no-hoper from South Africa and I got a couple of pints from the bar and found ourselves sitting with our training petty officer. 'Do you think it's fair P.O.,' I asked, 'that those with families at the passing out parade get to go home a day early?'

'It's not for me to say, young man, thems is the Navy's rules and regulations,' he replied, curtly.

'Thanks, P.O.,' I said, while thinking *no help at all.*

'Have another pint, Jock. Carlsberg, is it?' he asked. The P.O. was a cracking bloke, and one of the less draconian of the Sea Daddies.

The bar in The Raleigh Club on a Friday night after a passing out parade was a truly depressing place, full of men on duty weekend and left behind sprogs like us. Women were at a premium: a couple of matelot groupies, the duty cleaner and the bird behind the bar, who must've heard every chat up line from here to Casablanca. The no-hoper from South Africa, who had suffered the taunts of post-pubescent naval recruits for six weeks solid, lit up a cigarette. I fancied one.

'Can I have one of yer fags?' I asked.

'Yeah, sure,' he said. 'But I thought you didn't smoke.'

'Ah, no, not really, but one wee fag cannae dae any harm, can it?' I shrugged.

'Guess not,' he shrugged back.

'Careful, Jock, don't want you missing the train in the morning,' said someone, but I can't remember who.

I did make that train, but what I didn't realise was that first terrible hangover never taught me anything.

Jock Blair jerks my out of my lament. 'So, this is where ye are, instead of helpin lug the shore cables?' He's sniffed me out near the 15-ton crane, tucked away on the port quarter deck.

'Sorry, Chief, I just feel a bit tired,' I shrug, feeling the cold seep through me.

'Tired, my arse, ye were skivin,' Jock Blair says, hands on hips, his favoured fighting stance.

'Yes, Chief,' I admit, looking down at my well-bulled boots, wishing I was somewhere else.

'Well, they're done now and you're off on leave, but mind you're still on Domestics when ye get back. Enjoy yourself, an don't come back with a dose,' Jock Blair adds, almost with sincerity.

'Aye, Chief, Ah'm sorry aboot the shore cables,' I mutter.

'Aye, awright,' he says, waving me away. I'm thinking this is as close as we're going to get to an acknowledgement of what we've shared over the last four months. At this rate, we're going to have to star in *Falklands War 2: The Sequel.*

Back down in the mess after Jock Blair's reprieve, I hastily empty my locker, dodging all the huggers and kissers. I can hear them chatting incessantly about fuck all in particular, in fact anything and everything apart from where we've been and what we've seen. I leave them to their pointless conversations and slip out without a fuss. I hate all the emotion of saying goodbye – and I'd see most of them in three weeks anyway, so what was the point in interrupting their precious intimate moments just to say cheerio?

My suitcase and kitbag weigh a ton, but I practically skip over the gangway. A limp sun casts weak shadows of footsteps as I bound across and think about the air stewardesses on my flight to Edinburgh.

The Modern World

1982

'A single tae Edinburgh please,' I nod, looking around the sterile airport terminal.

'Have you booked it, sir?' says the posh woman behind the check-in counter who's clearly out of my league. Her blonde hair is up in a bun with curls corkscrewing down either side of her face, which makes me think of the SAS sliding down ropes from a helicopter. I need to get out more.

'Naw, Ah didnae think ye needed to,' I reply, sheepishly.

'No, sir, you don't, but it can be safer if the flight is full,' she says, formally, looking over my shoulder at a queue forming behind me.

I feel the blood rushing to my face, realising she's the first woman I've spoken to since those two women hugged me back in Stanley. 'Aye, right, Ah'll remember that next time,' I promise, a bit disappointed that my eyes meet a British Airways scarf where her cleavage should be.

I look around nervously at the queue as the posh woman writes out a ticket coupon. I don't want to look at her again in case she fancies a bit of sailor in the baggage hall. Behind me are a couple of middle-aged gaggling women. It'll be just my luck to get a seat next to them. One of them might even start playing footsie.

I wedge into my tiny seat, read the in-flight laminated safety guide, and double-check the space where the life jacket should be.

'Our estimated journey time is one hour, so please sit back and enjoy the flight. The cabin crew will shortly be going through the safety demonstration and we request that you give them your full attention. On behalf of British Airways, we'd like to thank you for flying with us today,' announces the stewardess, caressing the mouthpiece of the intercom.

I end up sandwiched between two boring businessmen with not a word between them. The stewardesses don't give me a second glance and I don't even get to see the clear blue sky. An entire hour of my life goes by without incident.

'Goodbye, sir,' clips another posh woman, this time a brunette wearing a forced smile, framed by a neat bob.

'Thanks very much, bye,' I say, underwhelmed by the whole experience. I get a fleeting image of the helicopter winchman from my day out in Stanley and find myself smiling.

The Edinburgh rain rouses me into a sprint down the steps and across the tarmac to the baggage hall in 32 seconds. The hall smells a bit like my high school's foyer, but so far no Adidas bags.

The carousel snakes its way round the middle of the bright, artificially shiny hall of Edinburgh airport. People congregate around the metal and plastic shapeshifter, trollies on guard. The push and shove begins as the annoying beep beep signals the movement of baggage.

Some impatient travellers nudge their trollies a little closer to the carousel. Others, seeing they're getting left behind are having none of it and shuffle forward. Someone has lit up a cigarette, making my nostrils sting. The bags and cases jostle their way round the carousel like orphans waiting to be picked up and given a home. My case, with all its jingoistic ramblings written on the side, seems to be bellowing Me! Me! Me! My huge man-eater of a kit bag follows. No-one notices.

It seems flying home in uniform isn't such a good idea.

I scuff the smoking bloke's elbow accidentally with my kit bag and he lets out an expletive in a posh Edinburgh voice as his ciggie falls on the floor. Probably some naval officer's dad.

'Sorry, mate.' I nip, a flash of anger spurting from nowhere. The man looks me up and down and decides I'm not worth it.

Time for a taxi. Maybe I can share it with a gorgeous stewardess and get waylaid into spending a sex crazed afternoon in a hotel.

'Where huv you just come from, then?' says the taxi driver glancing in his rear-view mirror, his shiny balding head mottled with liver spots. A huge scar across his crown suggests he came second in a bar fight.

'Portsmouth . . . Portsmouth,' I repeat, my first effort having been drowned out by a passing car's horn.

'On leave?' the perceptive taxi driver enquires.

'Yeah,' I reply, champing at the bit to ramble on about my four-month rollercoaster ride around hell, but stopping myself in case I sound like a bragger.

'That was some carry on down the Falklands,' the taxi driver says, quizzically. 'You weren't down there, were you?'

'No,' I answer, quickly, not really knowing why I've said what I've said.

'Just as well, eh?'

'Aye.'

He obviously hadn't bothered to read my suitcase hieroglyphics.

We cross over the Forth Road Bridge. The magnificent rail bridge runs parallel. The emerging sun bounces light off the millions of rivets that hold the giant, unique structure together. I marvel at the idea that it was built using hard, manual labour under horrendous conditions with the threat of serious injury or death on a daily basis – and all for a pittance. Little did some men think that, when they waved goodbye to their wives and kids to set off to help build it, they might not return home.

A train crosses, dwarfed against the giant iron girders. Soon enough though, the bridge is replaced by jagged cliffs as we head onto the motorway and into Fife. We're getting closer. I feel tense; unaccustomed as I am to coming home from a war, there will be the small matter of conversation. Would we all pretend that it didn't happen? Talk about the weather, what I want for my tea, how I had grown, the garden looking nice, and Mrs Ewing, the 80-year-old woman from next door, still being senile.

My stomach is churning. My mum and dad haven't been getting on for quite some time. Dad hit the bottle after being made redundant and he's taking more of his frustrations out on my mum. To be fair, he never needed much of an excuse to make all of our lives hell from day one.

'Brightening up now,' chirps the taxi driver.

'Yeah, could be nice,' I reply, happy that I've put him off his war footing.

It's time to talk to him anyway. 'Left at the next roundabout please, mate.'

A short break in conversation follows as I sit on the edge of my seat and watch him perform the manoeuvre. I then gauge what the perfect time will be to give him the next direction, the tension building up slowly as each bend and junction brings me nearer to my house. After what seems like an age, I issue one more instruction.

'Left here, mate, and follow the road round,' I say twice, wondering if he's a bit deaf or if it's just that I hate the sound of my own voice enough to sabotage it.

He hangs a left into Stevenson Avenue, where I had spent all of my short life before joining the Navy. Little has changed. One long winding street of about 100 houses, mostly well coiffured, peppered by the occasional unruly tenant, identified by a junkyard instead of a garden and a cage of monkeys instead of a fireplace.

Lazily, the driver stays in fourth gear and chugs up the hill, the engine threatening to cut out with every crawling yard. We pass Ivan Bishop's house, number 11, one of my mates from school. His garden is not so much a junkyard as a small farm. Ivan's dad, a self-professed gamekeeper rescues animals that he doesn't shoot and eat, including Goosey the one-eyed goose and a sparrowhawk with a broken wing that graduated from the garden and made a home on top of the TV. I once went to the toilet in Ivan's house and discovered a bath full of brown trout. Ivan will be on holiday from his second year of university. I can't remember if it's Oxford or Cambridge he's at; Cambridge I think, or maybe even Canterbury. Maybe we could meet up for a pint. Ivan likes cider.

We round the bend and, straight ahead, sits my house, draped in soggy flags and bent-out-of-shape bunting. There's no-one out in the street, which feels a bit eerie for four o'clock on a Saturday afternoon. Maybe everyone's watching the wrestling. The white ensign above our front porch hangs limply from my bedroom windowsill, worse for wear from too many soakings, the single word 'David' scrawled across it in smudged royal blue ink.

The taxi stops underneath the streetlight that has illuminated much of my life, including my skull-rattling fall as a toddler. I get out. The driver helps lug my kitbag out of the boot while I wrestle with the suitcase. I hand him a £20 note. He looks at me and smiles.

'Have a good night tonight,' he says.

'Thanks very much,' I reply, wondering briefly what he thought about my earlier denial about the Falklands.

My house is set back from a square where my pals Alan, John and I had played and fought as kids. I learned to ride a bike here when I was five. It was Mum who had coaxed and cajoled me into keeping my balance as I pounded the pedals. *Come on, you're nearly there, look! Aw, nearly. One more time, that's it . . . Aw, nearly. Right, have a wee rest and I bet you'll be able to do it afterwards.* And she was right. I took off, riding that bike for all I was worth, pedalling as if my life depended on it, round and round the square. I dumped my bike and ran into the living room, beaming. "Dad, I've learned to ride my bike! Watch me, Dad! Dad!" But all that greeted me was silence followed by the snapping of a fold in his newspaper.

Now, the square is the domain of parking spaces. Our football pitch, baseball ground, Action Man playground and cycle track is no more.

The path from the taxi to my house across is about 100 feet. I hoist up my kit bag onto my shoulder and grip the tattooed suitcase. I signal to the taxi driver that I don't need a hand with the luggage even though I'm buckling under the weight. Pride, eh? I gingerly make my way along the path, past three or four of my mum's closest neighbours: Mrs Campbell, who took me in when I lost my key on the way home from school, Mr and Mrs Cunningham, who dropped off a bin bag full of war

294

comics when I'd been in bed with flu, and Mrs Walker, who regularly told us off for our football going into her garden. Poor Mrs Walker.

The path from the square merges into my own garden path, bordered by irises on one side and on the other a lawn with a crew cut. My mum often took some of her frustrations out on the grass. I look up to see the council-yellow front door open and my mum appear behind it.

'David!'

I flinch at the explosion of my open-armed, lipstick-wearing mum about to pounce on me. She crushes me with a hug, almost bursting my eardrum as she bellows, 'Welcome, home son!' into my right ear. I step back, startled, but she catches me on the edge of the front door step and holds on for all she is worth. Her watch catches my chin and I grimace. You go all that way to fight a war, come back without a scratch and your mum maims you with her first big hug.

'Oh, God, I can't believe you're here!' When she finally lets me go, I almost fall off the step, nearly pulling her glasses off. Her eyes are welled with tears, but she smiles through. I can smell the mixture of lipstick and cigarettes and it smells great. We've argued about cigarettes in the past but at this moment, I'm just delighted to see her happy. She takes off her big tortoiseshell rimmed specs and wipes her eyes.

'It's great tae see ye, son,' she says, her face resembling a mum looking at her new born.

'Aye,' I sniff. It's all I can manage on the emotional front.

The smell of baking emerges from the kitchen. The cars may have taken away my playground, but the council will have to bury my mum with her girdle[*].

Through the hallway, I perform a strange, shuffle-like dance with my mum into the living room, before she slips away to the kitchen as if she's suddenly forgotten something.

Dad snaps shut his newspaper and emerges from his armchair. He hovers, unsure, unsteady. 'Well done, son,' he manages.

'Thanks,' I scrape out.

It's hard to forget how much he put me down when I failed my first Navy entrance exam. He said I'd be no good, and after I broke my heart coming back from the careers office – nearly three years ago now – he was ready to rub salt into my wounds. I try to look at him through different eyes. I try to tell myself that I've survived a war intact, that family conflicts are peanuts compared to the thought of being blown up by an unseen enemy 8,000 miles from home.

I look down at him and force a smile, but immediately sense tension between him and my mum. I think back to the terror-filled nights we shared when I was growing up. Noses pressed up against the condensation-soaked windows, lit by the midnight moon. My sister, asleep in the back bedroom, Mum and me waiting . . . waiting . . . waiting for the silence to break, the segs from his shoes piercing the pavement: tap, tap, tap, tap, scrape. Tap, tap, tap, tap, and then the final scrape as he clattered against the single step, put his key in the lock and turned it; the signal for all hell to break loose. Now, he prowls around, looking for any sign of weakness, like a shadow on a lung.

---

[*] Scottish term for a stovetop griddle for making scones and pancakes

Mum appears with a tray full of fresh scones, her face red from the heat of the oven. Dad and I sit down on opposite sides of the living room, sizing each other up while Mum fusses with crockery and cutlery, setting everything down on the coffee table. 'There's plenty more where that came from, eat up, ye're lookin a wee bit thin,' she says, handing me a plateful of scones. Of course I wasn't looking any thinner than I normally do, but I succumb to the pressure to eat four scones and a pancake, closely followed by a plate of soup and another scone.

'Ah'm gonnae go down tae the swing park later an see who's there,' I announce.

'What?' Mum blurts out, shocked that I didn't want to stay in all night and regale them with war stories.

'Ah'll no be oot aw night, dinnae worry. Ah jist want tae see if Alan's aboot,' I explain.

She scrunches her face. 'Well, mind an look after yersel when ye're oot,' she sighs, anxious not to let me see her disappointment, but it's obvious.

I look over at my dad for signs of life, but the only flicker in his eyes is reflected from the muted television, which he has deigned to turn down for my benefit. When I go, he'll reach for the sound button and commence his worship of all things pixelated.

I stand up and brush some crumbs from my uniform. Realising no-one's planning to take my photograph, I head upstairs, ditch it and get ready to head to the swing park. In one minute and 38 seconds, I'm back downstairs. I poke my head round the living room door.

'That's me away then,' I announce.

My mum springs off the sofa, spilling some of her tea. I step forward and reach out to steady her. 'Aw, ye're lookin great!' she gushes, even though I'm clad in a basic jeans and T-shirt combo I'd last worn when I left school. 'Enjoy yersel, son!'

Dad shoots us a cursory glance, but refuses to comment. He picks up his paper, having managed three whole words since my return. Who knows, maybe tomorrow he'll manage four.

As I approach the swing park, Alan and John are playing it cool, almost as if they had a conversation about how they should act when I show up. I spot Wendy coming out her front door, heading our way. I imagine ten seconds before this, her curtains would have been twitching.

'Hi, Alan. Alright, John?' I say, flatly.

'When did you get back?' John asks, biting at a scraggy nail.

'Just the now. I flew up fae Portsmouth tae Edinburgh an got a taxi.'

'How was it?' Alan asks, leaning against the frame of the swings.

'No bad.'

They both stare at me as if I'm a museum exhibit. Wendy sidles up and plonks her ample arse on one of the swings before resuming her well-worn crossed-arm pose. I imagine in ten years' time that she'll be waiting at her back door, baseball bat in hand, for her husband to return from the pub. Wendy is a great listener. That's how gossips get all their material.

'Ye're back then,' she drones, finally acknowledging my existence.

'Great to see you too, Wendy. Sorry, I forgot a stick of rock,' I retort, flashing her a cheeky grin.

'Where's yer tan then?' she questions, beginning to swing, her shoes occasionally scuffing the concrete.

I'm just about to give her one of my legendary comebacks when John dives in. 'The French lassies are back,' he says, puncturing the awkwardness. I perch on a swing, the three of them looking at me as if I'm about to sprout horns.

'Are they comin up tonight?' I ask.

'Ah think so,' says Alan. 'There's a new one, an she's gorgeous.'

'Great!' I reply, and start swinging.

'You'll not get off with her,' Alan mocks. Alan – who's been my best pal since primary school – has clearly failed in the chat up stakes with the new girl. I know this because Alan has always failed in this area . . . with all girls!

'Don't you be too sure. Ah've got stories tae tell,' I tease.

Wendy, who's acted as a natural minder for any girl I've fancied down the swing park, harrumphs and rolls her eyes, something I'm used to her doing while I'm talking. The difference this time is that I couldn't care less.

I gain height on my swing and I'm flying. The warm, damp air rushes past me, the swing shaking as it's pushed to its limit. I start laughing. John and Alan just ogle me, their faces registering uncertainty, maybe even mild panic. Scraping my shoes hard on the white-pocked tar, I judder to a sudden halt.

'Fuck,' grunts Wendy.

The French girls are on the horizon. This time, there are three, one more than usual, as Alan intimated. The two who've been coming every summer for the last three or four years have broken free of their shapeless childhood years and now appear sophisticated and demure as they glide towards us. The oldest, and always the most serious, casts me a lingering look, which registers as *I remember you, but there's something different; dangerous even.*

'Bonjour,' I say, full of it.

'Bonjour, Davide,' says French girl number one, whose name I still find too difficult to pronounce.

I slip off the swing and kiss them both on both cheeks. They giggle, taken aback by my forwardness. Alan and John's reflex is to burst out laughing, while Wendy tuts loudly, but I dismiss them all as immature, maybe even jealous. Then I set my eyes on the new arrival and, suddenly, I feel a rush of heat to my face.

'C'est l'amour n'est-ce pas?' the serious one says to French girl number two, whose name I also can't pronounce.

I haven't a clue what she's said, but it sounds like she was taking the piss. I feel like I've face-planted into a field of nettles, but I can't stop gawking at the new girl. The great thing is, she doesn't seem to mind. Then Wendy jumps in, 'Stick your tongue back in, why don't ye?'

Alan and John's jealousy radar is full on. I can feel their resentment with my own radar: even they can't fail to notice that there's a spark between me and French girl number three. I've survived intense bombing, electrocution and a minefield. Falling in love should be a walk in the park.

I hand her the chain of one of the empty swings and she takes it, no hesitation. She looks straight into my face. No words, just the summer breeze caressing her corkscrew brown curls. I steal a look down at her athletic, toned body. Her smile registers that she's noticed me noticing. I smile back. She lifts herself onto

300

the swing and rocks back and forth. Then her eyes leave me. For now.

But I have a plan.

Worlds Apart

1982

The following morning, Mum and I are conspiring in the living room as I wolf down a bowl of corn flakes.

'Are you sure you can afford it?' Mum asks, her frown threatening to knit her eyebrows together.

'Of course. I saved a fortune,' I boast. 'Now get down to the travel agent.'

'He'll no want to go,' she cautions, and I'm thinking maybe she'd prefer to go alone, but my plan won't work if they don't go together.

'I think he will,' I say. 'Have you seen the way he looks at me? He'll come round.' I give her a nudge with my elbow and instantly feel the awkwardness it generates between us.

'No chance,' she says.

I reach for her hand. She recoils, stunned by my intimacy. To think this woman has cleaned every colour of shit from my arse, but now she feels shocked when I touch her.

'What?' I say, bending down to look her into her green eyes, flecked brown with worry.

'Nothing,' she says turning away to gaze out the window.

This is Mum's stock answer when something is up. I'm too wrapped up in my own scheme to change course now though. Selfish, call it what you like. I'm on a mission.

'It'll be fine,' I assure her. 'Once you're down there, there's tons of bingo and the beach is amazing.'

'Aye, son,' she says, her shoulders slumping as she fishes a cigarette from the pocket of her apron.

'Did you have a good time last night?' she asks, angling for some gossip.

'French girls are back,' I reveal. 'And there's a new one.'

'You be careful,' she warns, sparking up a cigarette.

I give her £500 to drag my dad down to Blackpool, a decent wedge, I reckon. To be honest, I'm feeling suffocated by the attention, especially all the baking. I'm stuffing myself with cakes, scones and pancakes just to keep up with Mum's frenzied endeavours, but I'm also taking her offerings down to the swing park. I feel like a Spanish conquistador, offering food to the locals in return for . . . for what? Friendship? Acceptance? Validation? Fat chance, this is Fife. If you do anything here worth a fuck – paint a picture, go to war, get on *Top of the Pops* – you're shunned, seen as being up your own arse, too big for your boots, best to keep your head down and be as bland and resigned as everyone else. *Dinnae stand oot, pal, you'll only get knocked doon.* That could be Fife's motto. I reckon my dad could have written it, along with his other favourite mantra, *Keep your nose clean.* What the fuck does that even mean?

Françoise, that's French girl number three's name, loves my mum's scones. When she gets flour stuck on her nose, I point at it, and then she points to her nose and laughs, and then I laugh. When she laughs, her almond eyes light up, giving me a tickle in my stomach and a tingle a bit lower down. When we laugh together down the swing park I feel a collection of muffled groans all around us. *Fuck em*.

Mum has finally persuaded Dad to go on holiday. Ya beauty! Part one of the plan is sorted. I should've thought of a wanky militaristic title like Operation Sunburn, but never mind. A whole week with the house to myself! Partaaaaaay! Part two of the plan is to get closer to French girl number three.

When the night of the party comes, I feel like I'm going to throw up. As I look at myself in Dad's shaving mirror, there isn't much of a difference between the scared kid who went to the first year school disco with two bits of bum fluff on his face and the man-child who stares at his still spotty face but with a bit of a tan from the Equator and worry lines from the South Atlantic. I reach for the razor and think back to that first year disco, where Darren Haldane ruined my night. Mum was up out of her chair, thinking I had set fire to myself, but I told her not to worry. Just a change of shirt that's all, no drama. The reality was I cried in the toilet, frustrated at not being able to land one on that fucking reject with his little fuck of a brother, but they were at least six inches taller than me. Oh, and they also knew how to fight, so I was at a distinct disadvantage.

Things happened that night. Call it a miracle, cos it certainly felt like a miracle. I ran back to school, clad in a banana yellow shirt with blue houses on it. I danced like a maniac and when the slow dances came on, nearly every single one of the gorgeous girls from my year danced with me. It was the first time I had cupped a girl's bum and my fledgling penis wasn't complaining. I snogged most of those girls and hoped the night would never end. Lurking in the dark sat Darren Haldane, sniffing out fear and desperate for a fight. The next day, I fantasised that Darren Haldane would be bent double, clutching his groin, while Motorcycle Girl stood over him in her patent leather biker boots, hands on hips, oozing superhero sexuality. Motorcycle Girl and I never got near a date. I just wasn't ready for the grown up thing back then. I think I'd have been happier putting a picture of her up on my wall and practising kissing my own hand than talking to and getting to know her.

I'm praying that tonight, with Françoise, it will be different.

I purchase a half bottle of rum from the corner shop and wheel out Mum's dusty drinks trolley, which harbours vodka, whisky and advocaat. I had tried advocaat and lemonade one Hogmanay and loved it, but it'd never wash in the Navy, so I became hooked on beer.

Mum would be proud of my hosting skills. I even rustle up some crisps and nuts. Dad has a dozen tins of export in the cupboard so I think that should be enough to go around. The Frenchies drink beer, well two of them do. I don't actually know what Françoise drinks.

Since I got back, I've blagged my sister's old room, which gives me a perfect view of the swing park, ideal for seeing who's hanging about and who I might not want to bump into. I size up my clothes options on my sister's double bed. I've picked out jeans and a black T-shirt, and leather trousers and a white, flouncy shirt like Tony Hadley wore on *Top of the Pops*. I'm no Tony Hadley though. I dab on some quality aftershave, courtesy of Smurf, and my crew cut takes care of itself.

John turns up first, his shock of bleach blond hair contrasting sharply with a sunburnt face; there's even some skin peeling on the tip of his freckled nose and his eyelashes look almost white. His bony arms protrude from a maroon short-sleeved shirt and he smells like he's nicked some of his dad's Old Spice. He looks over his left and right shoulders, scoping out the square for parents or nosey neighbours – because at 17, he's underage and his dad's teetotal.

'Alright,' John says. 'Anyone else here yet?'

'Nut,' I reply, dismissively, looking over his shoulder too, hoping to catch a glimpse of the French girls.

'Oh,' he says, shifting from one foot to the next. 'Is it Blackpool they're away to?'

'What?' I say, still looking over his shoulder.

'Your mum and dad? Did they make it down?' he says, bluntly, poking me in the ribs.

'Aye, it'd no be much of a party with my mum and dad hingin aboot. Ye comin in or whit?' I step back and do that sweeping hand movement you see bouncers do at a nightclub.

'What have you got?' John conspires, scanning the living room.

'Vodka, whisky, rum, beer . . .'

'Whisky,' John interjects, his greyish-blue eyes widening.

'It's Bell's whisky,' I enthuse.

'Well, that'll have to do if you don't have any single malt,' he shrugs, zoning in on my mum's print of *The Crying Boy* on the back wall (the Woolworths version). There's a knock at the door. I leave John, whisky in his hand, looking unsure where to sit.

I open the door and it's Alan. I suspect he's been watching John from his bedroom window so he wasn't first to arrive. I wonder if they're uncomfortable in my presence. Alan's alabaster skin is the kind that posh people have in aristocratic paintings. His blond hair hangs listlessly, cut into a perfect bowl, his coal black eyes, which are recessed into his symmetrical, chubby face, reminds me of a snowman. Unlike John, he's brought something, but it isn't much. A tatty white carrier bag hangs down by his side. *Christ, do these people not know about bringing something to a party?*

'I brought a few records and some Sweetheart Stout,' Alan says, holding up the carrier bag, as if the contents are the elixir of life.

'Did ye bring *One Step Beyond?*' I ask, trying to keep a straight face. *One Step Beyond* by Madness had been our dancing-like-maniacs-in-our-bedrooms record, strictly no girls allowed. Those days feel like several lifetimes away now.

'Ah can go and get it,' Alan suggests, willingly.

'Naw, it's alright,' I reply, raising a hand. Alan seems wary. Maybe he still fancies his chances with Françoise.

The three of us stand awkwardly in the living room, a homage to all things beige and brown, now enhanced by the gold-coloured drinks trolley. John seems rooted to the spot, so I pour him another large whisky.

'Alan?'

'Whit?'

I motion towards the drinks trolley.

'Oh, aye, em, just a vodka,' he says, as if he's been drinking vodka all of his life instead of Dandelion & Burdock.

John sips his whisky, winces, looks around again, then burps. 'French lassies no here yet then?' he enquires.

'They're coming,' I say, a little too quickly. I wonder if I sound a bit desperate. I pray to the same god I prayed to a few months ago, the god in charge of Argentinian bomb droppers, that the Frenchies will appear.

'Are Wendy and Lynn coming?' Alan pipes up.

Wendy and Lynn are founder members of the swing park gang. I used to fancy Lynn (her hips mesmerised me in tight black jeans) and I'm sure she fancied me back, but Wendy always managed to play gooseberry. She might try playing that part again tonight, but that isn't happening.

My heart does a quick Fosbury Flop as the door goes again. I check myself in the mirror and catch the reflection of Alan and John screwing their faces up in unison. I straighten my T-shirt and realise my palms are sweating, so I wipe them on my jeans. I swing open the door and my face falls as French girls number one and two hold up a couple of bottles of wine. Okay, at least they've brought something, but not the thing. Not that Françoise is a thing. I rub my hands on my jeans again, wondering where all this sweat is coming from.

'Eez there a problem?' says French girl number one, looking puzzled.

'No, no problem, come in,' ushering them in. 'Help yourself to a few crisps and that.'

The two Frenchies sit on the sofa as far away from Alan and John as humanly possible. I get them a beer each from the dusty drinks trolley and force a smile.

'Your mother?' French girl number one says, looking around. Perhaps in France, parties come with parents.

'Eh?' I say, wondering if she's seen my mum in the town without my dad and they haven't gone to Blackpool after all.

'She eez on oliday?' she asks.

'Aye . . . aye, she is . . . with my dad,' I say, pacing about. 'They're away together.'

She leans towards French girl number two and they do a bit of that conspiratorial whispering thing. Then they start giggling. My throat is dry so I reach for a beer and crack it open. French girl number one breaks off and looks up at me, pointing her beer at my face. 'Oh, Davide, don't be sad,' she teases. 'Françoise is going to be here soon.'

'What are you talking about? . . . Oh, Françoise, cool. Well, if she comes, she comes,' I say, doing a terrible impression of nonchalance. They piss themselves laughing, and this time I join in, glancing out the window.

'Who else is coming?' John asks, swirling and nosing his whisky like he's on a distillery tour.

'Just a few more of the swing park gang,' I say.

'So, Wendy and Lynn then,' Alan sniffs, excavating a handful of nuts from the bowl.

Half way through The Jam's *All Mod Cons*, Françoise turns up. She's managed to achieve that French thing of making skinny blue jeans and a high-necked cream chiffon blouse look sexy. Alan regurgitates a dry roasted peanut as she enters the living room. John knocks back another whisky, now delighted to be squeezed between the two other Frenchies. The whisky must be taking effect, cos he's wearing a grin that screams *I've lost my inhibitions*.

I'm desperate to keep a clear head. I haven't sailed 8,000 miles to fail at the last hurdle. Alan is sulking in the chair near the telly. He looks like he's going to switch it on, but I throw him a cutthroat gesture and he plonks his arse back down. Without Lynn and Wendy here, he comes closest to sabotaging the party, a kind of *It's my ball and I'm not playing so neither are you* vibe going on between us.

The door goes again. *Shit.*

'Well?' Wendy booms on the doorstep, feet planted and arms folded in full battle mode as she pretends to wait to be invited in.

'Oh, aye, in yiz come then. Hiya Lynn. It's great to see you.'

'Hello, David,' she says, sensually, her velvet voice stirring a familiar feeling in my trousers. Maybe this is going to be complicated, or maybe I'm just delusional.

Part of me is desperate to say *You two are surplus to requirements and neither of you fancy Alan or John, so why don't you just have a wee drink to be sociable and then fuck off home.*

Wendy clocks Françoise and gives her the *How the hell do you make jeans and a blouse look so sexy?* once over. Lynn tries to ignore her. I get them some drinks, trying not to spill them as I gaze at Françoise.

As it starts to get dark, John is dancing with Wendy and I wish I had a camera. It's like watching Reagan and Khrushchev waltzing.

To think, one summer ago, we'd all been a gang, roaming the streets in the early hours of school holiday summers, causing mischief; just low key stuff like ripping up bedding plants from old people's houses and sticking our willies into empty milk bottles, just to show we could. We'd then return to our tents in our back gardens and giggle until the sun came up. We had our fights, but we tolerated each other. Sometimes mutual loathing is the basis of a friendship. One night, we did the empty milk bottle trick and Alan couldn't get his willy in it any more.

I feel sorry about the bedding plants though.

Lynn is now talking to Alan, a Kodak moment if ever there was one. The two Frenchies aren't as immature as Wendy and, probably feeling they're surplus to requirements, they stand up and kiss us all goodbye. I gulp down a Bacardi. The permutations are getting fewer and Françoise is looking at me a bit perplexed as if to say *What next?*

The Bacardi makes my eyes linger on Françoise longer than normal and I can't help smiling. She smiles back and then comes over and sits on the arm of my chair. Unsure what to do next, I look at the reproduction of *The Crying Boy* hanging over the mantelpiece. This painting is more famous than *The Mona Lisa* in Scottish homes but about a million times cheaper. I glance at John and he's kissing Wendy's hair! If they ever find out what they've had been up to tonight, there'll be carnage. I make a mental note to tell them tomorrow. No such chemistry exists between Alan and Lynn, just the mutual appreciation of lots of free booze and a comfy sofa with no parents kicking about.

After another four or five albums and a few spillages, everyone has drifted off home, leaving me alone with Françoise. Have I underestimated my friends? Written them off as immature and spiteful, desperate to ruin any notions I have of having fun? Is this what paranoia feels like? Their lives have also changed, but I'm too wrapped up in myself to notice. It hasn't been just a few months –

311

it's been over a year since I spent any time with them. Perhaps they were worried about me? Maybe they'd avoided my mum, scared to speak to her in case they said the wrong thing. After all, ships had sunk on an almost daily basis in the Falklands. What could any friend of mine say to my mum about me being at war that would make her feel better?

Miraculously, a few hours later, Françoise and I are lying side-by-side on my sister's double bed, holding hands. The early morning summer light that used to get me up for my milk round flickers through the sprawling beech tree at the back of our garden and brushes over Françoise's nakedness, dappling her olive skin like little fingers.

As the light stretches across the bed, I look at her breasts. She turns and looks at me like a doting mother protecting her child. I lean over and kiss her salty lips; crisps probably. I stretch my hand across her firm stomach and up to her breasts. I play with her nipples, but probably a bit too hard as her body tenses, so I retract my hand and go a bit lower. Our lips never part, like two frantic, needy limpets, or one frantic, needy limpet and one who just goes with the flow. I think back to those social and health classes in first year for direction. I wish there was a Haynes manual for sex, like they have for fixing cars. The social and health stuff about how to avoid diseases and not get girls pregnant is about as much use as wheels on a submarine. The cumulative effect of all these thoughts sends conflicting signals to my penis and I realise that things are floundering down below. *Why is masturbation so much easier?*

Our lips seem welded together, but so do Françoise's legs. As the room brightens, all hope of losing my virginity fades, and with it comes the ability to relax. Our lips finally separate and I begin to breathe normally again. Françoise gives me a look that says *You're sweet, but this isn't going to go any further. Well, not tonight anyway.*

I'm actually relieved. I know I shouldn't be, in a *teenager nearly loses virginity to gorgeous smouldering French babe* kind of way, but the pressure I placed on myself was enormous and now a weight has been lifted. I lie back, stare at the ceiling and smile a wry smile. There'll be plenty of time to shake off the virgin tag. After all, I've survived a war. Surely the worst stuff of my life is over? I think of nights down the pub with Scouse and Jacko. I'm old enough now, though nowhere near tall enough, to get served in a pub without showing my ID card, which I have to admit is a buzz, especially now that I'm a hero. Most people probably won't even remember the war in the Falklands, but I'll never forget it.

I let out a huge sigh as I think about my pals and how I'll have to apologise to them for being selfish and arrogant at the party, and then we can go and get really pissed. I consider getting up and knocking their doors, but the digital alarm clock says 04.59, so best to get some sleep. Oh well, at least I get to sleep with a beautiful French girl, which is probably a lot more than most of my classmates can say. *Jesus, I'm actually sleeping with a French girl!* Wait till I tell Scouse, he'll be jealous as fuck. Then, I feel Françoise's hand brush across my chest, before venturing downwards.

I hear the flap of the letterbox squeak open and immediately leap up, grabbing my head and doing that lizard thing with my tongue, flicking it in and out of my mouth and trying to moisten my alcohol and crisps dried lips.

Françoise has gone, leaving her petite imprint in the bed. I lean over and smell the brushed cotton sheets. Strands of her hair cling to the pillow. I hope we'll see each other again soon. I worry that she's gotten into trouble with the people she's staying with; perhaps the other two Frenchies have manufactured a cover story, like the usual alien abduction one I used to use when I was five minutes late and my dad was waiting. When your dad is going to thump you anyway, what's the point in coming up with something plausible?

I think back to when he first set eyes on me when I returned from The Falklands. He still wanted to be the man, but I clocked the same hollowed-out look in his eyes that I'd seen in the survivors of *Antelope*. Part of me actually feels sorry for him, but I know that – like a cornered animal – he'll come out fighting one day.

I nurse some tea and toast, pick up the *Daily Record*, which had recently rattled through the letterbox, and turn on the telly. There's a snippet on about Maggie Thatcher and a possible victory parade, then some reporter mentions that a Royal Marine is to be charged with bringing home an Argentine machine gun. Bloody hell! The Navy had pinched helicopters, anti-aircraft guns and ammunition and no-one thought of sending them to jail. I think about my own little souvenirs and swallow hard.

Shit! I gulp down my tea before taking the stairs two at a time. In my bedroom, I fish out my battered suitcase from under my sister's bed and pop it open. Wrapped in the sweatshirt that the big Welsh Guard had swapped me for some dry socks are a field dressing, my dog tags and three bullets. They look so different to the first time I saw them, when I'd been puttering around the ship in the wee small hours, helping to defend the hull from imaginary Argentine frogmen. I'm not sure why I kept them; they'd been allocated, along with a spare magazine, and somehow they weren't missed. Well, when your bosses are busy stealing helicopters and stuff, a few stray bullets don't go amiss, do they?

I thunder down the stairs and out into the back green. The ground around Mum's plants is hard. A couple of days of baking sunshine has welded her begonias and geraniums to the earth. I retrieve the kettle from the kitchen and pour leftover lukewarm water near the pampas grass and let it work into the soil. I grab a trowel from Dad's shed and use it to scrape at the mud, which starts to give way. As I scoop out the last of the hole, a piece of grey plastic catches my eye. Attached to it is a pair of plastic feet and a tiny blob of bubbled plastic. This could be the soldier I torched with Mum's lighter a couple of summers ago. I scrape away more of the hardened soil, using more water from the kettle to soften the surface. As more earth gives way, more soldiers are revealed, most with limbs missing, some with their heads burned, or melded to arms or legs.

I dig a bit more, closer to Mum's geraniums. I scrape and score frantically, having used up all the water from the kettle. The earth cracks and I realise I'm forcing the trowel hard and fast into the compacted ground. It starts to break up like the trays of toffee we used to make at school. Then I find him. Tommy. The little green soldier who had led the brave attack on the machine gun nest when I was an 11-year-old kid. His twisted body is almost unrecognisable, mud baked onto his face and stump of a leg, which I'd ripped off after Dad destroyed my little plastic plane when he came home that day from work. I was laying out all my soldiers in battle formation on the living room carpet, a ritual that took an hour, but on this day I was distracted by Mum calling me through for my tea. My dad's bike was broken and he'd been forced to walk to work. He caught me out by coming through the front door. Before I could shout "Dad, mind ma stuff!" I heard the snap of broken plastic. I ran through to the living room and cried "Dad!" as he held up the little plane I'd spent hours building and painting. I went to grab it off him, but he raised it out of my reach and said "Shouldn't have been there in the first place."

I hold up Tommy, or what's left of him. The sheen of his uniform has dulled, his rifle is bent in half and his stand, clinging on to a single leg, caked in dirt. *Poor bugger.* As I start cleaning him up with a thumb, a spot of mud on his head darkens, the saltwater of a solitary tear helping to break it up. *Shit! Where did that come from?* I sniff and wipe my eyes before placing him back in his grave. Before I cover him over, I reach into my jeans pocket, pull out three smooth, shiny rounds of ammunition and place them next to him. As I carefully claw a mound of earth into the little grave, I hear familiar voices. In 2.5 seconds, I'll see the faces those voices belong to. I know it'll be 2.5 seconds because when I was a kid, I timed my dad's entry through the close and out into the garden every single night. Someone someday will exhume Tommy and three rounds of ammunition and wonder what kind of nutter lived here. I look up into two concerned faces, both framed by varying lengths of blond hair. I smile, and their concern disappears in a flash of crooked teeth.

'Still playing with soldiers?' John says, mustering some hungover sarcasm.

'We're going to go down the swing park,' Alan adds.

He seems to be waiting for guidance as to what to do next, so I scramble to my feet and hold up my mud-caked hands. 'Just burying my dad,' I joke.

Going Underground

1985

'Iain? Fuck! Iain?'

'Dave!'

Iain 'Cheesy' Mould was the only sailor in basic training who called me Dave, which I hated, though not as much as Jock.

'Great to see you, man!' I blurt, going in for a man hug.

'Wow, really great to see you too! How's things?' he asks, enveloping me, as commuters dodge around us, heading for home and the promise of a train-free weekend.

'Wow, great to see you,' I say again, face flushing as I struggle to find better words.

'You too,' he confirms, a little too quickly.

We walk along Baker Street tube station platform. I size Iain up on the sly, wondering what things we have left in common from basic training.

'How's your brother?' I ask, peering past multiplying office workers on the platform.

Iain's brother, Andrew, had been on *Invincible*, miles from any of the shitty stuff in the South Atlantic, but I asked out of politeness and to fill any potential embarrassing gaps.

'Fine, yeah, fine,' Iain says, fidgeting with his comb-over.

I was aware that Iain might feel uncomfortable about perhaps being one of the few sailors who never sailed to the South Atlantic, apart from the crew on a few fishery protection vessels and a hovercraft called *HMS Speedy*, which lies rusting in a forgotten part of Portsmouth dockyard.

Iain had written to me when I was in the Falklands and we had agreed that the next time I was in London, we'd meet up. I had managed to avoid this up until now, but when the chance to go to Live Aid came up, I knew that Iain, the mega music fan, would be up for it. His parents live in a leafy suburb of north London, so we have a place to crash after a few beers. Unfortunately, it's miles in the opposite direction of Wembley, so we'll have an early start and I vow that I'll keep my drinking in check. Who knows, we might even bump into some posh totty at the local kebab shop.

The train crawls up to Amersham, 15 stops at three minutes a stop means 45 minutes of semi-forced conversation. I'm desperate to get to the pub so I can stop thinking about what to say next and just drink.

The pub in Iain's hometown of Amersham is at the dead end of the Metropolitan line, where commuters have no issue scrapping for an hour to get into London, or do mind, but can't afford the alternative, namely a mortgage for a one-bedroom three-by-two bedsit with noisy neighbours and an overgrown communal garden.

The pub's not so much spit and sawdust as spit and spit. Everything in this pub is hard and angular, including the punters. Either the budget didn't stretch to cushioned seats or the cushions have been ripped out and turned into projectiles for a barney.

'Your good health, Iain. Nice boozer by the way,' I say with a bit of flourish. I look around and make a mental note of the exits, something I've started doing recently.

'Really great to see you, Dave.' Iain's eyes sparkle with genuine enthusiasm and the knot in my stomach begins to loosen.

'Slange!' I say a bit too loudly, attracting a few malevolent glances followed by some unintelligible griping from one or two punters propping up the bar. We clink together our pint glasses harder than expected and I flinch at the sound.

Iain stood out in our class. For a start, he was a failed artificer foisted upon us from *HMS Fisgard*. He was the very thing I'd wanted to be when I first went to the careers office, but that single failed exam had led me to joining up for a semi-skilled job instead of an apprenticeship. Of course, my dad never let me forget about it.

Iain had introduced me to Bob Dylan, Pink Floyd, cod philosophy and motorbikes. He had a Honda Benly 200cc and sometimes he rode it down from Amersham to *HMS Collingwood* where we did our electrical training. I bought my Suzuki scrambler after seeing his bike. His bike had an electric starter and a top speed of 65 mph. My bike, however, rarely went above 50 and the faulty kick-starter would knacker my knee and leave me shore-side waiting for an operation.

'Great to see you,' I repeat, fighting to find something better to say.

'Yeah, you too,' Iain says, looking around for a spot to blend in.

'Does your mum not mind us staying at her place?' I enquire, looking back towards the bar in an effort to avoid what looks like a rugby scrum of regulars huddled round one of the few tables.

'They're away, so it's just you and me, mate,' Iain replies. 'Let's get a seat,' he adds, pointing to a corner that's a bit far away from the exit for my liking. The beer is taking its effect though, so I follow him.

'Can't wait till tomorrow,' Iain says, enthusiastically, settling into what passes for a chair.

'Should be a great gig,' I nod, noticing a bald-headed geezer over Iain's left shoulder is giving us his full attention.

The beer is flowing as the pub fills up and I think I'm doing okay. The conversation grows louder and faster.

'Fuckin should've seen it, man,' I bellow, regaling Iain with stories of my close shave as Standing Sea Fire Party when *Antelope* was evacuated and all the survivors were brought on board. 'I was head to toe in my asbestos fire suit with my BA on. I looked like a fuckin Yeti! Smelled like one as well.'

Guffawing at my own sick joke, Baldy is suddenly standing over me and in my face, but I can't make out what he's saying, but I'm mesmerised by his lips glistening with spittle. Iain scrapes back his chair, gets to his feet and attempts to calm things down.

'He's just a bit pissed, mate,' Iain says, submissively. A moment passes like someone has pressed pause on a cassette player, then . . . Baldy slopes back to the bar. I notice he's wearing a stripy blue and white T-shirt and a brief memory of Françoise enters my head and I catch myself smiling.

Iain sits down and leans in towards me. 'Dave. Mate!' he cautions, motioning his palms down towards the table.

321

'What? Aye, aye, I'll keep it doon, sorry,' I say, punctuating my chatter with gulps of beer.

'Should've seen those poor bastards from the *Antelope*, Iain, fuckin shame it wis. I reckon some of them probably wish they'd been killed. Abandoning ship, man, fuckin nightmare. All that way to fight in a war and you're knocked out in the first round.'

Iain tries to calm me down, but the four or so beers have kicked in and I'm out of control. I become aware of a few knuckle draggers eyeing me up, honing in on my Scottish accent. *Fuck em.*

'So, anyway, Live Aid, it's gonnae be fuckin magic! Maaaagic!' I scream, raising my hands like a kid on a rollercoaster.

Suddenly, my hair is soaking and beer is running down my face. My chair screeches as its pulled backwards, my heels flailing uselessly as I fight for purchase on the dirty, beer-stained floor. A thuggish, tattooed arm is round my throat, dragging me by the chin towards the exit.

Then it all goes black.

I'm outside on the pavement, flat out, sucking in oxygen from a mask. My left arm strains against a blood pressure cuff. My jaw is numb and my mouth swirls with a mixture of stale beer and blood. I cough into the mask as I struggle to catch my breath. I'm lifted into a sitting position and held under my armpits while I vomit.

I'm vaguely aware of a crowd in shorts and T-shirts, the chatter of a two-way radio and what must be a paramedic's latex gloves dabbing at my right eye. I have no idea where Iain is, but there's the wail of an ambulance in the distance.

The rest of the night resembles the jump cut footage of a film. A light shining in my eye. My name being called. The sting of a needle above my eye as stitches are sewn. The comfort of a pillow, then sleep.

***

The train rocks and rattles through the harsh London daylight like the teeth inside my swollen mouth. Iain's mottled face and neat-ish stitches mirror my own. He told me that when Baldy stuck a glass in my face, narrowly missing my right eye, he jumped in to save me and ended up in the back of an ambulance. I sustained a bruised jaw, two black eyes and a chipped tooth, which I worry with my tongue. I later learn that Baldy had been out on bail that night for putting two coppers in hospital.

The carriage is crowded apart from the two aisle seats next to us. I'm willing the bile in my stomach to wait until we're off the train. I'm not quite beyond embarrassment but throwing up in a crowded train looking like a hungover panda comes close.

We slug into Wembley as the 80,000 strong crowd whoops and cheers to the sound of Status Quo's 'Rocking All Over the World'. It's unbearably hot and noisy and the sweat from my head is stinging my stitches. Iain and I make a half-hearted attempt to get near the front, prodding and nudging a few yards forward before we settle for half-way up the pitch. Miraculously, I've been able to keep down the slice of dry toast that I had for breakfast. Everyone around us is jumping up and down and singing, but all I can think about is hiding my facial injuries from the Navy when I have to return from summer leave.

I try to focus on the bands while willing my body to get through the pain and nausea of my hangover. But it's

323

no use. As Spandau Ballet take to the stage, I turn to Iain and nod in the direction of the exits. 'Can I get your keys, mate? I've got to go,' I shout over the din of 80,000 revellers.

'But what about Queen?' Iain shouts back.

'Next time, mate! You stay!'

'What?'

'You stay!' I shout louder, wincing as I catch my tongue on my jagged tooth.

Iain makes moves to come with me, but I put my hand out. I turn and leave him there. There's no point in two of us suffering for my fuck up.

On the train, I scrutinise my reflection in the window and think about a film I saw about a year ago, *An Officer and a Gentleman*. Despite all the odds, Richard Gere's character, the son of drunk, makes it through naval officer training and ends up carrying a gorgeous Deborah Winger from her dead end factory job off into the sunset. But me, I get two black eyes, six stitches above my right eye and a tooth that clings to my bloodied gum like a rat on a lifeboat. Not exactly dating material, but I've survived. After all, it's what I do best.

Here Comes
the Weekend

1992

I relish Old Firm matches as a press photographer. This one is at the end of Comic Relief and will provide respite from photographing people wearing red noses. Saturday mornings at *The Sunday Mail* are spent dodging news jobs while waiting for the canteen to open before heading off to the match. The photo studio is far enough away from the newsroom and as long as you're nowhere near a phone, no-one can send you out on a job that might make you late for the footie. As I sit there pretending to be busy, I think back to some of the hidey-holes on board *Fearless*; places you could sit and think without being disturbed, or places to deal with your hangover. These places are few and far between, because you have to be out of tannoy range. The *Daily Record* and *Sunday Mail* also has a tannoy system, and whilst it's inescapable, I have an armoury of excuses for not hearing it.

The pervasive accountancy and management practices designed to promote high blood pressure and instability have made their way across the pond and are creeping into the Saturday shift system at *The Sunday Mail*. In previous years, you could turn up around lunchtime, do a football shift and disappear. Now, you're fodder for early news jobs that hardly ever make the paper, but it stops the Managing Editor from having to bring in a news photographer and pay them. Meanwhile, the shareholders and executives will still be putting their expensive lunches on a tab.

It's a cold, bright afternoon, but the rain that usually appears around half an hour before the start of a game hasn't materialised. Ibrox stadium is packed and it's only 2.30pm. I suppose you have to get there early if you're a real fan – to get your full complement of hatred in against the other side; like a cost benefit analysis for bigotry.

I like to arrive at least an hour before the game, but I get caught up in a news story; some crap that involves babysitting a reporter who's too scared to go to a dodgy neighbourhood by themselves and needs an insurance policy. Of course, my nine stone frame will struggle to provide the perfect bulletproof vest should it kick off, but it will at least give the reporter a ten second head start to get back to the car. Thankfully, after half an hour of the reporter listening to some poor unfortunate, we're speeding back to the office in time for me to grab a pie and beans and the least battered telephoto lens from the pool cupboard.

After wolfing down my grub, I discover that the sports reporter covering the Rangers Celtic match has already bolted to Ibrox (via the pub) so I have to take my own car. Well, at least all my equipment, including waterproofs, are there already because I'm always forgetting vital bits of kit. The only downside is the parking will be murder by now.

Once I arrive, I flash my photographer's pass at the car park steward. He points me to a spot that'll involve a cross-country run back to Ibrox to make kick-off. As I open the boot and wrestle with my gear, I can hear the buzz of the stadium in the distance. Impaled on its monopod, I hump the lens over my shoulder, which is as heavy as a drowned Labrador, and slalom my way through the sea of parked cars, trying not to bash the lens against the pristine paintwork of Porsches and Audis. I navigate my way through the police horse shit that peppers Edmiston Drive and weave among stray supporters who've had one last pint and are clutching their season tickets, looking at them with gooey eyes, like new fathers. The Ibrox tannoy blares out some crowd-rousing beats, startling them out of their booze-soaked dream world.

I fumble in my waterproof trousers' pocket for my pass and hold it up to another burly steward for inspection. I'm waved into the stadium and the wall of noise hits me square in the chest. I take a deep breath and try to compose myself. The air smells of hot dogs, pies, beer farts and hatred. I feel like the four sides of the stadium are pressing down on me, but I spot a few friendly photographers' faces at the Broomloan Road end of Ibrox and head towards them. I smile and think of something funny to say as my waterproofs mark each step closer to them with a squeak. Unfortunately, I'm not liked by everyone in the group I'm approaching; for some, it's nothing more than friendly rivalry from other papers, but others either don't rate me or think I'm too young, or too funny, or too small, or too noisy – but I've got enough allies to make it worth the trudge.

I spot Henry McInnes, a *Sunday Mail* staffer who always has a word and a smile for me. I dump my camera case and lens on the blue painted surface behind the goal and hitch up my sweaty waterproof trousers. A ball skids

327

off the pitch and slams against my case, making me flinch, generating an ironic cheer from the Celtic fans behind me. I look up, their faces contorting into menacing glee. A Celtic player brushes past me, grabs the ball and passes it to his teammate, who lines it up for further target practice. Every kick towards goal is met with a cacophony of noise. I walk over to Henry.

'Alright, David?' he says.

I cup my ear to catch the soft burr of Henry McInnes's question as the noise from the fans bounces around the walls of the stadium.

'Aye, no bad,' I reply. 'As long as it doesn't rain, eh?'

'Fingers crossed,' he smiles, crossing his fingers as the decibel levels tingle my ear drums and I feel a stab of adrenaline in my gut. I turn and signal with a wave that I'm off, take a deep breath and head up to my end of the park to cover the Celtic attack for the first half.

Photographers talk incessantly about the weather, especially bad weather and how it affects cameras, lenses, glasses, motor drives, you name it. A sudden shower can ruin your whole day if you don't have a chamois leather, and if your lens hood isn't good enough, a bright day will cause flare in your lens resulting in not being able to see anything. There's no such thing as good weather for a photographer, unless you're on holiday.

I look up at the sky again. It's mostly blue but, like my mood, it is capable of sudden change. I hope the match will be half decent and that if there's a pitch invasion I manage to get a great picture without getting my head kicked in or tripping on the heel of my baggy waterproof trousers, which are now sticky with sweat.

I lump my cumbersome lens with its monopod over my shoulder and head for the far end of the stadium.

Henry picks his spot and, as second photographer, I take the opposite side. As I walk past the dugouts of the main stand I can't believe what I'm witnessing. The Rangers fans in the terrace have their hands raised in Nazi salutes and are singing about a battle where their great, great, great, great grandfathers had been the heroes (even though some of them would have to have been cooks or accountants).

Some might argue that their arms aren't high enough for it to be a Nazi salute, but I know what I see. And as if that isn't bizarre enough, they're all wearing blue plastic noses - thousands of them, chanting sectarian abuse, supporting their own version of Comic Relief.

I know I should be recording this hideous image, but because all the other photographers are ignoring it, I do too. It bothers me, but I tell myself that I might cause a riot if someone spots me clicking away. Regardless, I feel like a coward.

It still bothers me when the teams run out to a wall of noise. My heart judders and my hands and feet feel numb.

I've covered these games loads of times and while they aren't exactly sweetness and light, I manage to block out the noise and concentrate on getting the best shots.

This time is different though. With each crunching tackle, I feel my heart flutter and the sweat trickle down my face. My chest tightens and my left arm feels like it's being gripped by an invisible force. I try to concentrate and focus through the telephoto lens, but my vision's fuzzy and I'm terrified that I'm about to have a heart attack. I put the camera down and try to regulate my breathing, but I'm fighting a losing battle. I tap one of the other photographers on the shoulder and shout that

I'm not feeling well and have to leave. He mouths some words back to me along with a puzzled expression, but I'm already heading for the exit. I have no idea what's happening and as I turn to see those blue-nosed supporters screaming at the opposition, one of them singles me out and shouts, 'You're going the wrong way!'

I almost trip over my waterproofs in my desperate need to get out, but as the cacophony of hatred recedes, my heart rate decreases and I manage to catch my breath.

Once I make it back to the car, I fling the gear into the boot and sit in the driver's seat, staring at myself in the rear-view mirror. I check my pulse and a memory of doing the same during the war in the Falklands invades my consciousness. My pulse is rapid, like it belongs to a fullback sprinting down the wing. I check it again and again until it eventually slows, but then it trips and fires up again and I try to tell myself I'm okay, but I don't feel okay at all. I slump back in my seat and try to calm down, but my thought process has already locked onto the fact that something serious could be wrong with me.

We've Only Started

2015

'It's just what you love, what you hate, and what you would do if you were God,' Stuart explains, plopping the well-thumbed joke writing book onto the table between us. He gives us a look that says 'Capiche?' then turns and heads for the stage, where people are already tuning up guitars.

I look at the other guy sitting opposite me, dwarfed by the cavernous hall of the Orbiston Neighbourhood Centre. He's biting his nails and doing that knee jangly thing while his eyes dart around the hall like a kitten that knows a rock-filled bag is imminent. *Why do we do this to ourselves?*

Strangely, the thought of someone shitting themselves more than me calms me down. I've already scanned the room for exits – emergency or otherwise – so I know how to escape if my panic overwhelms me. Judging by the behaviour of this guy, if it's possible to spontaneously combust with panic, he should be at least smouldering by now. I race through a few pages of Stuart's book and write down a few ideas. My mum has just had a heart attack after being attacked by a seagull, so that's my opening joke.

Stuart says we only have to do two minutes on stage and there are only eight other people in the gigantic church hall, so if I bomb, only eight people will tell their friends – and they'll tell their friends – and maybe some neighbours – so the fallout will be in the 200-300 range. It's highly unlikely to make the local paper and I don't even live here, so minimum collateral damage for yours truly.

'Awright?' I look up to find Stuart looming over me. It feels like his eyes are boring right through me and picking up the church notices at the back of the hall. He registers my fear level and his stare softens to a glare.

'You okay for the two minutes?' he asks, leaning back from the desk to create some breathing space. The other guy signals his readiness with a strangled cough and half-raised hand. The nails on blackboard sound of his chair makes me flinch, but I'm doing this even if it kills me.

'I'm ready,' I reply, standing up and clutching my crumpled notes with a sweaty, white-knuckled hand. I'm sharing the stage with a stack of chairs and some stuff left over from a Nativity play, but it still feels vast.

Shaky-leg guy gives it his best shot, but I time his set at one minute and 23 seconds and I really hope I can make the full two minutes. I'm surprised at how competitive I've become. As I make my way to the stage, I pass the slumped shouldered figure of shaky-leg guy on the bottom step.

'Well done, mate,' I console, attempting to pat the guy on the shoulder, but somehow I miss and pat dead air instead. He seems transfixed by the click laminate flooring and doesn't respond.

'Okay Davy, you're up,' Stuart beckons from the stage, arm waving like a traffic cop after an accident.

I stride the stairs at the side of the stage. A few minutes ago, I was ready to bolt, but I'm so annoyed that someone's called me Davy that I'm on the stage before I know it, looking down on my audience, entirely made up

332

of the other performers. I was hoping for at least a volunteer dinner lady peering through the door at the back of the hall.

'Hullo, Wembley!' I boom, channelling my inner Michael McIntyre. There are a few nervous titters and I'm thinking, *That's eight seconds, just 112 seconds to go.*

Two minutes later (I run over by 18 seconds), there's a mixture of polite clapping and bemused faces, but I've just done something I'd have thought entirely impossible only a few months ago. I exit stage right still with the mic, slump back into my chair and take a few deep breaths.

Stuart bounds over to me and grabs the mic. 'Why did you do that "Hullo, Wembley" thing?' he asks, folding his arms around it protectively, a scowl forming on his forehead.

Uh-oh.

'Don't know, Stuart,' I stutter. 'One day I might say it for real.'

'Aye,' he grunts, 'but no the day.'

In the world of put downs, it's a belter. I think back to when my dad said I'd amount to nothing and my nose stings. I pinch it in a vain attempt to stem my eyes from welling up and turn my attention to the blurry notices on the far wall.

'Might have a wee gig for ye though, Motherwell Miners' Bowling Club in a fortnight . . . if ye're interested.'

I sniff hard and clear my throat before turning back. 'Fine' is all I can muster, but inside I'm screaming *Fucking awesome!*

Sound Affects

2015

The bass booms and my heart judders. The waves of panic rise. The blood scurries to my vital organs, leaving my hands and feet tingling. I'm struggling to breathe – and my chest is being crushed by the writhing mass of middle-aged white men belting out the opening lines of The Jam's 'Eton Rifles' in terrifying tribal precision, thumped out by Bruce Foxton's band, From The Jam.

'David! Daaaaaaaavid!' I twist round to see Becky's contorted face, her glacial blue eyes wide with fear. 'We should go, it's too loud,' she yells above the thudding bass, her hands pressed hard against her ears.

'It's alright,' I scream back as a flailing elbow catches me in the ribs. I'm not giving up my position right down the front for anyone.

'Too loud!' she protests.

As I turn away, the bass invades every part of my body. Nerve endings in my feet and hands tingle. I search helplessly for the exits, knowing I'm not going to go until the end of the gig, because I can't deal with the shame of letting my favourite band down and the embarrassment I'd feel being watched by all the other fans seeing me leave.

I turn back to the stage and spot a photographer I know in the pit. He's wearing ear protectors and, for a split second, I think about asking him if he has a spare pair. But I don't. I lean over the barrier that separates the crowd from the photographers and I see one kneeling beside his camera gear. He's picking out a pair of orange ear protectors from a bag. I know that a pair of these could be a life saver, but I turn my attention back to the band and sing the words to every single song until the lights come up.

***

It's Christmas Eve, three months after the gig. The ringing in my right ear is constant, though it's got nothing to do with jingle bells. My hearing test came back revealing no significant hearing loss, but I'm still called into the dimly lit consultant's room at the hospital. Sitting across from me at the side of his desk, the consultant sifts through my auditory readout. His face is mellow with years of projected concern. He looks up at me with a smile.

'The good news is there's no damage to your auditory nerve,' he says, his voice soothing as he nonchalantly squares some paper on his desk.

'I'm really struggling with this, Doctor,' I reply, even though I know he's a Mr, but I feel his title doesn't match his expertise.

He looks out of his window for a moment before turning back to me. He leans forward and presses his hands against mine as if we are praying together. His jaw softens, eyes crinkled at the edges. 'Everything will be okay,' he whispers.

I feel like I'm ten years old. He lets go and leans back into his chair. I take this as a signal that the conversation is over.

I spend the next five days screaming, crying and ranting against the sheer fucking unfairness of life. Becky stares at me, her car crash of a husband sitting on the bottom stair, physically vibrating with anxiety. And all this while we try to do Christmas.

I torture myself with questions. *Why didn't I leave that gig? Why didn't my wife force me to leave? How can I be so stupid? Why do I sabotage my life like this?*

And then I begin to think of killing myself.

I run various scenarios through my head and thank God Scotland doesn't do guns, then wish to fuck we do, because a single bullet would do silence forever.

Some of my suicidal thoughts make me laugh, like the ones that involve planning. I'm so lethargic I can't commit to anything that involves a spreadsheet and I'm not great with heights, so bridge jumping is a no-no. Stuff with blood, like slitting my wrists, is out, and there's a chance a rope could fail and leave me with brain damage *and* tinnitus. I've been off the booze for four years, so I'd see it as a failure if I take a vodka/pills cocktail. Running all this over and over in my head and finding so many excuses convinces me that killing myself isn't the answer. I need to find a reason to live.

Then my phone rings. It's Stuart.

That's Entertainment

2015

Applause rings around the Motherwell Miners' Welfare Bowling Club. The female comedian with the skin-tight tartan trousers and shouty voice is taking a bow on the dancefloor in front of the stage, which has been commandeered by the bingo caller and his ball machine.

I'm on next.

There are 212 people here, 204 more than my last gig. I counted them to calm my nerves, though a few came and went to the toilet, some under their own steam, others with the assistance of Zimmers and the odd mobility scooter.

I've checked all the exits are clear.

Stuart takes the mic from the wacky-trousered shouty woman and launches into his compere spiel. I scan the crowd from the side of the stage, separated from them by a single table. I breathe in for four, hold for four and breathe out for four, then start again. My gut tightens as some feedback from the speakers pierces my ears, but I manage to tune out as Stuart goes into his laconic repertoire, which is mercifully short.

'Give him a big hand for his comedy debut, it's David Cruickshanks!' Stuart announces with a flourish, throwing his free hand into the air.

The mention of my name and serious, genuine applause brings my focus back to the room. Stuart looms large and hands me the mic. 'All yours,' he sings.

'Hullo, Wembley.!' I turn to see Stuart wince. *Fuck it, things can only get better.*

My comedy debut in front of a paying audience feels so much like a night on the booze with blank spaces where memories should be. All the watching faces blend into one, but I clock about five Zimmers in the 200+ crowd and think to myself *Some of these people might be fighting their own tinnitus to catch a punchline.*

Relax David, it's not like you're getting paid for this I remind myself, but my tingling feet suggest I've got as much chance relaxing as most of the audience has of getting to the toilet unaided.

Miraculously, I finish my 20-minute set without forgetting any of my gags.

And they laughed.

As I walk off the dancefloor to a decent amount of applause, I almost collide with Stuart as he reaches for the mic to announce the next act.

'Fuckin Wembley,' he snorts.

I shrug back. I'm too knackered to think. It's over and I'm still breathing.

Stuart turns back to the audience and goes into full showbiz mode. 'Give it up for David Cruickshanks!'

I slump into my chair at the side of the stage.

'Ye wurnae bad, eh?' says the wacky-trousered shouty woman at a significantly reduced volume.

Christ, praise indeed I think to myself, slumping even deeper into my chair. I concentrate hard on sucking in every ounce of the uplifting atmosphere of Motherwell Miners' Bowling Club – and think of the stories all of these people could tell. And then I think about my own story . . .

I've been physically and mentally abused by my dad.

Bullied by the school head case.

Bombed by the Argentine Air Force.

I've stuck two fingers up to a minefield.

Had my ears pummelled by a Jam tribute act.

My mind shot by PTSD.

Been attacked as a press photographer.

Beaten up in a boozer.

And I've just gone and put myself back in the firing line.

And I've survived.

Once again.

Epilogue

In October 2020, Craig Hardie, a good friend of mine and the fittest man I know, feels noticeably tired. Four months later, he dies from pancreatic cancer.

Craig's death forced me to face my own mortality and reminded me of how many near-death experiences I've had. I realised that, for a period of almost 50 years, I've dodged so many real and metaphorical bullets — so I started to ask myself, why? Why me?

In response, I've decided to chronicle my near-death experiences, listing them here in the hope of discovering something about myself in the process, and the reasons I'm still alive.

1969:   I slip on black ice yards from my house, fall and bang my skull. I'm rushed to hospital but, thankfully, there's no fracture. I'm kept in overnight for observation and ice cream.

1975:   I electrocute myself twice, once by poking a knitting needle into an electric fire, the other via a crude attempt to investigate the inner workings of an aquarium air pump. Unfortunately, the pump was attached to the mains at the time.

1976:   The school bully renders me unconscious in the playground for 15 minutes as he crushes my rib cage, just for a laugh.

1982:   The Argentine Air Force tries to bomb my scrawny arse out of existence for 100 days without success. I survive the war only to stray into a minefield during the peace. A month beforehand, when the ship is anchored off Ascension Island, I electrocute myself in the intense heat of the engine room while trying to replace a lamp.

1985:   On the eve of Live Aid at Wembley Stadium, I'm hospitalised and lucky to escape with my life after being brutally beaten up outside a pub in Amersham by a thug out on bail for putting two coppers in hospital. I'm saved by the intervention of my shipmate, Iain 'Cheesy' Mould.

1986-
1989:   I have 17 car accidents, two of them serious and one ending up with me having a brief stay in hospital. One car is a right off. My bosses at the Fife Free Press aren't impressed, something to do with paperwork. They never do send me on that driving refresher course though, something to do with budgets.

1989:   At a Fife Flyers ice hockey match, a puck doing approximately 97.3 miles per hour misses my head by a few inches and embeds itself in a wooden advertising hoarding. The crowd cheers.

342

1992: I'm 18 metres below the surface of the Caribbean Sea with hardly any dive training, and my regulator valve fails (the dive instructors tell you the regulator is fail-safe). In a blind panic, I head for the surface without looking up and miss the boat's hull by millimetres. Ten minutes later, I plunge back in and complete my dive.

1993: After I take his photograph, a drunk in Glasgow's Gallowgate chases me with a knife. Luckily, I'm a good runner and manage to lose him.

1997: Two days before I leave the *Daily Record*, I'm driving home on the motorway after photographing a Spice Girls concert at the SECC. Someone launches a half brick from one of the bridges over the Stepps bypass, which smashes through my windscreen. Thankfully, it catches the rear-view mirror on the way in and lands on the back seat. The police can't believe how lucky I am.

1997: Six minutes after leaving my rented house in Solent Road in North West London, my Lycra clad body is spread-eagled over the bonnet of a moving car. My bike is not so lucky; it goes under the wheels.

1998: I'm driving down the main road from Belfast to Enniskillen with a reporter in the front seat and actor Shaun Williamson, of *Eastenders* and *Extras* fame in the back. Sitting next to him is his dad, who announces he wants his son to see the town where he grew up.

Now that the peace agreement has been ratified, it's possible to visit, safe in the knowledge that 'the troubles' are over. At 1pm, the reporter suggests we stop at Omagh for lunch. For whatever reason, we don't stop, preferring to carry on to Enniskillen for the photoshoot.

When we arrive, Shaun is mobbed by the Enniskillen townsfolk and we're all treated to fish and chips in exchange for what seems like hundreds of autographs. After tea, we pop into a local pub, just in time to view the horrific scenes of the Omagh bombing blaring from a television in the corner of the bar.

Including two unborn children, the Omagh bombing killed 29 people and injured a further 220. Who knows what would have happened that day if we had stopped for lunch in Omagh.

Even If I was a cat, I'd be long dead by now, so I'm hoping the reason I'm still alive is because I have something valuable to give back. Maybe it's this book, or the work I do with veterans, or maybe it's my ability to make people laugh.

If life is a rollercoaster, then I'm the exhilarated and terrified kid who gets back on it the second it ends.

Whoever or whatever it is that's keeping me alive, I hope it doesn't end anytime soon.

Glossary

back-classed   **53**
failure to complete a task, or sickness
lasting five days or more, resulting in
the recruit going back one week
in basic training

bimbling / bimble   **51 / 80**
walking / walk

bogies   **25**
nasal mucus rolled into tight balls,
like organic Blu-tack

bootnecks   **148**
Royal Marines

briney   **101**
brine

bull / bulling   **53 / 280**
polish / polishing

burberry   **154**
a traditional rain jacket exclusive
to the Royal Navy, not to be confused
with the designer brand

close up   **77**
report to the designated area

dead man's click   **194**
when the trigger clicks
but there are no rounds left

dhoby / dhobied 74 / 268
wash / washed

dhoby-dust 134
washing powder

dogwatch 68
a four-year period of senior service

dogwatch/morning watch 235
dogwatch: 1600-2000hrs after a full day's
work; morning watch: 0400-0800hrs,
followed by a 0800-1200hrs regular
working day

doubling / double 51 / 55
jogging / jog

Eager Beaver 82
informal term for a military tractor

Exocet 130
French-built anti-ship missile

fairy 203
Air Engineering Mechanic

fizzog 45
face

flashed up / flashing up 110 / 176
started / starting up

flying stations 175
when the ship's flight deck is
out of bounds to all personnel
except the flight crew and
flight deck personnel

focsle 130
forward part or 'pointy end'
of the upper deck of the ship

for'ard 173
towards the front of the ship

galleon 206
a 19th century three-masted ship

gash 169
rubbish

genny 120
generator

girdle 296
Scottish term for a stovetop griddle
for making scones and pancakes

GPMG 148
General Purpose Machine Gun

greenie(s) 63
electrician(s)

Pucara 184
an Argentine ground-attack
and counter-insurgency aircraft

reggy 221
a regulator in charge of naval discipline

rig 207
uniform

scare charges 155
underwater grenades

set, a 118
a beard and moustache

shore cable party 285
electrical engineers tasked with
connecting shore electricity to the ship

skids 226
underwear

slip anchor 274
pulling up the anchor in readiness to sail

Snow Cats 82
small, tracked vehicles

spittoon 259
a large, circular, silver-coloured ashtray
that sits on the floor

Acknowledgements

As someone in their sixth decade of life, I acknowledge the enormous debt of gratitude I owe to so many people who have shaped my life and writing:

My mum, Margaret, continues to be my biggest cheerleader and her boundless enthusiasm is infectious.

My wife, Becky, has continued to navigate us through choppy waters and has steadied the ship more times than I can remember. She deserves all the credit for coming up with the book's title.

My best friend, Chris Boyne, sadly no longer with us, was the best stand-up comedian I knew, despite never gracing a stage.

My 95-year-old pal, Hugh Martin, a top fisherman and electrician, and is the best inventor never to have applied for a patent.

Alan White, John Pratt, Ivan Bishop, Alan McCreadie, Allan Fowlis and Joanne Carroll – my Stevenson Avenue gang.

Baz White, my friend Alan's dad, who was the catalyst for my career in the Navy. His pragmatic calmness and warmth towards me showed a different side of male behaviour.

My history teacher, John Brown, who showed interest in me, faith in my academic ability, and almost convinced me to go to St Andrews University. It nearly worked.

Bob Berwick. The best fire station janitor and graphic artist ever.

My naval family and the entire ship's company of *HMS Fearless* in 1982. My comrades who – armed with humour, tough love and lots of alcohol – got me through one of the most traumatic periods of my life.

Glenrothes Camera Club former president, Bob McCrae, who cancelled his Saturday to develop my first ever news photo, which appeared in the *Glenrothes Gazette*.

Fife Free Press Chief Photographer, Bill Dickman, who saw my raw potential, stamina and perseverance, and moulded me into an award-winning press photographer.

All press photographers who are constantly misrepresented as cold-hearted, door-stepping doom-mongers. Most are warm, witty, intelligent, caring and thoughtful, and I consider it a privilege to have worked alongside them.

My former *Daily Record* and *Sunday Mail* colleagues: photographers Alan Peebles, Kenny Ferguson, Ian Torrance, Andy Hosie, William Thornton, Mark Runnacles, Richard Parker, Eric Craig, Jack Hamilton, Martin Wright, Roy Cameron, Eric Rutherford, Bill Fraser, Bert Paterson, Robert Paterson, Derek Ironside, John Gunion, Bill Fleming, John Dempsie, Bert Purcell, David Robertson, David McNeil, Ronnie Anderson, Henry McInnes, Robert Hotchkiss and Craig Halkett; and reporters Anna Smith, Cara Page, Brian 'Brogues' McCartney, Fidelma Cook, Elsa Mc Alonan, Fiona Black, Kenny Rattray, Gary Ralston, Mandie Appleyard, Ian Leckie, John Dingwall, Billy Sloan, Alex Gordon, Bill Leckie, David Leggat, Maggie Ritchie, Mike Ritchie, Charlie Beaton, Fiora Jackson, Keith Jackson, and so many others.

Gerda Gordon, an unflappable IT guru, and the amazing staff at the *Daily Record* library.

Andrew Watson, a great long-time friend in and out of photography, and a top bloke.

Andy Allan, a man of integrity, wisdom and good humour, and an unrivalled picture editor.

Trudi Wallace and Terri Craig, my fashion shoot partners in crime.

Anne, Billy and Amy Davidson, who took me in to their house for a few weeks while I found my feet in London. Three months later, I was still there!

Claire Cisotti (nee Gannaway), who championed my photography career in London and did it with such class.

Paul Hackett, a brilliant photographer and snappy dresser, who let me watch Scotland play in the World Cup from his Dalston pad.

Tony Grundy, who championed my writing, but sadly never got to see this book.

The Jam's Paul Weller, Bruce Foxton and Rick Buckler, who provided the soundtrack to my formative years and the inspiration for my chapter headings.

My fellow Glasgow Caledonian MATV class, including Linda Duncan McLaughlin, Michael Elisabeth Richardson, David Cosgrove and Will Murray.

My MATV tutors, Anne Marie Di Mambro, Chris Dolan and Dr Catriona Miller. Scottish drama writing is indebted to this hugely talented trio and never have so many writers owed so much of their careers to the knowledge and experience of so few.

My dad, a man who never got the chance to exorcise his own demons.

My sister, Christine, who has her own story to tell.

Stuart Doig from Fool On, a charity that uses comedy to combat anxiety.

My editor, Dickson Telfer. I have never met an editor more dedicated to the success of his author. Dickson has cajoled, encouraged and suggested changes that have enhanced and improved this memoir, and always with a smile and a desire to understand the language and traditions of The Royal Navy. Dickson probably has more knowledge of Jack-speak than the average sailor. His enthusiasm is boundless and his dedication borders on the obsessive, and that is why I will be holding onto him for dear life.

My publisher, Razur Cuts Books, for taking a punt on a complete unknown.

Gillian Gardner, my proof reader, for her honesty, forthrightness and attention to detail.

This book would never have existed without a chance conversation with *Herald* photographer Stuart Paterson, who sadly died in 2013. Stuart confided in me that a therapist had told him that writing down his experiences of trauma might be a way for the brain to process and reframe it. He was right.

About the Author

Since fighting in the Falklands and working as a press photographer for national newspapers, David Cruickshanks has become a qualified mental health Peer Support Worker and spends his time helping others deal with PTSD and PTSD-related mental health challenges.

He holds a Masters in Writing Television Fiction and a Diploma in Creative Writing, and has written sketches and gags for the BBC Radio Scotland shows *Lewis Macleod's Wired News* and Des Clarke's *Breaking the News*. His future plans include developing his stand-up comedy career and performing to bigger audiences.

David lives in Strathmiglo, Fife, with his wife, Becky, and spaniel, Maggie.

BOOKS

razurcuts.com

@razurcutsmag
@TheUnrealDavidC